*Guide to*

# *KODAK 35 mm Films*

EASTMAN KODAK COMPANY
ROCHESTER, NEW YORK 14650

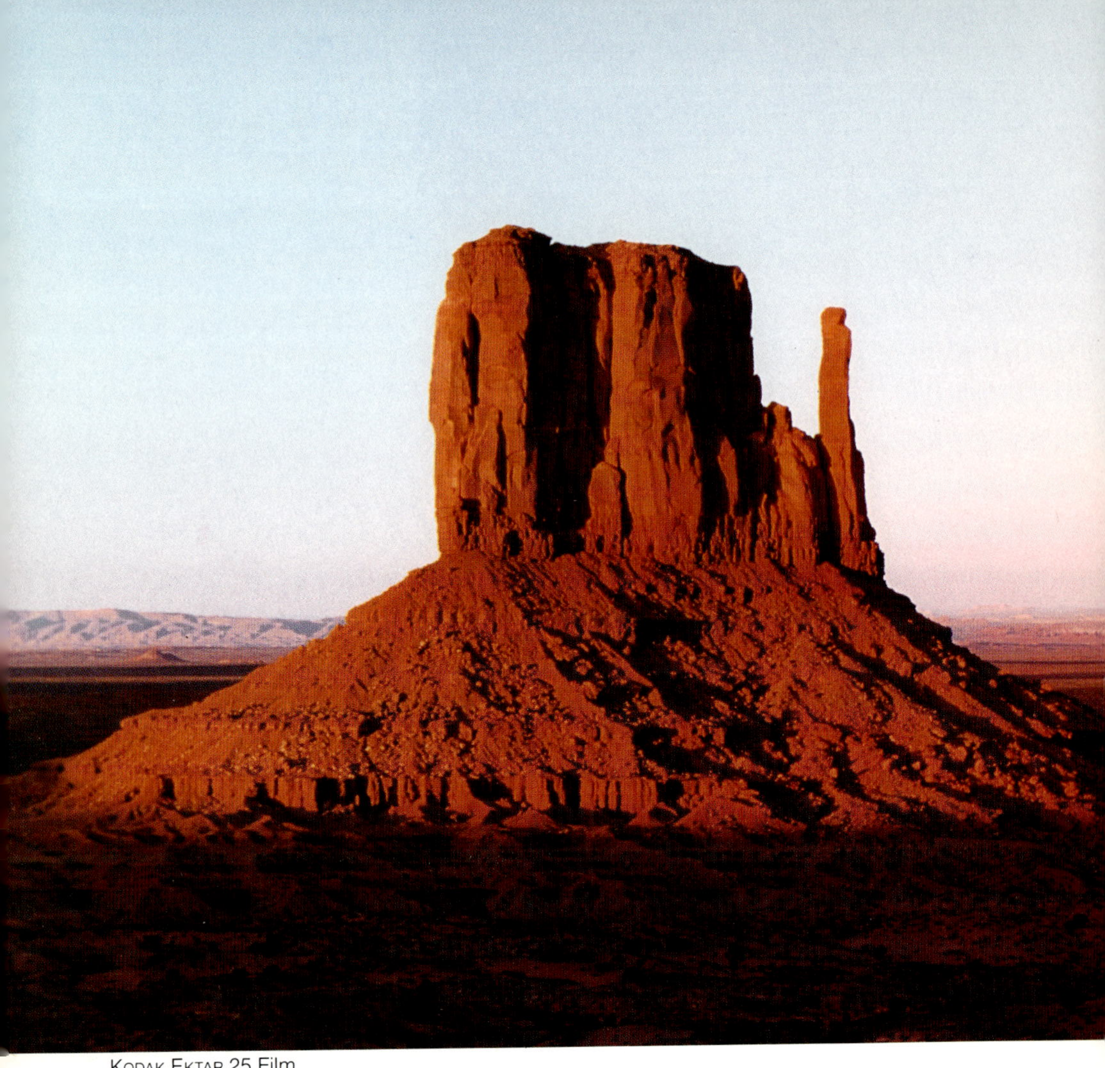

KODAK EKTAR 25 Film

Modern photographic films are truly remarkable in the ways that they capture the events of our lives. The uses of film in our society are almost endless. Because film is such a vital part of the photographic process and so profoundly affects the quality of your pictures, you need a film that gives results of consistently high quality. Kodak films meet this quality requirement.

Kodak is noted for being in the forefront of the industry and for making remarkable advances in film technology. The company is constantly performing research to achieve perfection in the manufacture of film to provide the greatest possible benefits and value to customers.

Kodak films are manufactured with a wide variety of characteristics so that you can choose the best film for the type of photographs you want to take. To select the best film for your needs, you should be familiar with the characteristics of the films that are available. The purpose of this book is to acquaint you with Kodak 35 mm films for non-professional use.

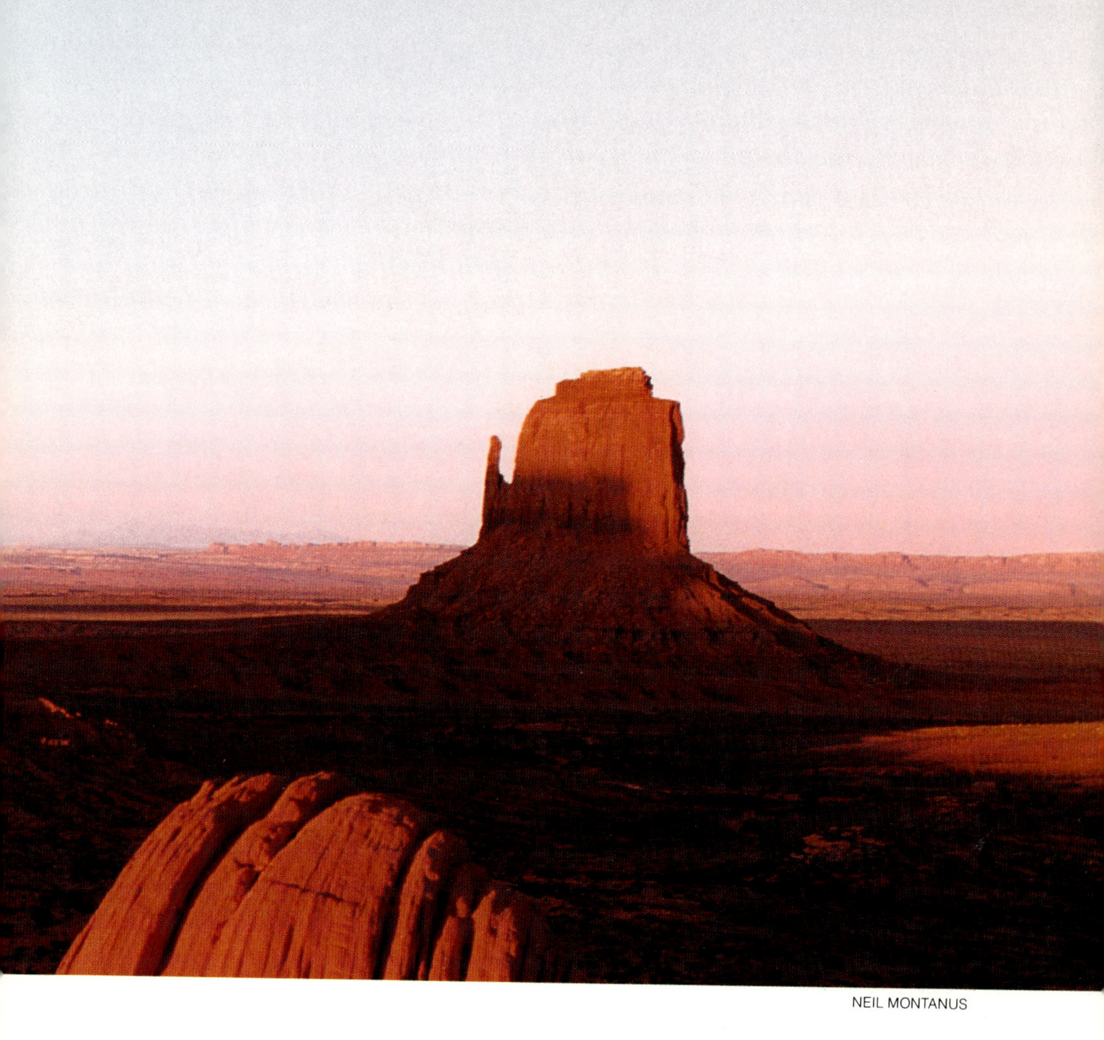

NEIL MONTANUS

The book has two parts—a text portion and a Data Sheet section. The text explains what you'll want to know about selecting the right film, exposing it properly, having it processed, and storing it. The Data Sheet section gives you details for each film, such as film speed, sizes available, recommended filters, reciprocity data, and film characteristics. The information here will help you make photographs that you will be proud to show to your friends.

For comprehensive information on professional roll and sheet films, you may want to purchase KODAK Publications No. E-77, *KODAK Color Films and Papers for Professionals,* and No. F-5, *KODAK Professional Black-and-White Films.* These books are available at stores that sell photographic products. In most countries outside the United States, Kodak books are usually sold in bookstores.

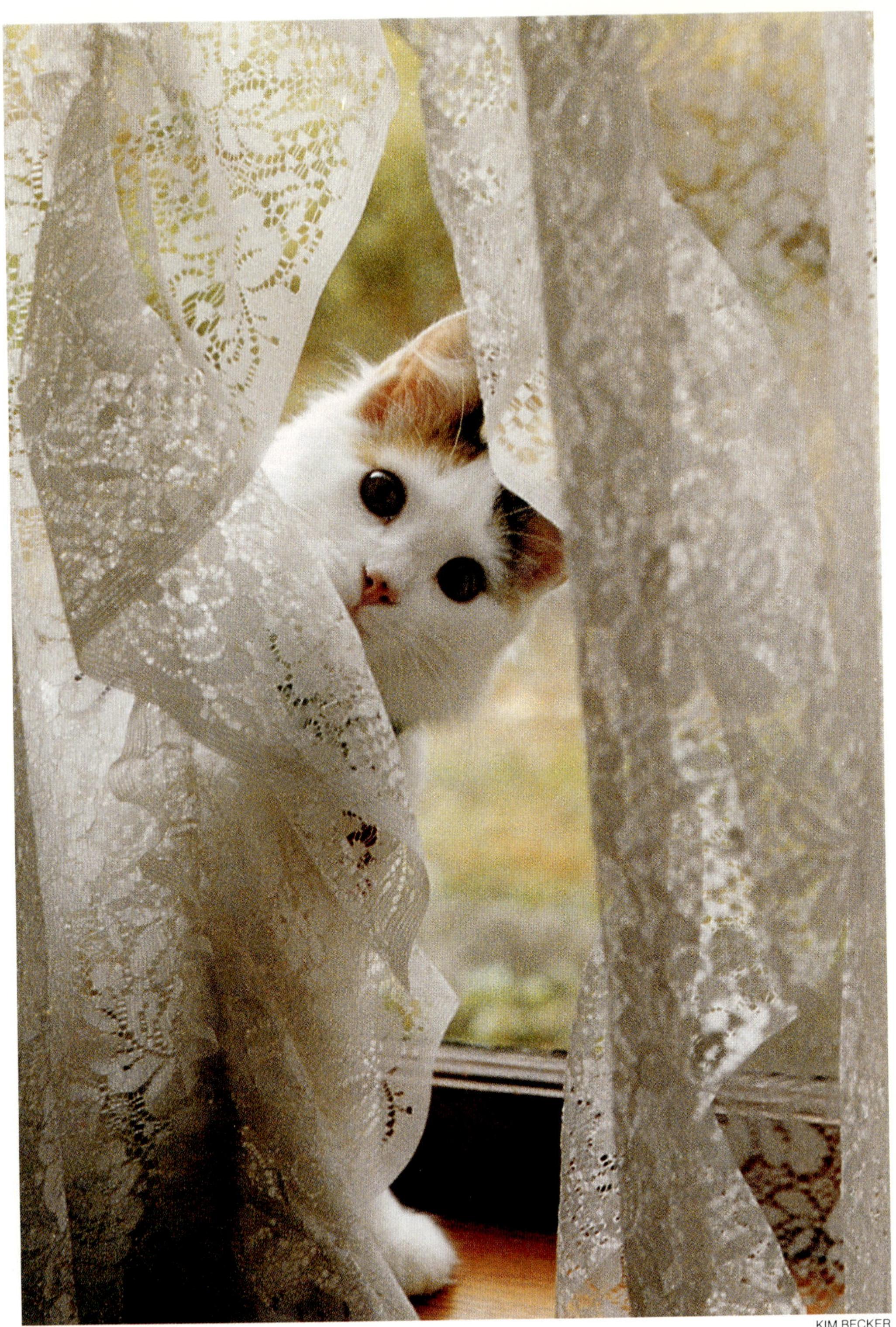

KIM BECKER

KODACOLOR GOLD 200 Film

# CONTENTS



---

Front cover photo by Don Cochran
KODAK EKTACHROME 64 Film

KODAK Publication No. AF-1

Second Edition, 1990 printing

Library of Congress Catalog Card Number 90-80634
ISBN 0-87985-660-2

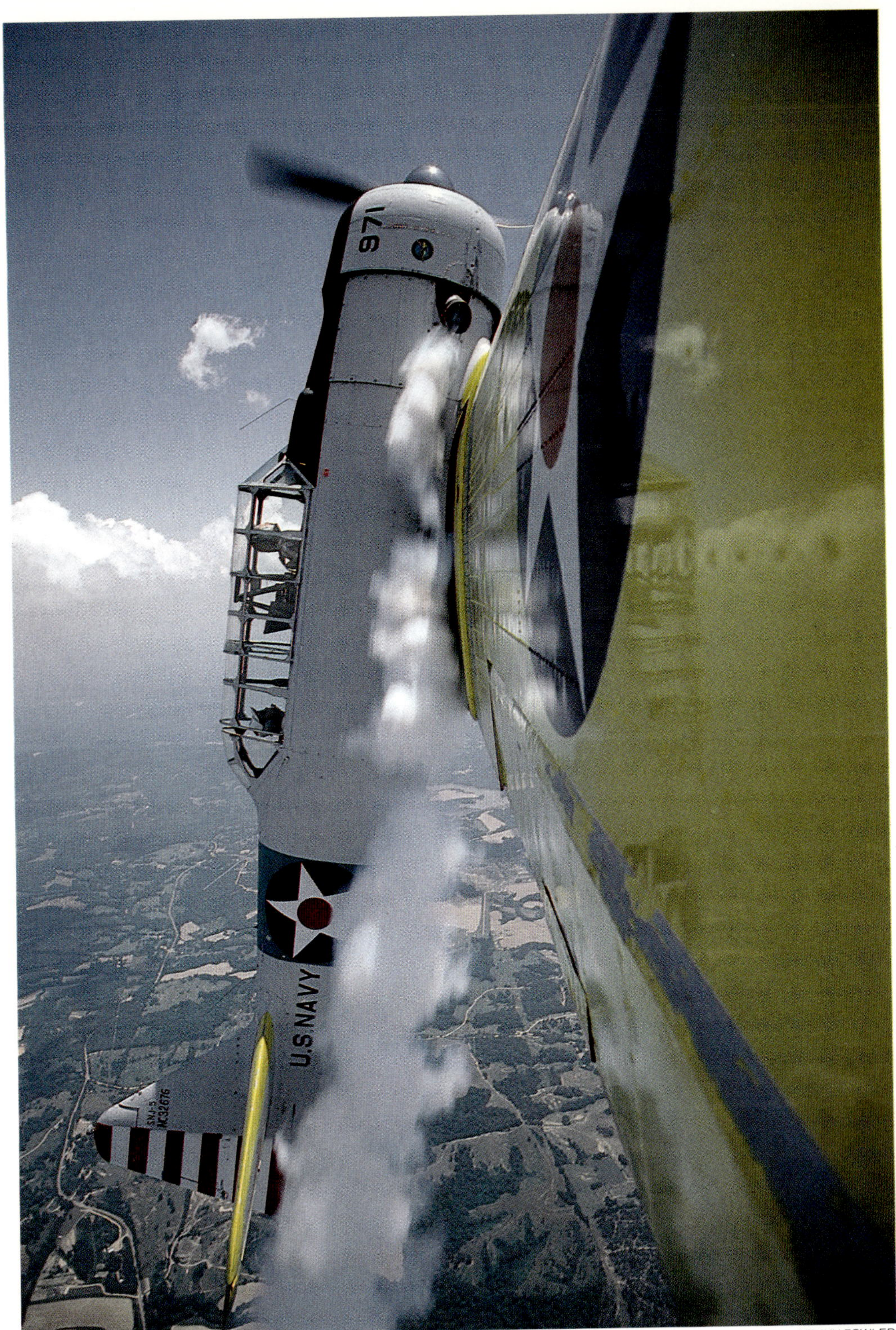


BENNY FOWLER

KODACHROME 64 Film (Daylight)

# CHOOSING A FILM

Your first consideration in selecting a film is the type of pictures you want—color prints, color slides, or black-and-white prints. Kodak makes several 35 mm films with different characteristics for each type of picture. The kind of pictures each film produces is printed on the carton. You can also obtain other kinds of pictures from your negatives, slides, or prints through processing labs (see page 52). The information in this book will help you select the best film for your needs.

Kodak 135 films are wound on spools and loaded into magazines. These films are 35 mm wide and have no backing paper. They are available in 12-, 24-, or 36-exposure lengths.

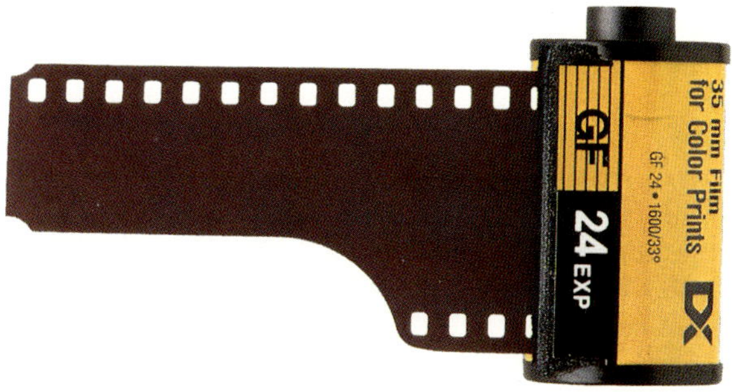


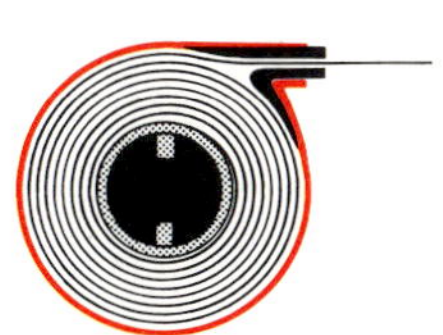

**A 135 magazine.** The illustration on the right is a cross-section view of a magazine loaded with film.

## DX ELECTRONIC FILM CODING

Electronically readable codes known as DX codes are printed on most popular Kodak 35 mm films and magazines. These codes enable many 35 mm cameras to perform certain functions automatically. These cameras set the camera exposure system for the speed of the film. They may also sense the length of each roll and signal the user to rewind the film after the last exposure, or trigger the camera to rewind automatically. They may be able to adjust the exposure system for over- and underexposure tolerances, depending on the exposure latitude of the film. For example, most color-negative films have wide exposure latitude, and color-slide films have narrower latitude. The information that the camera obtains from the DX codes may be displayed in the viewfinder or in a window on the camera body. Magazines and most film cartons for coded films have the designation "DX."

With many cameras, a carefully positioned line of print on the film magazine—identifying film type, film speed, and number of exposures—will show through a window in the camera back. You can then see whether or not the camera is loaded with film and see what type of film is in the camera.

Electronic coding of 35 mm film magazines is called "camera auto sensing," or CAS. This code looks like an abbreviated checkerboard and acts as a miniature electronic circuit board. It appears on the magazine surface as two rows of bright metal or insulated patches that line up with electrical probes in the camera. What any particular camera does with the information on the magazine depends on what the camera manufacturer designs the camera to do. See your camera manual.

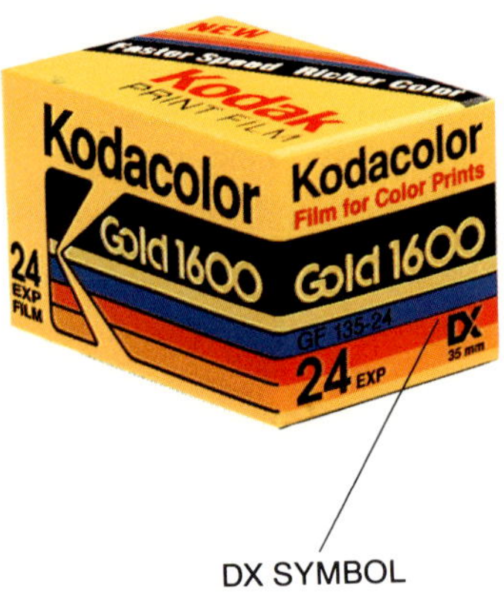


DX SYMBOL

A bar code on the film magazine and latent-image bar codes that are visible on the film after processing are designed to help the photofinisher. These codes make it easier for photofinishers to sort, process, and print films. This helps to shorten handling time, minimize errors, and improve finished picture quality for increased productivity and better service to customers.

You can use DX-encoded 35 mm films in 35 mm cameras that do not sense codes. Be sure to set the camera for the correct ISO film speed; also set (or keep track of) the number of exposures in the magazine.

Some compact automatic (non-single-lens-reflex) cameras will not read the DX codes for very-high-speed or low-speed films, and will not expose them correctly. See your camera manual or write to the camera manufacturer to find out the range of speeds your camera can read and expose correctly.

**ELECTRONICALLY READABLE CODES**
**FOR *KODAK* 35 mm FILM AND MAGAZINES**

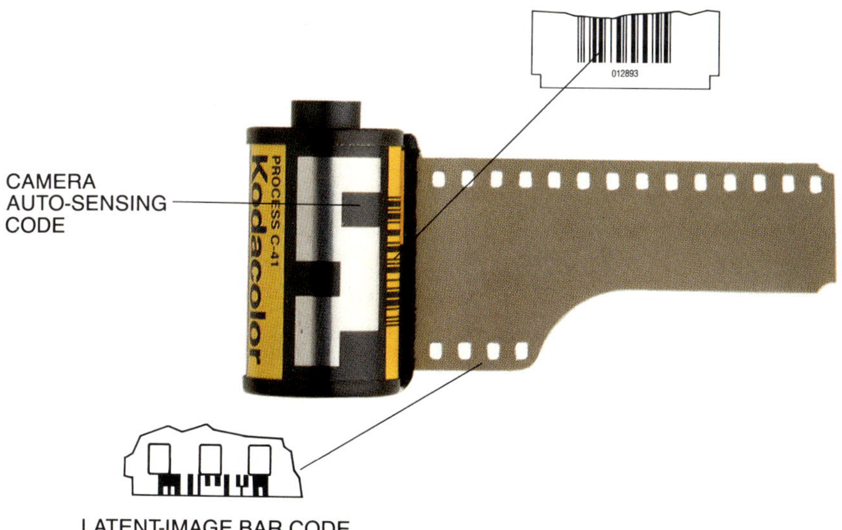


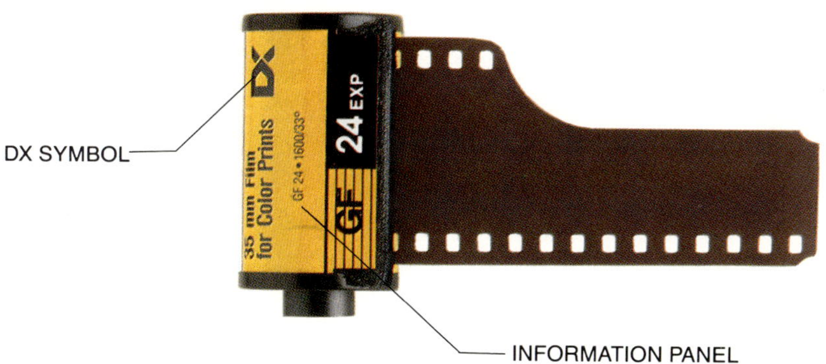


DX codes and the bar code on the film magazine are electronically readable codes that are included on most popular Kodak 35 mm films and magazines. A bar code on the film magazine and latent-image bar codes that are visible on the film after processing are designed to help the photofinisher. Films with the codes are packaged in boxes bearing the symbol "DX."

# CHOOSING A FILM

Each Kodak film is designed specifically to produce only one kind of picture—color prints, color slides, or black-and-white prints. Most film cartons tell you the kind of pictures that each particular film makes. (For the sizes available, see pages 116–119.) Color films give you a great deal of versatility; you can obtain color prints from slide film, color slides from print film, and black-and-white prints from both. See page 52.

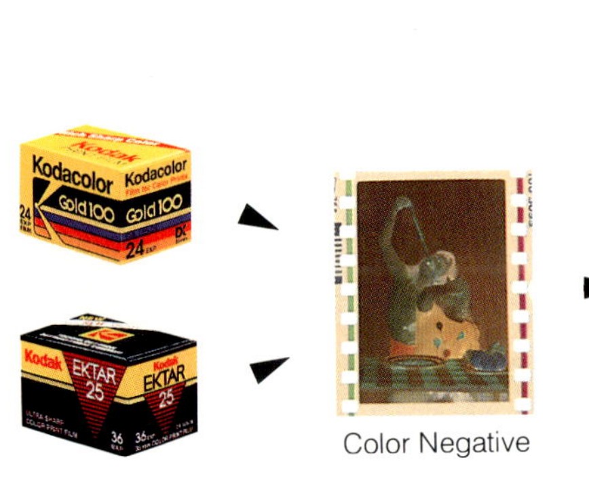


Color Negative

KODACOLOR GOLD and KODAK EKTAR Films are for color prints.

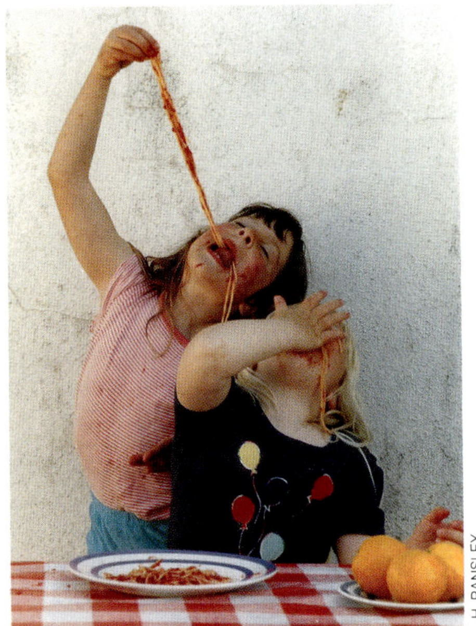


Color Print

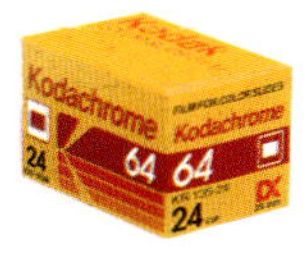


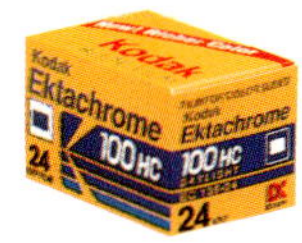


KODACHROME 25, 40, 64, and 200 Films, and KODAK EKTACHROME 50 HC, 100 HC, 160, 200, 400, and P800/1600 Films are for color slides.

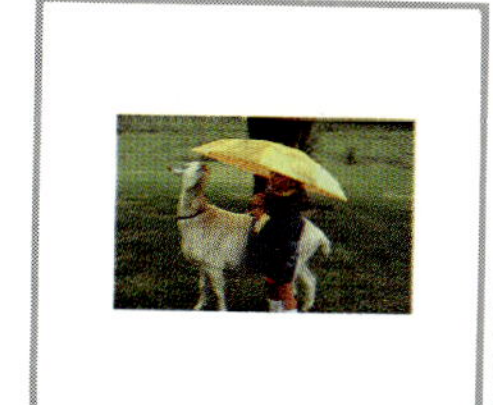

LINDA NEWBURY

Color Slide

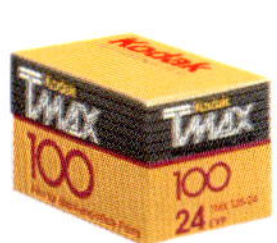


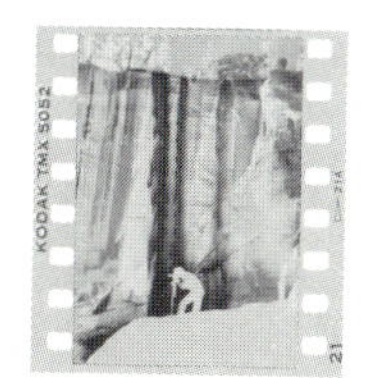

Black-and-White Negative

KODAK PLUS-X Pan, TRI-X Pan, and T-MAX Professional Films are for black-and-white prints. Other black-and-white films for special purposes are described on page 61.

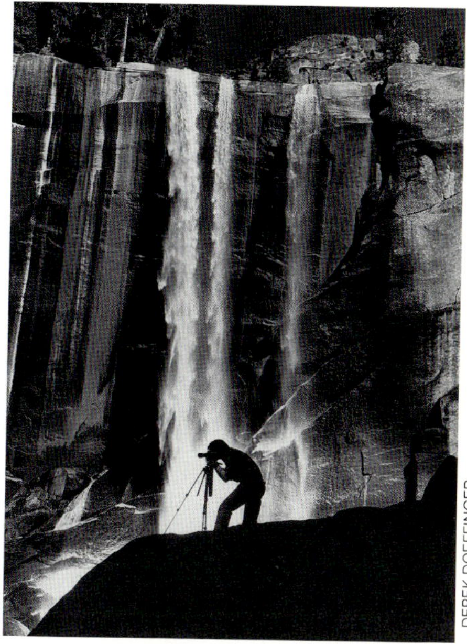

DEREK DOEFFINGER

Black-and-White Print

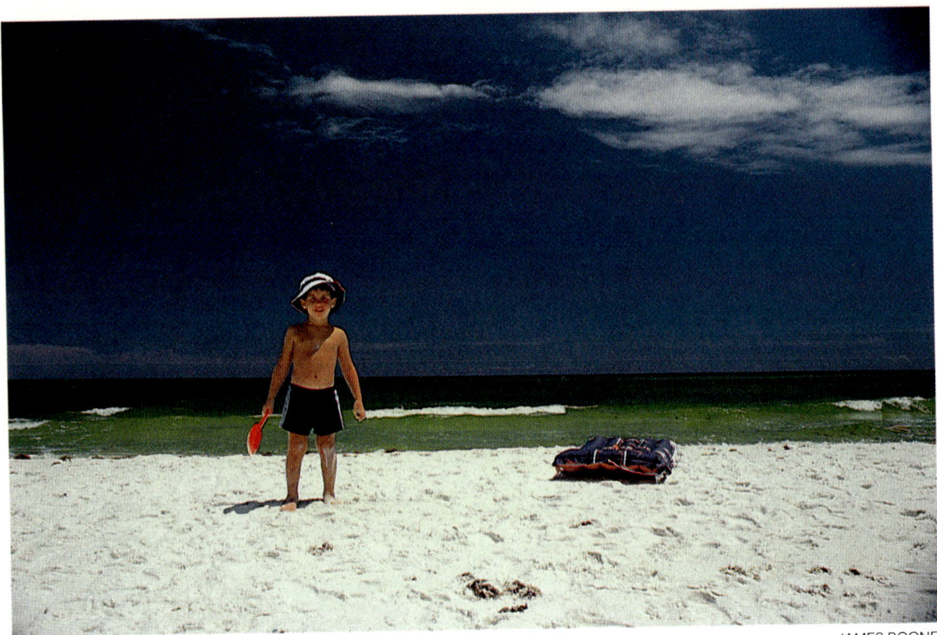

KODACHROME Film

JAMES BOONE

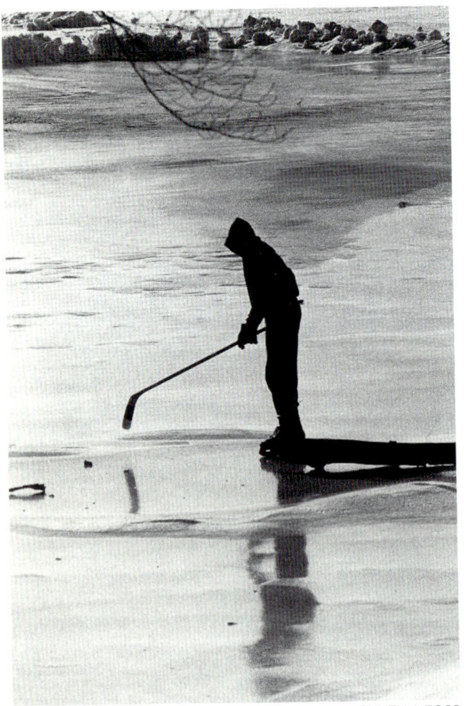

KODAK T-MAX 400 Professional Film

CYNTHIA FOSS

**To choose a 35 mm color film—** You'll want to know (in addition to the kind of pictures it makes) the film speed and the type of light source for which the film is balanced. Also, you'll want to have some idea of the color quality and the definition (see page 49) of the pictures it produces. If you do your own darkroom work, you'll want to know if you can process the film yourself.

**To choose a 35 mm black-and-white film—** Selecting a black-and-white film is simpler than selecting a color film. Unless you need one of the films designed for special purposes, your main considerations are film speed and the quality of definition you'll get in your pictures. (Definition is explained on page 67.)

# *KODAK* COLOR FILMS

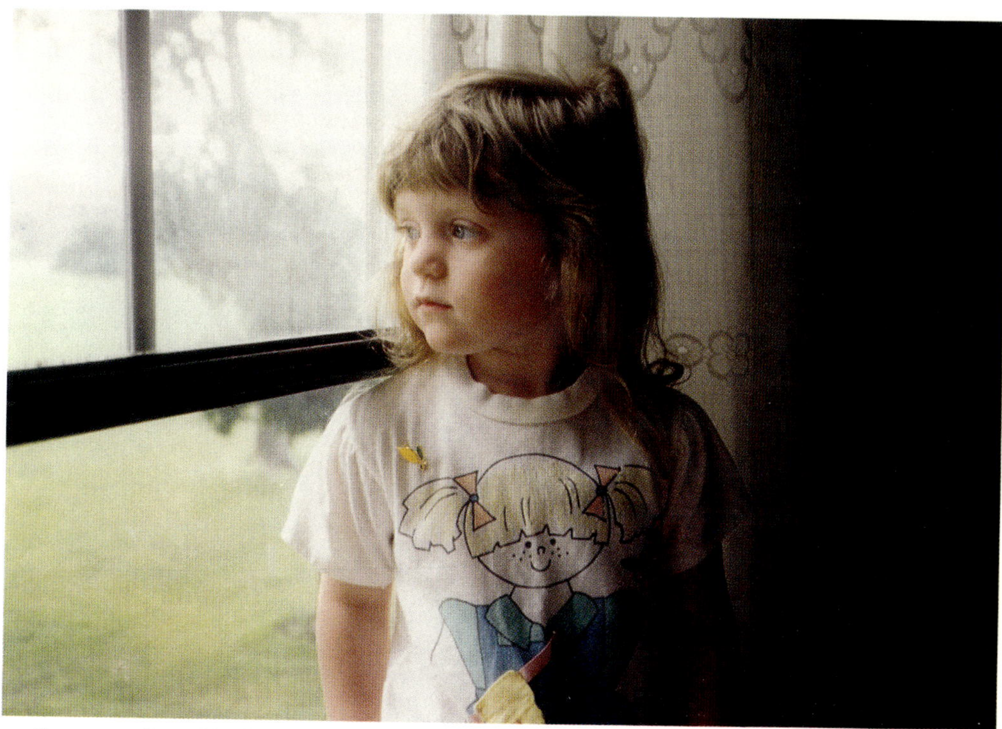

KODACOLOR GOLD 200 Film JONI GUSTAFSSO

You can use KODACOLOR GOLD 200 Film for some existing-light scenes that aren't too dimly lighted. It offers twice the speed of KODACOLOR GOLD 100 Film.

Color films for still cameras are available in two general types. One kind produces color negatives, which are primarily used to make color prints; the other kind produces color slides.

In color negatives, all the tones and colors of the original scene are reversed: Light tones are recorded as dark tones, dark tones are recorded as light tones, and the colors are the complementaries of the colors in the scene. Kodak color-negative films have built-in masks that help improve the quality of prints made from them. These masks give the negatives an overall light orange-tan color cast. All the color relationships are properly reproduced when the negatives are printed on color photographic paper. You can also have color slides made from your color negatives; see "Prints or Slides from Your Negatives, Prints, or Slides" on page 52.

The second kind of color film gives you color slides. During processing, the image on the film is reversed from a negative to a positive to produce a color slide or transparency that you can project onto a screen or look at with a viewer or an illuminator. Your film is processed, mounted, and returned to you as slides (or as unmounted transparencies if you prefer). You can order prints or duplicate slides from your slides or transparencies; see page 52.

Kodak color-negative and color-slide films are designed either for general use or for professional use. Most films for general use are manufactured for the needs of photographers who take pictures for recreation, such as photo hobbyists and people who take only casual snapshots. These photographers often have the film in their cameras for relatively long periods at varying temperatures; they usually don't have the film processed as promptly as professional photographers do. Casual photographers usually buy smaller amounts of film; storage conditions are less significant than for the professional. General-use films produce excellent quality as long as you don't subject them to extreme temperature conditions and delays before exposure and processing. See the section on storage of Kodak films beginning on page 102.

The names of most Kodak color films for professional applications include the word "professional." Professional films suit the needs and working habits of professional photographers, who require greater precision for commercial photography, process their film soon after exposure, and usually purchase large amounts of film at one time. To achieve this precision and meet these needs, professional films require refrigerated storage, prompt exposure, and prompt processing.

The most important difference between films for general use and those for professional use is the more rigid requirements for storing and handling professional films after the film leaves the factory.

You'll find a comprehensive table of condensed information for Kodak color films on page 116.

## FILMS FOR COLOR PRINTS

The most important considerations in selecting a film for color prints are film speed and definition. Film speed refers to the sensitivity of the film to light; it is described in greater detail on page 81. Definition refers to sharpness and graininess characteristics, and is discussed on page 49.

Kodak manufactures two families of 35 mm color-negative films for nonprofessional use. The family of KODACOLOR GOLD Films offers dramatic improvements over earlier KODACOLOR Films in speed, grain, and sharpness. The ISO speeds of the four films are included in the film names—KODACOLOR GOLD 100, KODACOLOR GOLD 200, KODACOLOR GOLD 400, and KODACOLOR GOLD 1600 Films.

A new family of color-negative films has been introduced by Kodak. They are KODAK EKTAR 25, EKTAR 125, and EKTAR 1000 Films. These films, designed for the advanced amateur photographer, set new standards for sharpness and clarity in their speed classes. They offer an exceptional means of creative expression for 35 mm camera owners who are avid photo hobbyists.

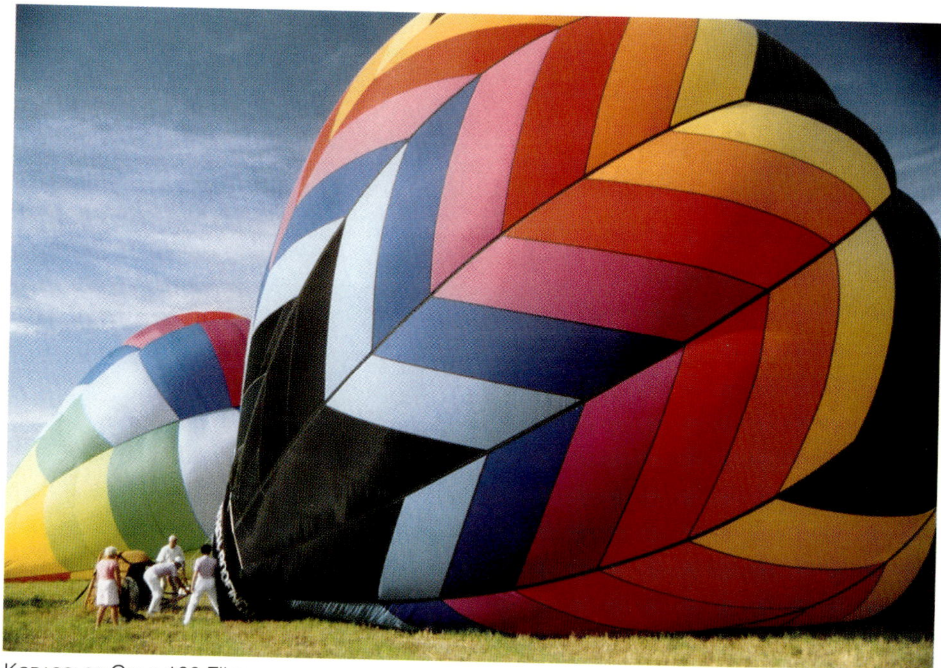

KODACOLOR GOLD 100 Film

JOAN KEROSKY

KODACOLOR GOLD 100 Film is an excellent general-purpose color-negative film when you want superior image quality. The speed is well suited for bright daylight as well as flash subjects.

**KODACOLOR GOLD 100 Film** is the sharpest color-negative film in the family of KODACOLOR GOLD Films. It features extremely fine grain and extremely high sharpness, which provide exquisite detail in prints and allow a high degree of enlargement. Color accuracy is unsurpassed. This film is excellent for general picture-taking when you want maximum image quality.

KODACOLOR GOLD 100 Film has a medium speed of ISO 100 and is intended for exposure to daylight or electronic flash. The speed is well suited for general lighting conditions, as well as for beach and snow scenes in sunlight. The film has wide exposure latitude, which produces satisfactory results even with moderate over- or underexposure. It is also available in 120-size rolls.

**KODACOLOR GOLD 200 Film,** with a medium speed of ISO 200, offers most of the qualities of KODACOLOR GOLD 100 Film but with twice the speed. The film has high sharpness and extremely fine grain. Its superb color rendition and contrast are similar to those of KODACOLOR GOLD 100 Film. The film is designed for picture-taking in daylight or with electronic flash. You can also use it for some existing-light scenes that aren't too dimly lighted.

The excellent photographic characteristics and speed of KODACOLOR GOLD 200 Film make it the ideal multi-purpose film. You can also use it when you want to stop subject movement, use zoom or telephoto lenses, or require more depth of field under relatively bright conditions. The film features wide exposure latitude. It's also available in 110 and 126 cartridges.

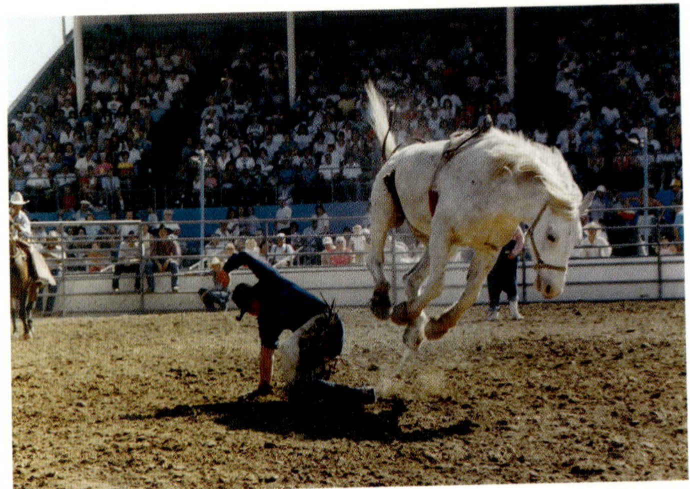

KODACOLOR GOLD 400 Film is an excellent high-speed film that lets you take pictures that would be impossible with a slower-speed film.

KODACOLOR GOLD 400 Film

DICK KREGER

**KODACOLOR GOLD 400 Film** is a high-speed (ISO 400) film for photographing fast action or low-light situations. It incorporates KODAK T-GRAIN Emulsions, which allow it to offer both high speed and extremely fine grain. Use this film in daylight, with electronic flash, or in existing light.

KODACOLOR GOLD 400 Film is intended primarily for situations in which you need high film speed. It extends your picture-taking opportunities and lets you take pictures that would be impossible with a slower-speed film. For example, you can use it to photograph subjects without flash by using the natural existing light, to stop action, or to use zoom or telephoto lenses in reduced light levels.

KODACOLOR GOLD 400 Film provides excellent flesh tones and rich color saturation. Special sensitizing characteristics let you obtain pleasing pictures under a variety of light sources, such as household tungsten lights or fluorescent light, without using filters over the camera lens. This film offers wide exposure latitude. It is also available in 110 cartridges.

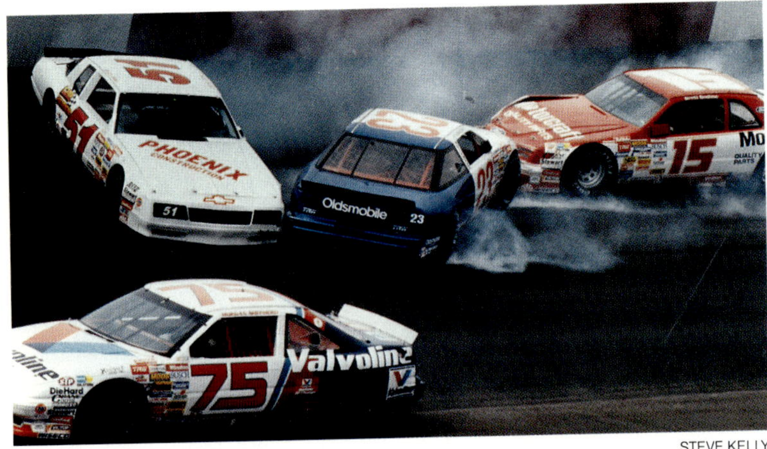


KODACOLOR GOLD 1600 Film

STEVE KELLY

KODACOLOR GOLD 1600 Film is a very-high-speed film that features the best color saturation of any 1600-speed color print film.

**KODACOLOR GOLD 1600 Film** is a very-high-speed (ISO 1600) film that features the best color saturation of any 1600-speed color-negative film. It incorporates KODAK T-GRAIN Emulsions, which permit a combination of very high speed and very fine grain. Designed for low-light and fast-action situations, it is also an excellent choice for hand-holding telephoto lenses, or for subjects that require good depth of field and high shutter speeds.

This film is color-balanced for daylight or electronic flash. You can also use it for scenes that are lighted by mixed light sources. It features better color reproduction under tungsten illumination than other manufacturers' comparable-speed films.

This film is intended for moderately low degrees of enlargement, such as 8 x 10-inch prints, from properly exposed negatives.

You can send KODACOLOR Films to photofinishing labs for processing and printing; or if you're a darkroom enthusiast, you can process these films and print the negatives on KODAK EKTACOLOR Papers.

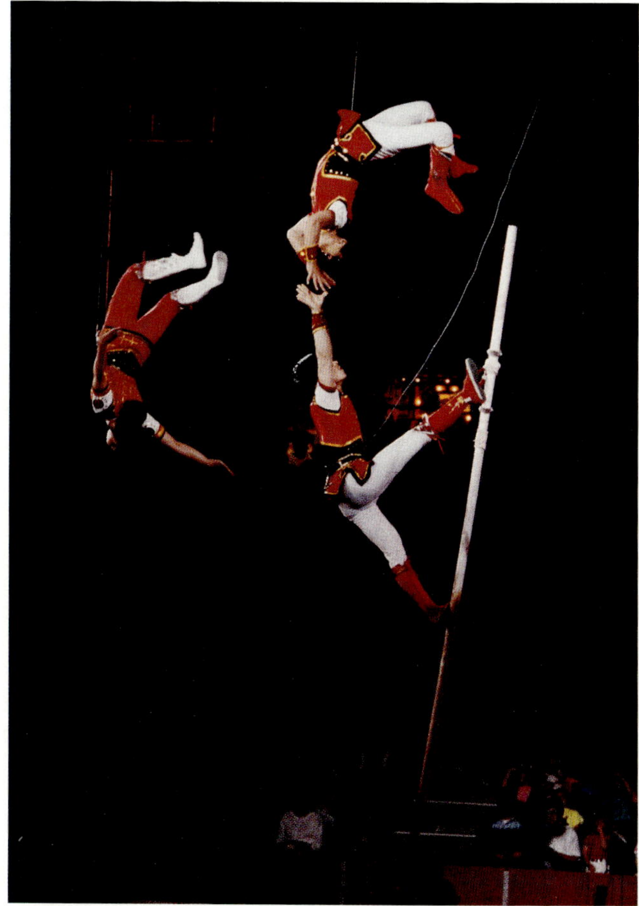

KODACOLOR GOLD 1600 Film — ERV SCHROEDER

Designed for low-light and fast-action situations, KODACOLOR GOLD 1600 Film allows shutter speeds fast enough for hand-holding telephoto lenses. Ringling Bros. and Barnum & Bailey Circus

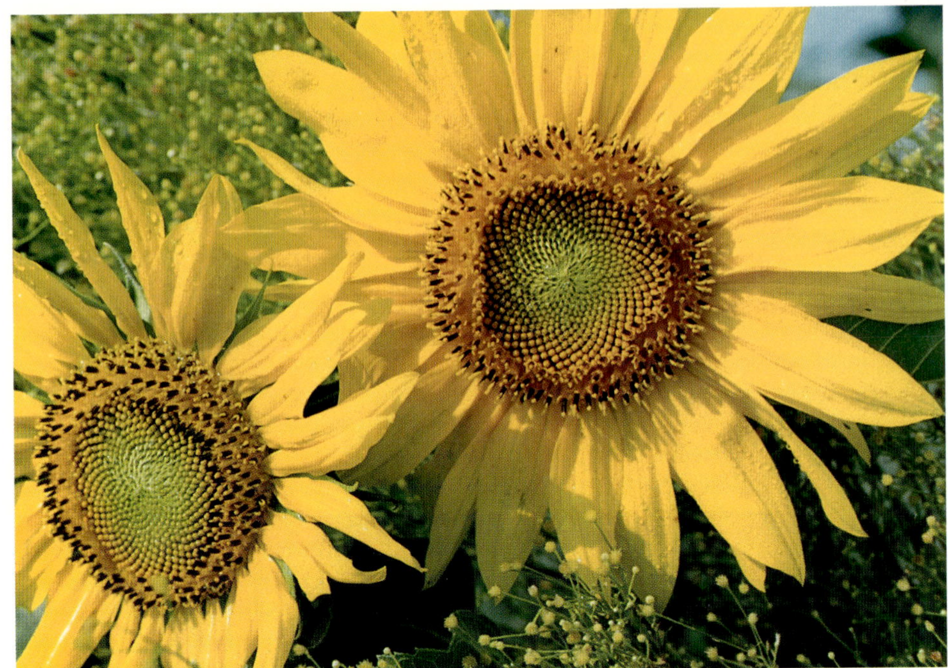

KODAK EKTAR 25 Film

STEVE KELLY

A technically advanced 35 mm film, KODAK EKTAR 25 Film allows an extremely high degree of enlargement with superb clarity.

**KODAK EKTAR 25 Film,** a member of the new family of KODAK EKTAR Films, is a technically advanced 35 mm color-negative film. It offers micro-fine grain, extremely high sharpness, and very high resolving power, which allow an extremely high degree of enlargement. It is designed for exposure with daylight or electronic flash.

This is the sharpest 35 mm color-print film ever made. It combines KODAK T-GRAIN Emulsion technology with new color-coupler chemistry, allowing you to produce very big enlargements with a level of sharpness and clarity never before possible from small color negatives. It is especially useful for portraiture, still lifes, landscapes, and any subjects that require the rendering of fine detail.

EKTAR 25 Film is designed for use in 35 mm single-lens-reflex cameras that allow you to set the film speed manually or that will *correctly* set the film speed automatically from the DX code on the magazine. (Some automatic 35 mm cameras do not read the DX code for ISO 25 film and will underexpose it.) This film requires more accurate exposure than other color-negative films.

A professional version of this film is available in 135-36 and 120 sizes.

**KODAK EKTAR 125 Film** is a medium-speed film that offers finer grain and higher sharpness than any other comparable-speed color-negative film, and yields enlargements of extremely high quality. Like the other two EKTAR Films, it incorporates T-GRAIN Emulsions. It has micro-fine grain, extremely high sharpness, and very high resolving power, which allow a very high degree of enlargement.

EKTAR 125 Film is balanced for exposure with daylight or electronic flash. You can also obtain pleasing results under moderately bright existing-light sources without filters. It has moderately wide exposure latitude, and gives satisfactory prints from negatives exposed at speeds from ISO 32 to ISO 250.

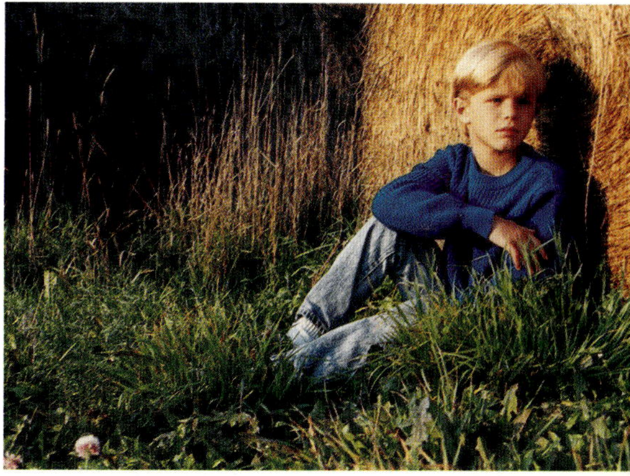

KODAK EKTAR 125 Film STEVE KELLY

KODAK EKTAR 125 Film is a medium-speed film that offers finer grain and higher sharpness than any other comparable-speed color-print film.

**KODAK EKTAR 1000 Film** has finer grain and higher color saturation than any other color-negative film in its speed class. It has very fine grain, medium sharpness, and medium resolving power. Its very high speed of ISO 1000 allows you to use higher shutter speeds to stop action or hand-hold telephoto lenses, or small apertures for increased depth of field.

The film is designed for exposure with daylight or electronic flash, but its improved sensitivity to tungsten light will provide pleasing results without filters in situations where the lighting is difficult to meter. Its wide exposure latitude allows you to produce satisfactory prints from negatives exposed at speeds from ISO 125 to ISO 2000.

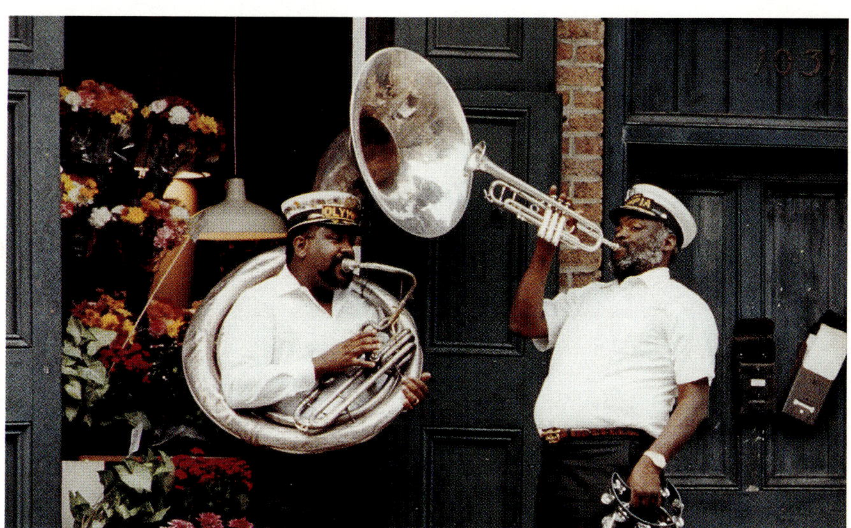

KODAK EKTAR 1000 Film STEVE KELLY

KODAK EKTAR 1000 Film offers improved, more saturated color than any other color-negative film in its speed range for brighter, clearer prints.

## FILMS FOR COLOR SLIDES

Kodak offers a variety of color-slide films with different characteristics so that you can select the film that meets your needs for the type of pictures you want to take. The most obvious differences in film characteristics are film speed and color balance. Color balance refers to the color quality of the light source for which the film is designed. See the discussion of color balance on page 36. Some of the other characteristics, such as color rendition, sharpness, and graininess, are more subtle—a critical comparison is often required to see the differences between films. Color balance, film speed, and personal preference are usually the most important factors in selecting a color-slide film. The following descriptions will help you choose a film to suit your needs.

**KODACHROME 25 Film (Daylight)** is a popular color-slide film noted for extremely high sharpness and extremely fine grain. The film features excellent color quality—pleasing flesh tones; clean whites and yellows; bright reds, greens, and blues. It provides good highlight and shadow detail. This film has a speed of ISO 25, and is for use in bright daylight or with electronic flash when you want the best possible image quality.

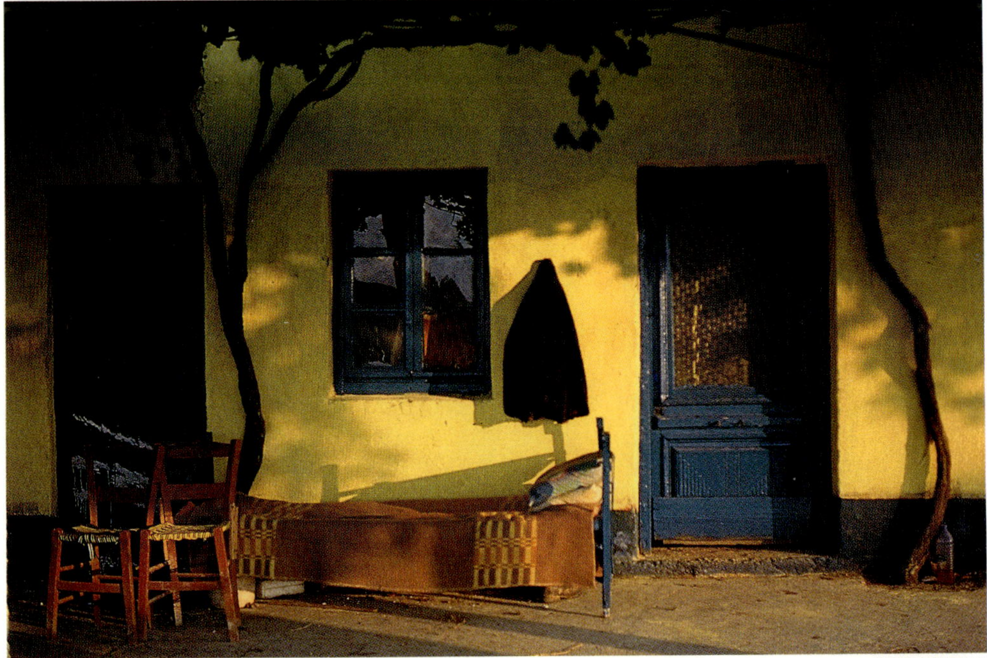

KODACHROME 25 Film (Daylight) JONATHAN RAISZ

KODACHROME 25 Film is a favorite for color slides because of its excellent color quality, extremely high sharpness, and extremely fine grain.

**KODACHROME 64 Film (Daylight)** is a good choice for all-around picture-taking when you want color slides. Its medium speed (ISO 64) lets you use higher shutter speeds or smaller lens openings under normal lighting conditions than you can with KODACHROME 25 Film, and it extends your picture-taking capability on overcast days, in the shade, or in somewhat subdued lighting. The film produces excellent color rendition with rich, saturated colors—bright reds, greens, and blues; clean whites and yellows; vivid blue skies; and pleasing flesh tones. The film shows good highlight and shadow detail.

KODACHROME 64 Film is almost as sharp and fine-grained as KODACHROME 25 Film. At normal screen-viewing distances, most viewers can't see any difference in sharpness or graininess. KODACHROME 64 Film is for use in daylight or with electronic flash. It is also available in 126-size cartridges.

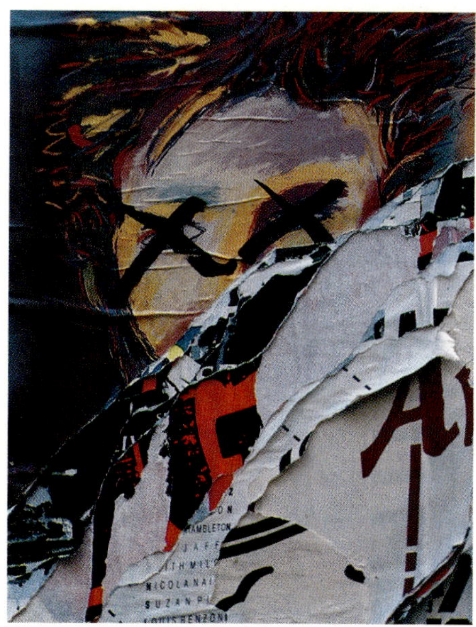

KODACHROME 64 Film (Daylight) SCOTT WEBB

KODACHROME 64 Film features excellent color rendition, and good highlight and shadow detail. Its medium speed (2½ times as fast as KODACHROME 25 Film) lets you use higher shutter speeds or smaller lens openings under normal lighting conditions, and extends picture-taking capability on overcast days, in the shade, or in subdued lighting.

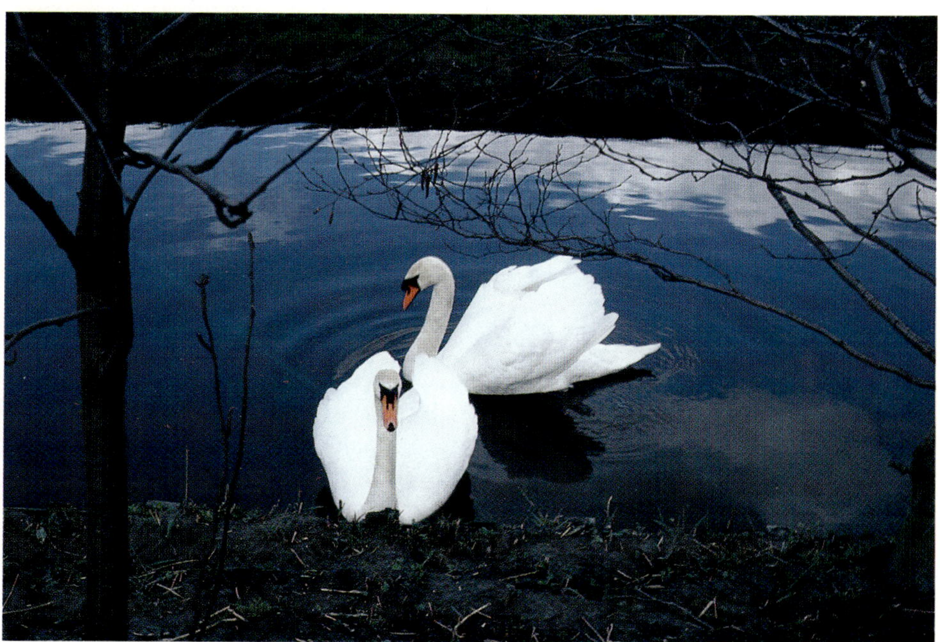

KODACHROME 64 Film (Daylight) FRANK VANDERWERF

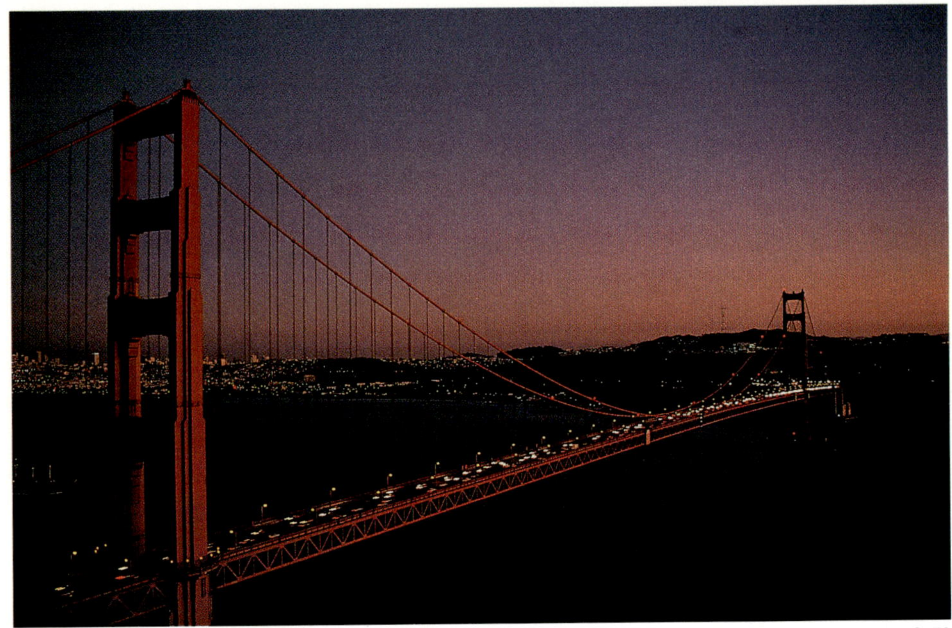

HERB JONES

KODACHROME 200 Film (Daylight)

KODACHROME 200 Film is the first KODACHROME Film with KODAK T-GRAIN Emulsion. With a speed almost three times as fast as that of KODACHROME 64 Film, it gives excellent results in many low-light situations.

**KODACHROME 200 Film (Daylight)** is the newest addition to the family of KODACHROME Films. It is the first KODACHROME Film with KODAK T-GRAIN Emulsions, and it features medium speed, fine grain, very high sharpness, and high resolving power. This film is designed for exposure with daylight or electronic flash, but you can also expose it with photolamps (3400 K) or tungsten illumination (3200 K) with filters.

With a speed almost three times as fast as that of KODACHROME 64 Film, KODACHROME 200 Film allows you to use smaller apertures for increased depth of field or higher shutter speeds for stopping action or hand-holding telephoto lenses. It gives excellent results in many low-light situations.

**KODACHROME 40 Film (Type A)** is designed for taking pictures with 3400 K photolamps. It has a speed of ISO 40 with this illumination. This film is valued for its excellent definition characteristics and its color rendition. The color balance of KODACHROME 40 Film and its snap, brilliance, and color fidelity make it an excellent film for making informal portraits, close-ups, and title slides, and for copying color originals. Its extremely high sharpness, extremely fine grain, and ability to record fine detail provide high-quality color slides. You can also take pictures in daylight if you use a No. 85 filter over your camera lens and expose the film at ISO 25.

Have your KODACHROME Films processed by a commercial lab. You can't process these films in your own darkroom; the process is highly complex and requires commercial photofinishing equipment.

**KODAK EKTACHROME 50 HC Film** is the newest member of the family of KODAK EKTACHROME Films. It offers very high sharpness and very fine grain, and produces vibrant colors similar to KODAK EKTACHROME 100 HC Film at a lower ISO speed. This film is designed for exposure with daylight or electronic flash. You can also expose it with photolamps (3400 K) or tungsten illumination (3200 K) with filters.

EKTACHROME 50 HC Film is a good choice for scenic photos, informal portraits, and colorful close-ups that show fine detail. It can be processed with other films in Process E-6 with no changes to the process.

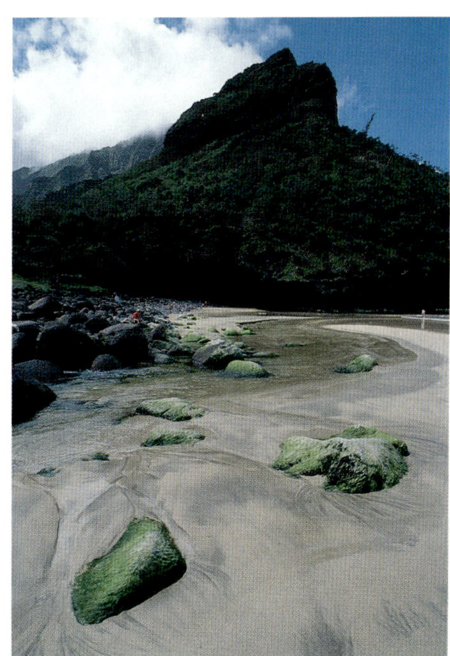

KODAK EKTACHROME 50HC Film JOHN GREEN

KODAK EKTACHROME 50HC Film, the newest member of the family of KODAK EKTACHROME Films, is a good choice for scenic photos.

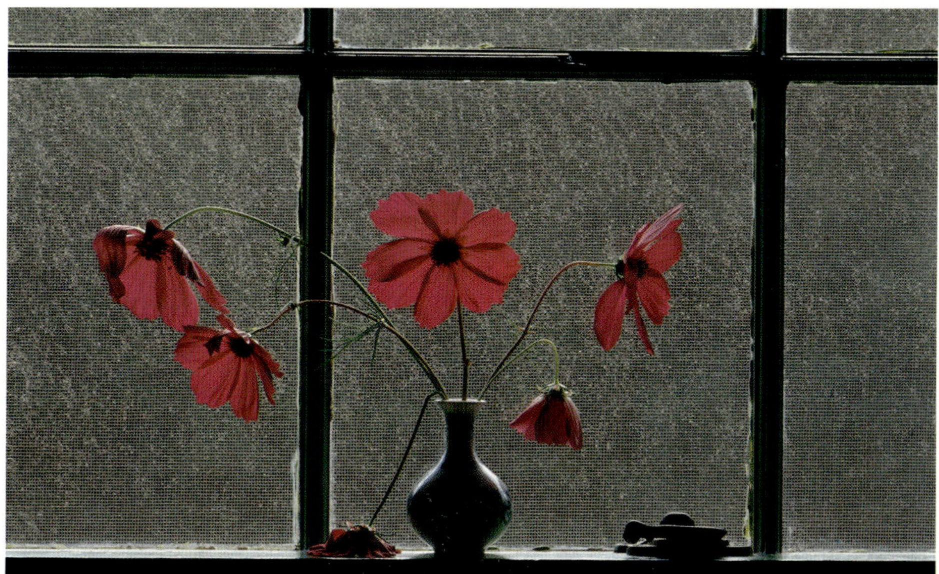

KODAK EKTACHROME 50HC Film DEREK DOEFFINGER

KODAK EKTACHROME 50HC Film produces vibrant colors similar to KODAK EKTACHROME 100HC Film at a lower ISO speed.

**KODAK EKTACHROME 100 HC Film** is a new medium-speed film that has higher color saturation than KODAK EKTACHROME 100 Film (Daylight), which it replaced. An excellent choice for both daylight and electronic-flash photography, it features very fine grain, very high sharpness, and high resolving power. This film accurately records colors while maintaining good neutrals and pleasing flesh tones.

If you compare this film with KODACHROME 64 Film, the KODACHROME Film is slightly sharper and finer-grained, but it's difficult to see the difference on the projection screen. EKTACHROME 100 HC Film provides higher speed while retaining high image quality.

Another feature of all KODAK EKTACHROME Films is that you can process them in your own darkroom or have a commercial lab process them.

A professional version of this film is available as KODAK EKTACHROME 100 PLUS Professional Film.

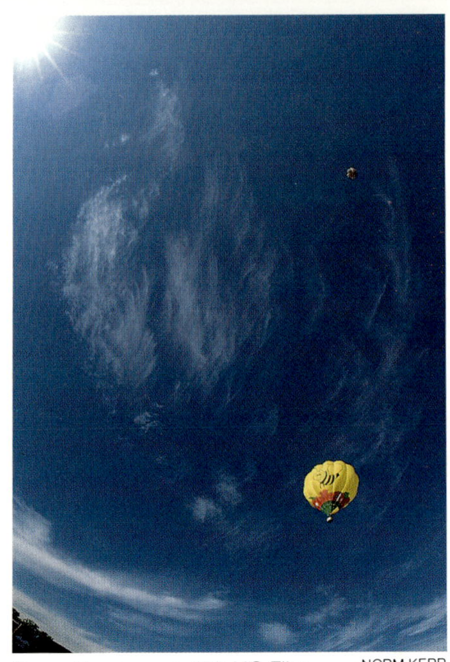

KODAK EKTACHROME 100 HC Film NORM KERR

An excellent choice for daylight and electronic-flash photography, KODAK EKTACHROME 100 HC Film gives rich vibrant colors.

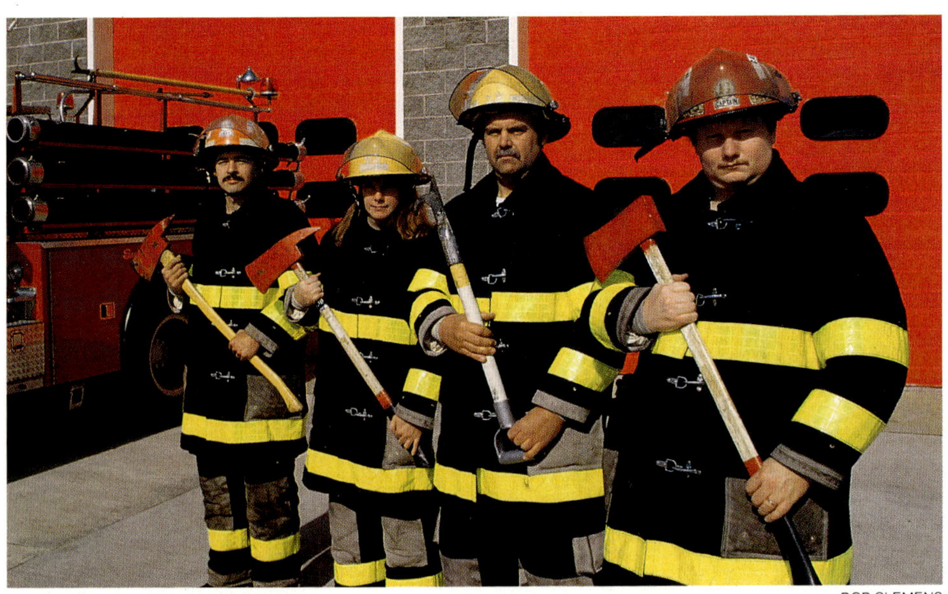

KODAK EKTACHROME 100 HC Film BOB CLEMENS

KODAK EKTACHROME 100 HC Film is an excellent choice for your slide shows; you can process all KODAK EKTACHROME Films in your own darkroom or have a commercial lab process them.

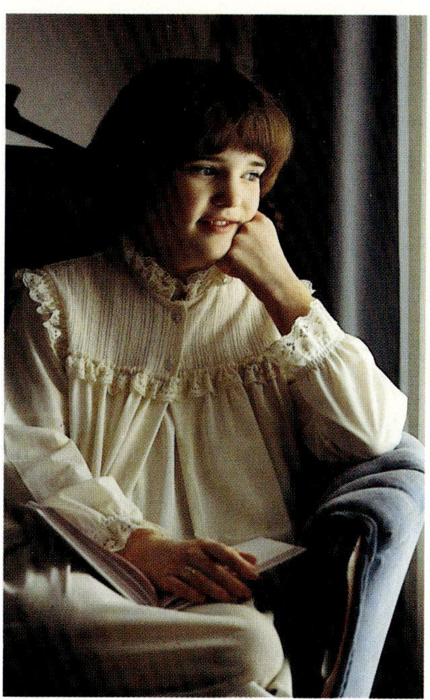

DON MAGGIO

KODAK EKTACHROME 200 Film is a good choice for taking color slides in the home by existing daylight. This film gives you very fine grain and pleasing color rendition as well as a fast film speed.

**KODAK EKTACHROME 200 Film (Daylight)** is a general-purpose color-slide film with twice the speed (ISO 200) of EKTACHROME 100 HC Film. It is a versatile film that lets you photograph under a wide range of lighting conditions from bright sunlight to existing light (if you have a relatively fast lens). It's also excellent for photographing subjects that require high shutter speeds or good depth of field, and for extending the flash distance range. It is designed for use with daylight or electronic flash.

EKTACHROME 200 Film is a good choice when you need a color-slide film with additional speed and very fine grain. It has grain nearly as fine as that of EKTACHROME 100 HC Film. The difference in graininess between the two films is usually not evident in projected slides viewed from a normal distance.

EKTACHROME 200 Film produces fine color quality with clean color separation between similar hues. Colors are slightly less saturated than those produced by EKTACHROME 100 HC Film.

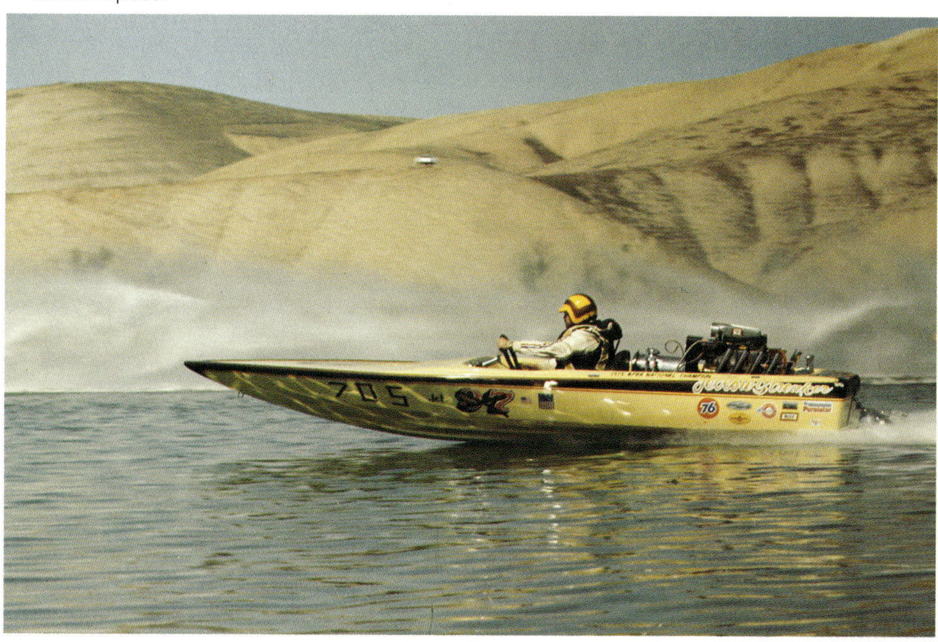


PETER GALES

When you want to photograph action in color slides and perhaps use a telephoto lens, a film with additional speed allows you to use the high shutter speeds you'll need. KODAK EKTACHROME 200 Film has the speed and high quality to give you excellent results.

**KODAK EKTACHROME 400 Film (Daylight)** is a high-speed film for use under lower light levels; for subjects that require good depth of field; and for stopping fast action in your pictures. Its high speed (ISO 400) lets you make hand-held shots when the lighting is dim (if your camera has an *f*/2 or faster lens). The film is good for making pictures with long telephoto lenses, which don't have large lens openings, or in situations where you need to use high shutter speeds to avoid the effects of camera motion.

The film is color-balanced for daylight or electronic flash. You can also use it to photograph subjects lighted by carbon-arc spotlights.

EKTACHROME 400 Film has high sharpness and fine grain, although the grain is not quite as fine as that of EKTACHROME 200 Film. The difference in graininess is not easily noticeable under normal projection conditions.

You can also expose this film at twice its normal speed (at EI 800) if you have the film push-processed. This lets you shoot pictures under dimmer lighting conditions or use faster shutter speeds to stop action. (You can also have other EKTACHROME Films push-processed for increased speed. See page 51.)

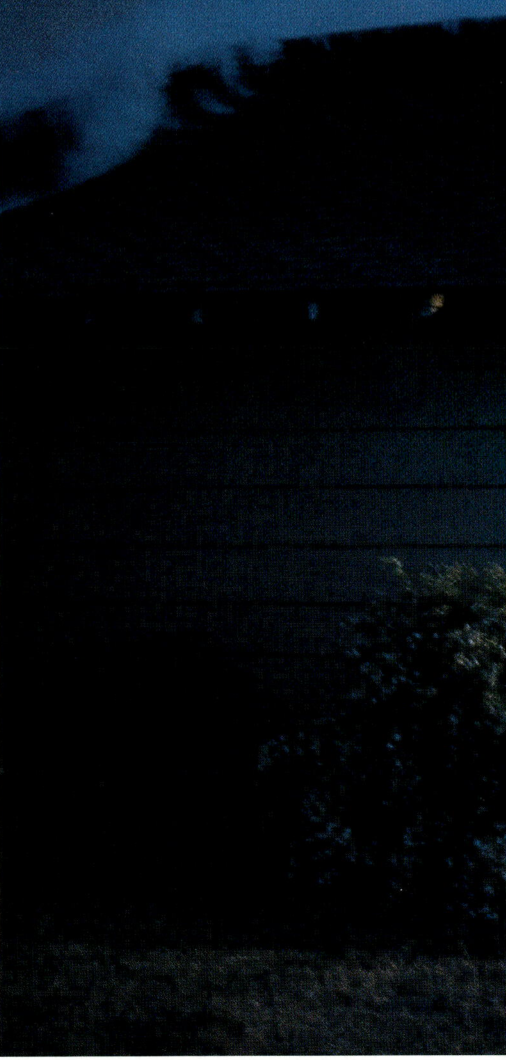

KODAK EKTACHROME 400 Film (Daylight)

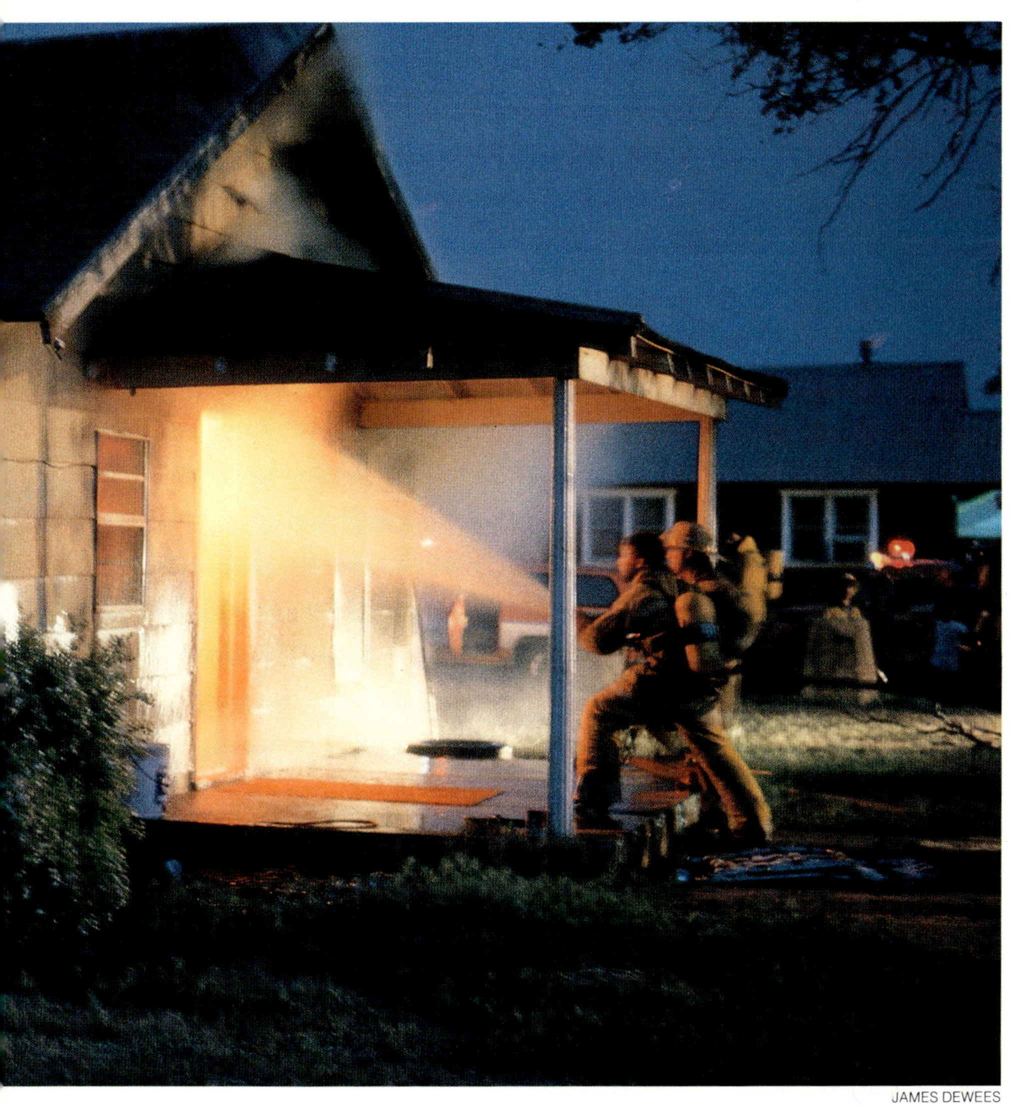

JAMES DEWEES

KODAK EKTACHROME 400 Film is a great film for taking color slides under existing-light conditions.

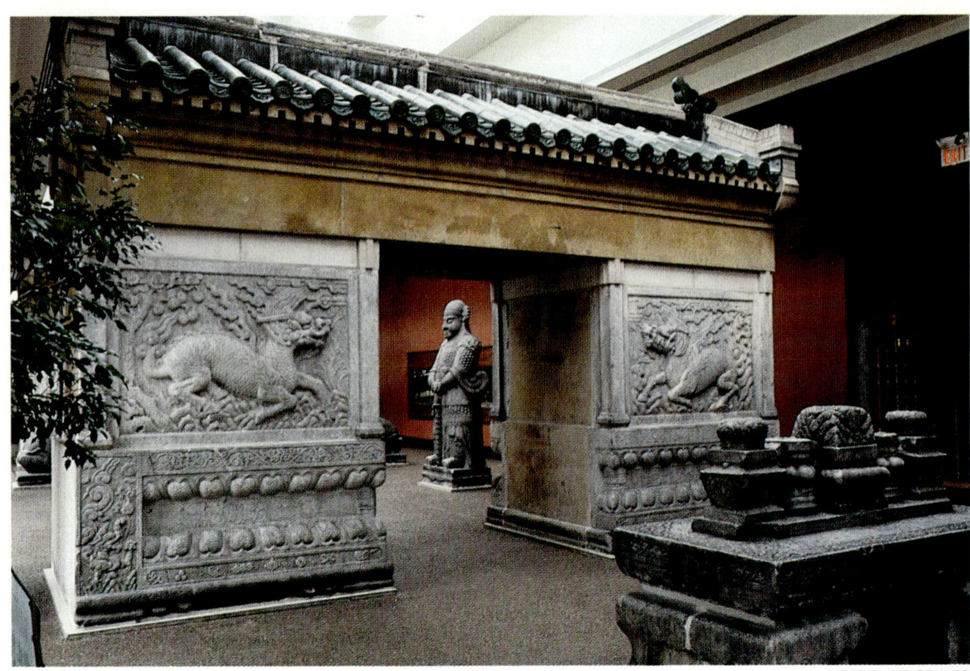

CAROLINE GRIMES

The photographer needed good depth of field with a hand-held camera in this museum dimly lighted by daylight. Exposing at EI 800 on KODAK EKTACHROME P800/1600 Professional Film (Daylight), which permitted a small lens opening, gave the desired effect.

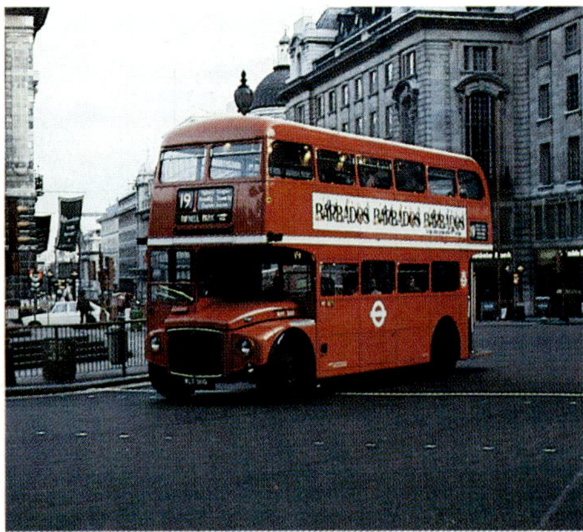


BRUCE NETT

The photographer used KODAK EKTACHROME P800/1600 Professional Film (Daylight) for the demanding conditions of stopping action in the dim lighting of late afternoon shadows. The film was exposed and processed at EI 1600.

**KODAK EKTACHROME P800/1600 Professional Film** is a color-slide film specifically designed for push-processing to a very high speed of EI 800 or EI 1600.* Although these speeds are recommended for best picture quality, you can obtain acceptable results when you expose the film at an even higher speed of EI 3200 or at a slower speed of EI 400. When you expose the film at EI 400, use a KODAK Color Compensating Filter CC10Y over the camera lens.

Use EKTACHROME P800/1600 Film whenever you need maximum speed in a color-slide film. It provides high sharpness and medium grain. Color rendition is similar to that of EKTACHROME 400 Film, but contrast is slightly higher. This film is color-balanced for daylight or electronic flash. You can also obtain good color rendition in slides taken of subjects illuminated by carbon-arc spotlights. EKTACHROME P800/1600 Film produces

*EI stands for Exposure Index. Use EI values in the same way as ISO speeds. See page 81 for more information.

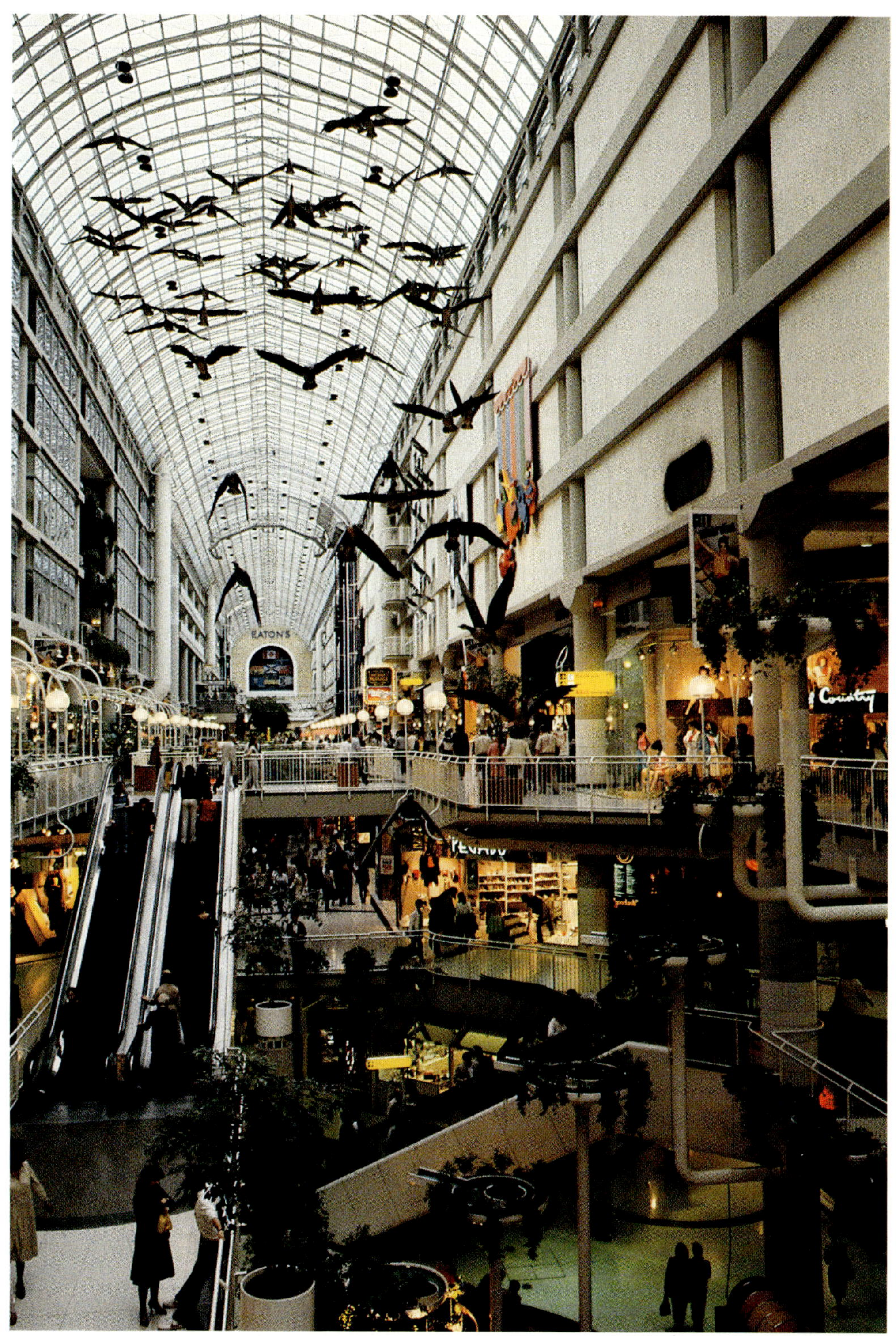


CAROLINE GRIMES

You can expose KODAK EKTACHROME P800/1600 Professional Film (Daylight) at very high speeds, making this film an outstanding choice for candid photography in dim existing lighting when you want color slides. The photographer used a film speed of EI 800 to take this picture.

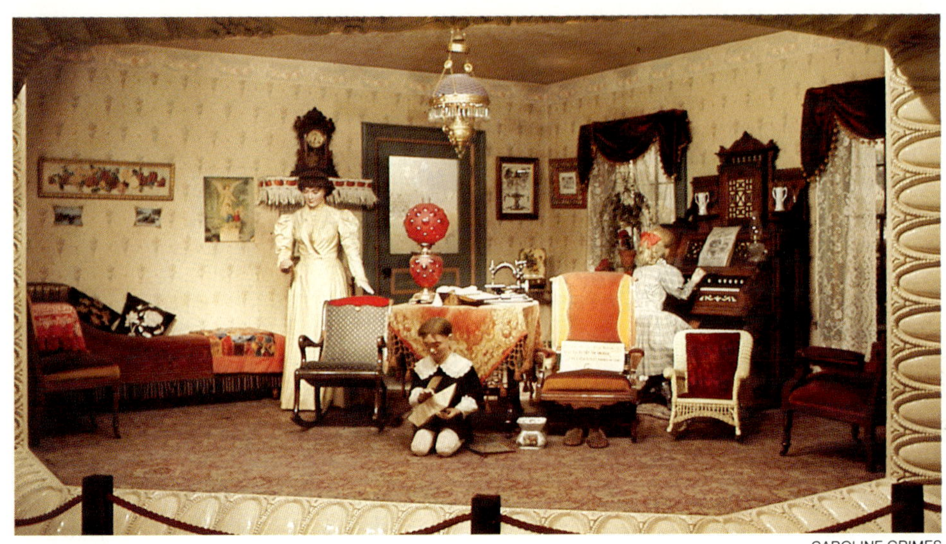

CAROLINE GRIMES

When the existing light comes predominantly from tungsten lamps, you'll obtain more natural-looking color slides if you use film balanced for tungsten light. KODAK EKTACHROME 160 Film (Tungsten). Museum of Science and Industry, Chicago, Illinois

acceptable results for noncritical purposes when you expose it to existing tungsten light. Slides made with tungsten illumination will have a yellow-red appearance, but many people find this pleasing.

EKTACHROME P800/1600 Film is an excellent choice for action and sports photography; for subjects in dim existing light; for photography with long-focal-length lenses that have small maximum apertures; or for using the smallest possible aperture for maximum depth of field. This film is also a good choice when you need to take flash pictures at extended subject distances.

Because EKTACHROME P800/1600 film is manufactured specifically for push processing, it provides significantly better quality at EI 800 and EI 1600 than that produced by push-processing EKTACHROME 400 Film to higher speeds. EKTACHROME P800/1600 Film has a higher maximum density (degree of blackness) to avoid the "smoky" shadow areas that other push-processed films may exhibit.

To tell labs how much to push-process a roll of EKTACHROME P800/1600 Film, indicate on the magazine the speed you used to expose the film, e.g., EI 400, 800, 1600, or 3200. A photo of the film magazine is on page 52. You must expose the entire roll at the same speed. If you plan to use the film at EI 3200, you should expose a test roll to see if the quality meets your requirements.

**KODAK EKTACHROME 160 Film (Tungsten)** is designed for exposure with tungsten lamps (3200 K) without filters. It gives excellent results with existing tungsten light, such as the light from household lamps. This film has excellent color rendition and sharpness. You can also use it to take pictures in daylight if you use a No. 85B filter over your camera lens and expose the film at ISO 100. EKTACHROME 160 Film distinguishes well between similar colors. Its color quality and sharpness are similar to those of EKTACHROME 200 Film (Daylight).

Under dim existing tungsten light, where you may need more film speed, you can expose this film at EI 320 and have it push-processed. See pages 51 and 52.

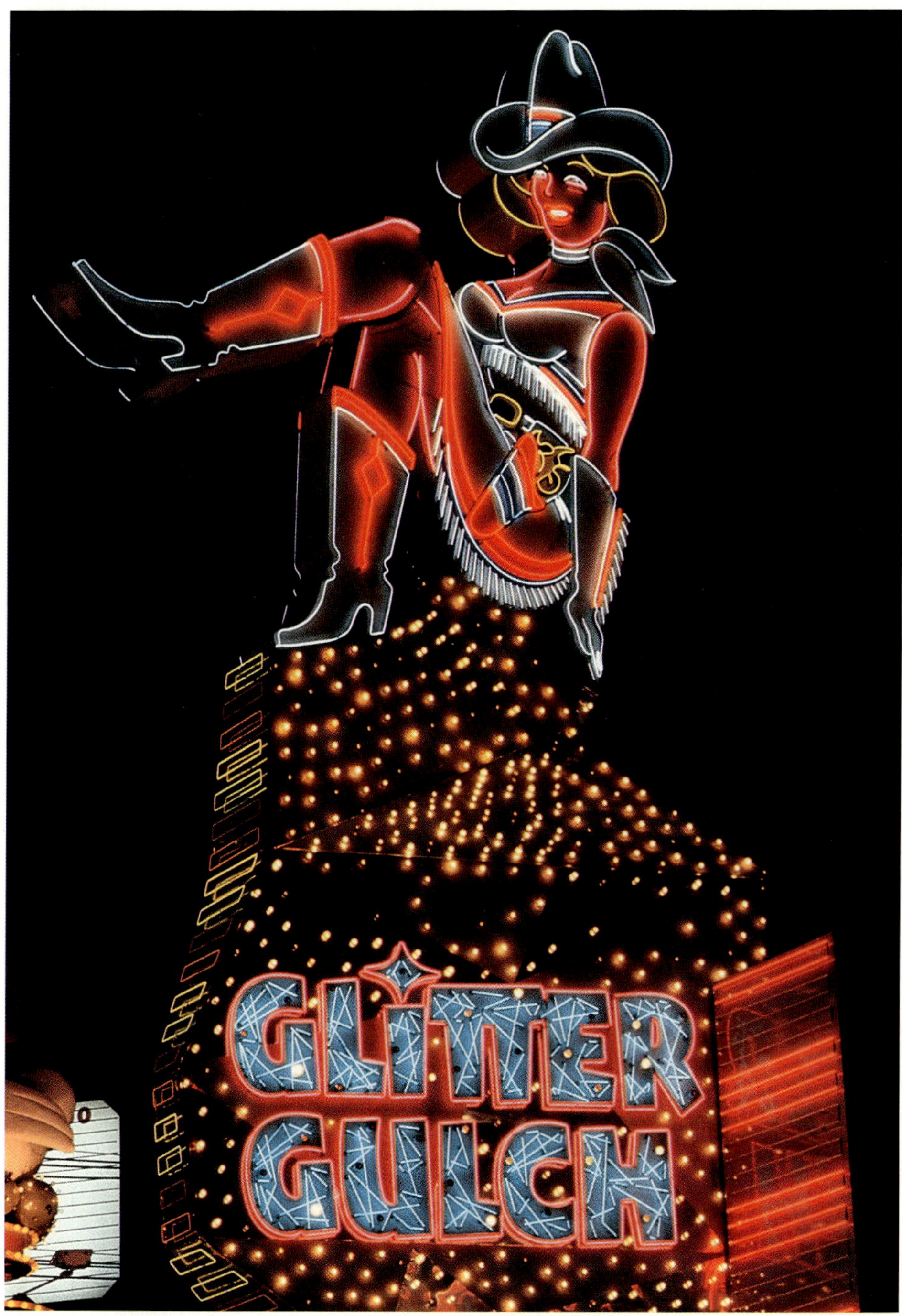


KODAK EKTACHROME 160 Film (Tungsten)

HERB JONES

You can use KODAK EKTACHROME 160 Film outdoors at night for pictures of illuminated signs, buildings, fountains, and street scenes. It also gives excellent results with existing tungsten light, such as the light from household lamps.

## Increased Film Speed with KODAK EKTACHROME P800/1600, 400, 200, and 160 Films.

An exceptional feature of EKTACHROME Films is that you can expose them at higher-than-normal speeds if you obtain special processing or push-process the films yourself. You'll obtain the best quality from EKTACHROME Films when you expose them at their normal speeds and have the films processed normally. Because quality is reduced slightly with special processing, it's seldom practical to pay the additional cost of the special processing for these films if you can use a higher-speed EKTACHROME Film at its normal rated speed.

However, if you can't switch to a higher-speed film, the higher speeds and high quality of these films with push processing offer many opportunities for color pictures that would otherwise be impossible. Increased speed is very helpful under dim lighting conditions—in existing light, for example. It's also helpful when you want to use higher shutter speeds to stop action and smaller lens openings to increase depth of field.

Push processing increases contrast and graininess to some extent. These changes, though, are not too noticeable on the projection screen, and overall quality is very good. Keep in mind that push processing to EI 800 or EI 1600 is the intended process for EKTACHROME P800/1600 Film and produces excellent results.

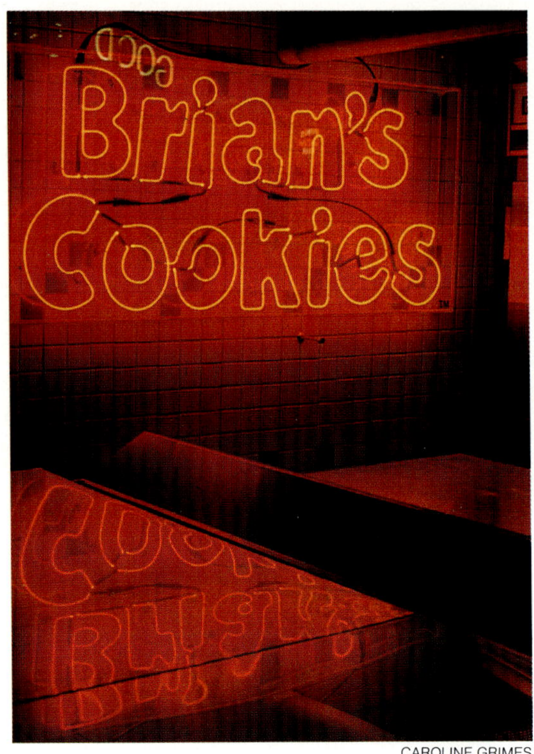


CAROLINE GRIMES

This colorful design was captured on KODAK EKTACHROME P800/1600 Professional Film with special processing (push 1) to EI 800.

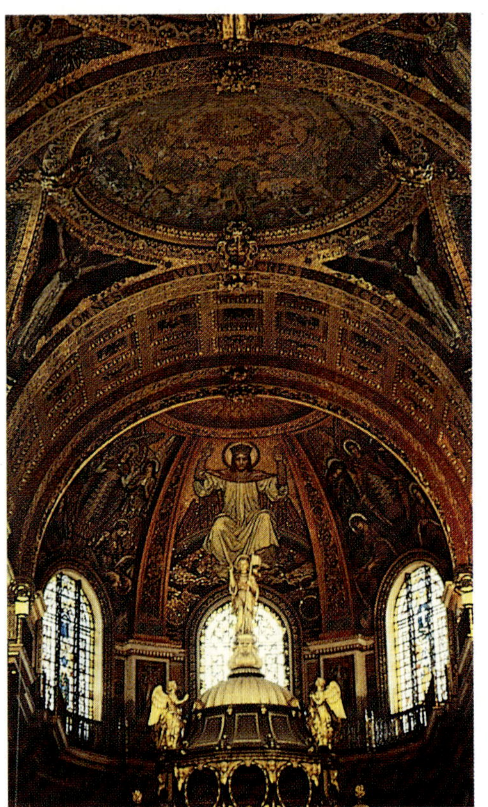

BRUCE NETT

KODAK EKTACHROME P800/1600 Professional Film with special processing (push 2) to EI 1600

## *KODAK* PROFESSIONAL COLOR FILMS

The following 35 mm films are designed for professional photographers; therefore, only brief descriptions are given in this book. If you have questions about these films, write to Kodak Information Center, Eastman Kodak Company, Rochester, New York 14650-0811. KODAK Publication No. E-77, *KODAK Color Films and Papers for Professionals*, (available from photo dealers or bookstores) includes technical data and other information on the films described here.

Because these films are intended for critical photography by professional photographers, they have more rigid requirements for storage and handling than Kodak color films for general use. Store unexposed professional color films in a refrigerator at 55°F (13°C) or lower unless different storage recommendations are given on the film carton or in the film instructions. After exposure, have these films processed promptly. See "Storage and Care of KODAK Films" on page 102.

These films are sold by dealers who sell professional photographic products.

**KODAK VERICOLOR III Professional Film** is a color-negative film intended primarily for professional use. It is designed for portraiture, wedding photography, and school pictures. The film has excellent skin-tone and color reproduction. It features moderate contrast and color saturation.

VERICOLOR III Film has a speed of ISO 160. It is designed for exposure times of 1/10 second to 1/10,000 second with daylight or electronic flash. It's also available in 120 and 220 sizes and in sheets.

**KODAK VERICOLOR HC Professional Film** is a color-negative film that's ideal for commercial illustration, outdoor portraiture, and other applications that call for increased color saturation. It's also useful for photographing outdoor scenes under low-contrast lighting conditions—e.g., on cloudy days or in deep shade. It is also available in 120-size rolls and in sheets.

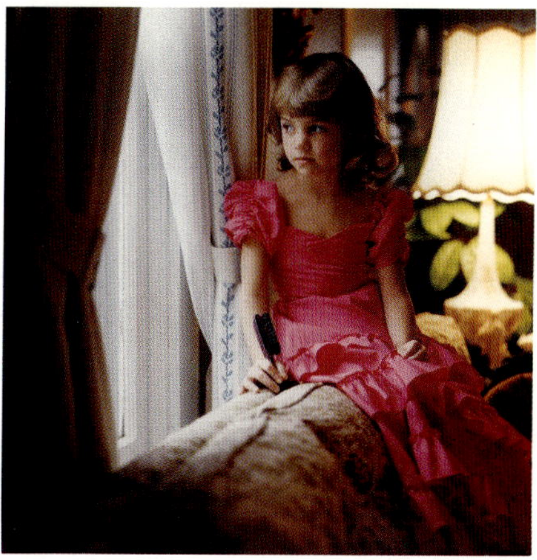

HENRY HITCHCOCK

KODAK VERICOLOR III Professional Film has excellent skin tone and color reproduction; it is designed for portraits.

**KODAK VERICOLOR 400 Professional Film** is a color-negative film that incorporates KODAK T-GRAIN Emulsions for extremely fine grain combined with high speed (ISO 400). Like those of KODAK VERICOLOR III Film, its moderate contrast and color saturation give excellent skin-tone and color reproduction. This film is designed for exposure by daylight or electronic flash. You can also obtain pleasing results in many types of existing light. Its speed and color reproduction make this film an excellent choice for environmental, commercial, and candid wedding photography. It is also available in 120 and 220 sizes, and in sheets.

**KODAK VERICOLOR Slide Film** is a special-purpose film for producing color slides directly from color negatives or for photographing artwork to make reverse-text title slides.

To make color slides from your color negatives, you can contact-print the negatives onto the slide film in a darkroom or use a 35 mm camera with a slide-duplicating attachment. To make reverse-text title slides, you can photograph text or artwork on a colored background. Or you can photograph a white background with a color filter over the camera lens.

The film is available in 135-36 magazines and in 35 mm 100-foot rolls. In the 135 size, the film is identified as KODAK VERICOLOR Slide Film SO-279.

**KODACHROME 25 Professional Film and KODACHROME 64 Professional Film** feature extremely fine grain, extremely high sharpness, and high resolving power. These professional color-slide films have color rendition, color balance, and other photographic characteristics similar to those of KODACHROME 25 Film (Daylight) and KODACHROME 64 Film (Daylight).

KODACHROME 64 Professional Film is also available in 120 size.

**KODACHROME 200 Professional Film** has characteristics similar to those of KODACHROME 200 Film (Daylight).

All three KODACHROME Professional Films are manufactured to tighter tolerances for speed and color balance than the non-professional films to meet the needs of professional photographers. To maintain these tolerances, these films, like other Kodak professional color films, require refrigeration before use and prompt processing after exposure.

**KODAK EKTACHROME 64 Professional Film** is a medium-speed (ISO 64) transparency film with excellent color saturation and soft highlight contrast. It is an ideal choice for commercial photography (especially fashion and product photography) when moderate color enhancement is needed. The film is also sold in 120 and 220 sizes and in long rolls and sheets.

**KODAK EKTACHROME 64 Film** is excellent for photojournalists or amateur photographers who use a lot of film under conditions that don't allow for refrigerated storage. It is available only in 50-roll Press-Pacs.

Both films have very high sharpness and very fine grain.

**KODAK EKTACHROME 100 Professional Film** offers outstanding color accuracy, excellent highlight detail, realistic neutrals, and excellent rendition of flesh tones. It features very fine grain, very high sharpness, and high resolving power. Its modified color sensitivity easily handles certain fabrics (azo-dyed) and colors that are difficult to reproduce accurately. EKTACHROME 100 Professional Film is also sold in 120 and 220 sizes, in long rolls, and in sheets.

**KODAK EKTACHROME 100 PLUS Professional Film** is a medium-speed color-reversal film that has higher color saturation than KODAK EKTACHROME 100 Professional Film. It is an excellent choice for use in advertising, illustration, and photojournalism. This film features very fine grain, very high sharpness, and high resolving power. It is also available in 120 and 220 sizes, long rolls, and sheets.

**KODAK EKTACHROME 200 Professional Film** is the professional version of EKTACHROME 200 Film (Daylight). The professional film is excellent for architectural and industrial photography under low levels of daylight. It has the same speed and other characteristics as the general-use film. The professional film also comes in 120 and 220 sizes, long rolls, and sheets.

**KODAK EKTACHROME 160T Professional Film** has the same speed (ISO 160) as the general-use EKTACHROME 160 Film (Tungsten). It is excellent for subjects in low levels of existing tungsten light. This film is also available in 120 size and in long rolls.

**KODAK EKTACHROME 64T Professional Film / 6118** is a sheet film that's ideal for producing high-quality images of products, artwork, and titles with tungsten light. It has excellent color saturation.

**KODAK EKTACHROME 50 Professional Film** is designed for photography with tungsten lamps (3200 K). The fine color quality of this

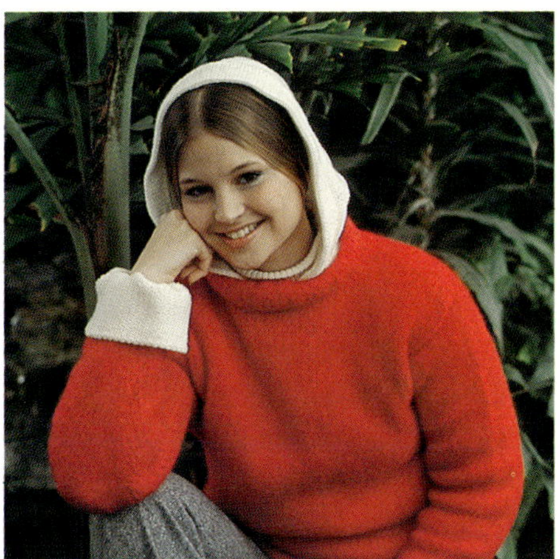

Original slide

KODAK EKTACHROME Slide Duplicating Film 5071 (Process E-6) is a superb film for copying original color slides. Sometimes you can make the duplicate slide better than the original. Here the duplicate was cropped for improved composition.

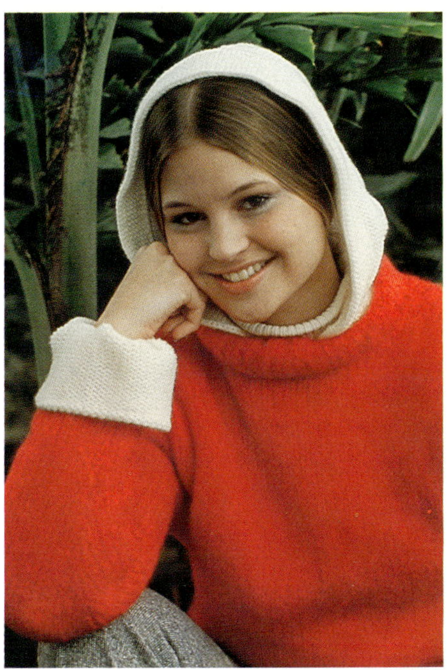

Duplicate slide DON MAGGIO

tungsten film makes it an excellent choice for informal portraits, close-ups, and title slides, and for copying color originals. You can also use this film in daylight with a No. 85B filter. This film is also available in 120 size and in long rolls.

### Films for Duplicating Color Slides

When you want to make duplicates of original color slides made on such films as KODACHROME and KODAK EKTACHROME Films, you'll usually get the best results when you use a film specifically designed for duplicating. You can use conventional color-slide films for making duplicate slides, but the duplicates made with such films usually have contrast that's too high, some loss of color saturation, and loss of image sharpness. If you have an original slide with contrast that's too low, you can often duplicate it on a conventional color-slide film, such as KODACHROME 25 Film (Daylight), with good results.

Sometimes when an original slide is less than ideal, you can make improvements when you make duplicates, e.g., cropping for better composition, correcting under- or overexposure, correcting color balance, or combining two or more images in one slide.

**KODAK EKTACHROME Slide Duplicating Film (Tungsten)** is a color-slide film for copying original color slides. The contrast and color-reproduction characteristics, very high sharpness, and extremely fine grain make this an outstanding film for making duplicates that are difficult to distinguish from the original slides. The film is intended for use at exposure times of about 1 second with tungsten illumination.

**KODAK EKTACHROME SE Duplicating Film SO-366 (Daylight)** is similar to EKTACHROME Slide Duplicating Films, but it is intended for short exposures with electronic flash. You can also expose it with daylight.

These films are not intended for general pictorial photography. Store unexposed film in a refrigerator at 55°F (13°C) or lower in the original sealed package.

### Films for Copying

Choosing a color film for copying originals such as photographs (prints), drawings, documents, and paintings is similar to choosing one for conventional subjects. The choice depends on whether you want prints or slides and on the type of illumination.

You can use any of the light sources recommended for the film, such as daylight, flash (used off the camera if necessary to avoid reflections), or photolamps. However, because most copies are close-ups, photolamps are usually the best choice; they let you control the illumination more easily, and you can use your exposure meter to determine exposure. See "Using Exposure Meters in Copying," page 98. If you use photolamp illumination, film recommendations for copying are the same as those under "Using Photolamp Illumination," page 48.

If your original is black-and-white, you can obtain good copies on color film. However, if you want a monochrome image that is a more accurate reproduction of the original or if you have many copies to make, it may be better or more economical to use black-and-white film. See page 61. Also, see the note about copyrighted material on page 61.

Copying is a specialized application of photography and can require special techniques. For an in-depth discussion of the subject, see KODAK Publication No. M-1, *Copying and Duplicating,* sold by photo dealers.

## COLOR BALANCE

Color balance refers to the ability of a film to reproduce the colors of a scene approximately as the eye sees them. Color films are balanced during manufacture for exposure to light of a certain

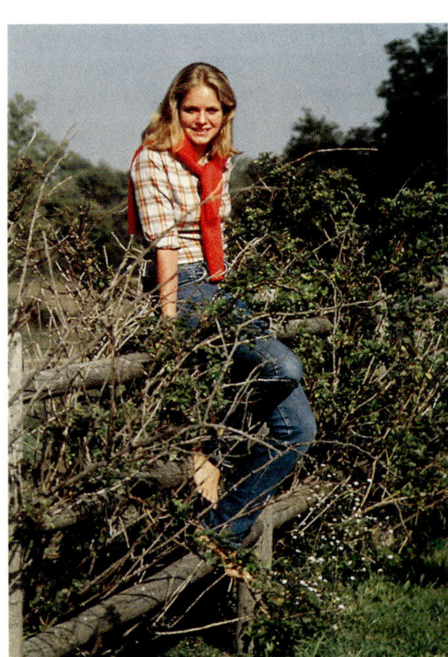

To take pictures outdoors with a film balanced for tungsten light, use a conversion filter for proper color balance. KODAK EKTACHROME 160 Film (Tungsten) with a No. 85B filter

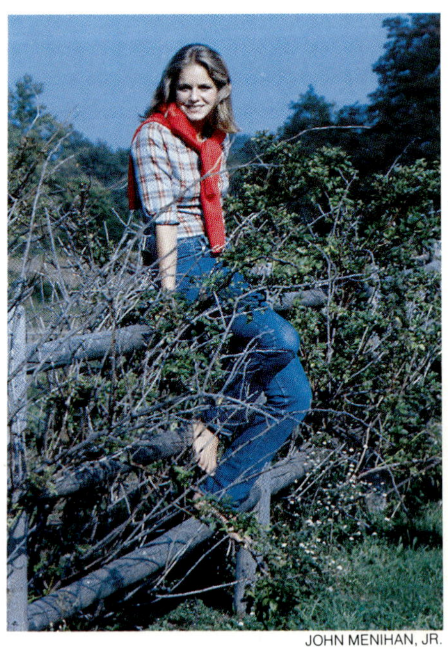

JOHN MENIHAN, JR.

If you don't use the recommended filter with tungsten film outdoors, you'll get this kind of bluish effect.

color quality, such as daylight, photolamps (3400 K), or tungsten lamps (3200 K).

You'll get the best results when you use a film with the kind of illumination for which it's balanced. Usually under these conditions, you don't need a filter to obtain correct color rendition. If you use a light source with a color quality different from that for which the film is balanced, you'll need to use the conversion filter recommended in this book or in the film instructions. You can get good results with filters, but most of them absorb light and reduce the effective speed of the film.

Because the film in a slide or transparency is the same film you exposed in your camera, the color rendition depends primarily on the light source and the filter you use when you take the picture. The color balance of prints made from color negatives exposed with the wrong light source usually can be improved when the prints are made. But if the negative is exposed with light sources significantly different from that for which the film is balanced, full correction may not be possible.

## FLASH PICTURES

You don't normally need a filter for taking flash pictures with daylight-type Kodak color films. The color quality of electronic flash is similar to that of daylight.

When you want to take flash pictures on a film balanced for tungsten lamps (3200 K), we recommend that you use a No. 85B conversion filter. With a film balanced for photolamps (3400 K), use a No. 85 filter.

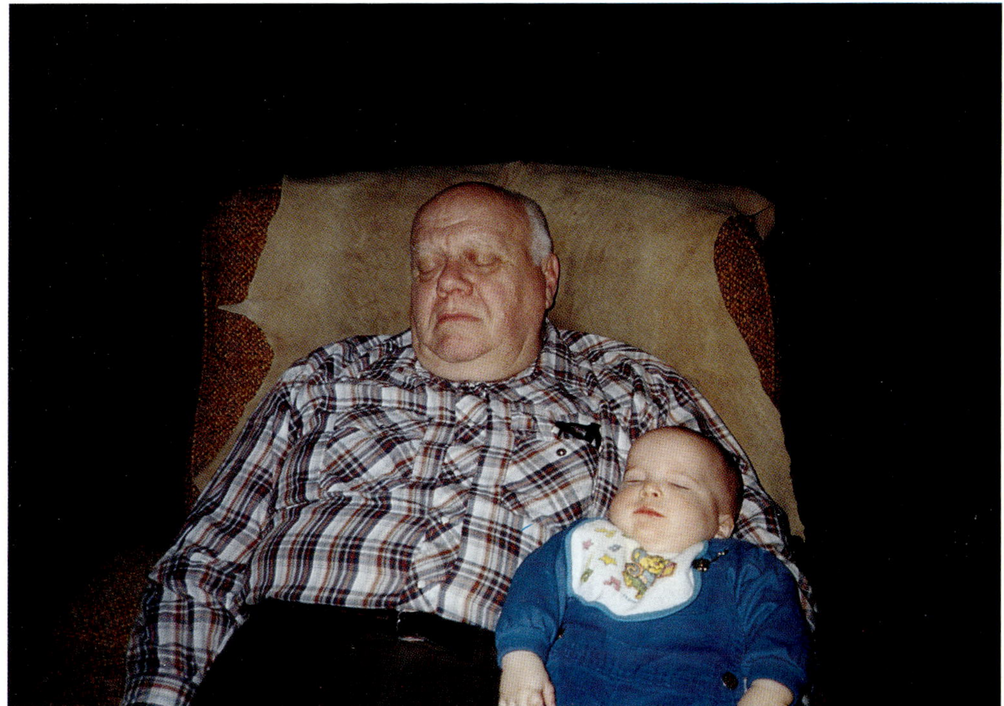

KODACOLOR GOLD 200 Film

GAIL BERGER

You can use electronic flash for taking pictures with daylight-type Kodak color films, as shown in this flash picture taken with KODACOLOR GOLD 200 Film.

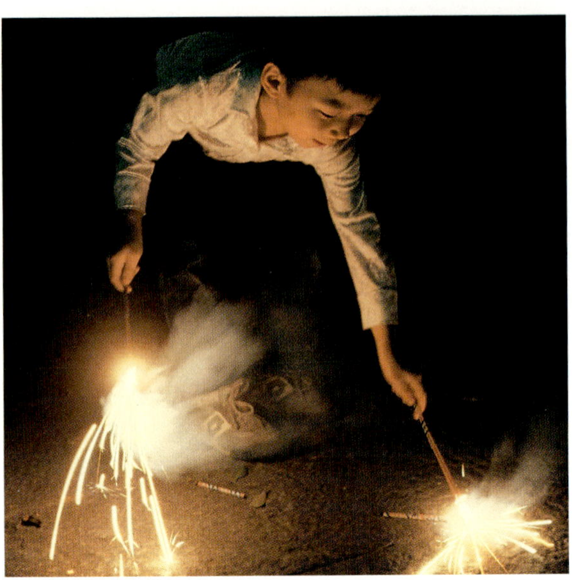

KODAK EKTACHROME 400 Film (Daylight) NORM KERR

You can use daylight film for existing-light photography outdoors at night. Your photos will be warmer, or more yellow-red, than pictures made on tungsten film.

## EXISTING-LIGHT PHOTOGRAPHY

Existing light, sometimes called "available light," includes artificial light present in a scene, lighting indoors or outdoors at night, daylight indoors, and twilight outdoors. Technically, daylight conditions outdoors, including bright sunlight, are existing light. But when we define existing light for photography, we are referring to lower levels of light than you would encounter in most daylight conditions outdoors.

Actually you can use all Kodak color films for taking pictures by existing light if you don't mind putting your camera on a tripod or some other firm support and using slow shutter speeds or time exposures. But your picture-taking will be much easier and more versatile if you can hand-hold your camera and use shutter speeds of 1/30 second or higher. This may require an *f*/2.8 or faster lens and a high-speed film, because existing light is often quite dim.

Take advantage of the speed of today's fast films and lenses by taking candid pictures with a hand-held camera. Excellent films to use are KODACOLOR GOLD 1600 and KODAK EKTAR 1000 Films for color prints, and KODAK EKTACHROME P800/1600 Professional and EKTACHROME 400 Films for color slides. KODACOLOR GOLD 1600 and 400 Films have a special sensitization that produces pleasing results under various kinds of existing light without filters.

If you're using color-slide film, the choice between the daylight film and the tungsten film depends on the type of lighting, the amount of film speed required, and your personal taste. Daylight film is better for indoor scenes illuminated by existing daylight. You can also use it to photograph performers illuminated by carbon-arc spotlights. When you're photographing subjects indoors with fluorescent lighting, daylight film will give the best results; however, the color rendition of the slides will usually be greenish, depending on the type of fluorescent lamps. See "Filters for Fluorescent Illumination" on page 45.

You can use daylight film for existing-

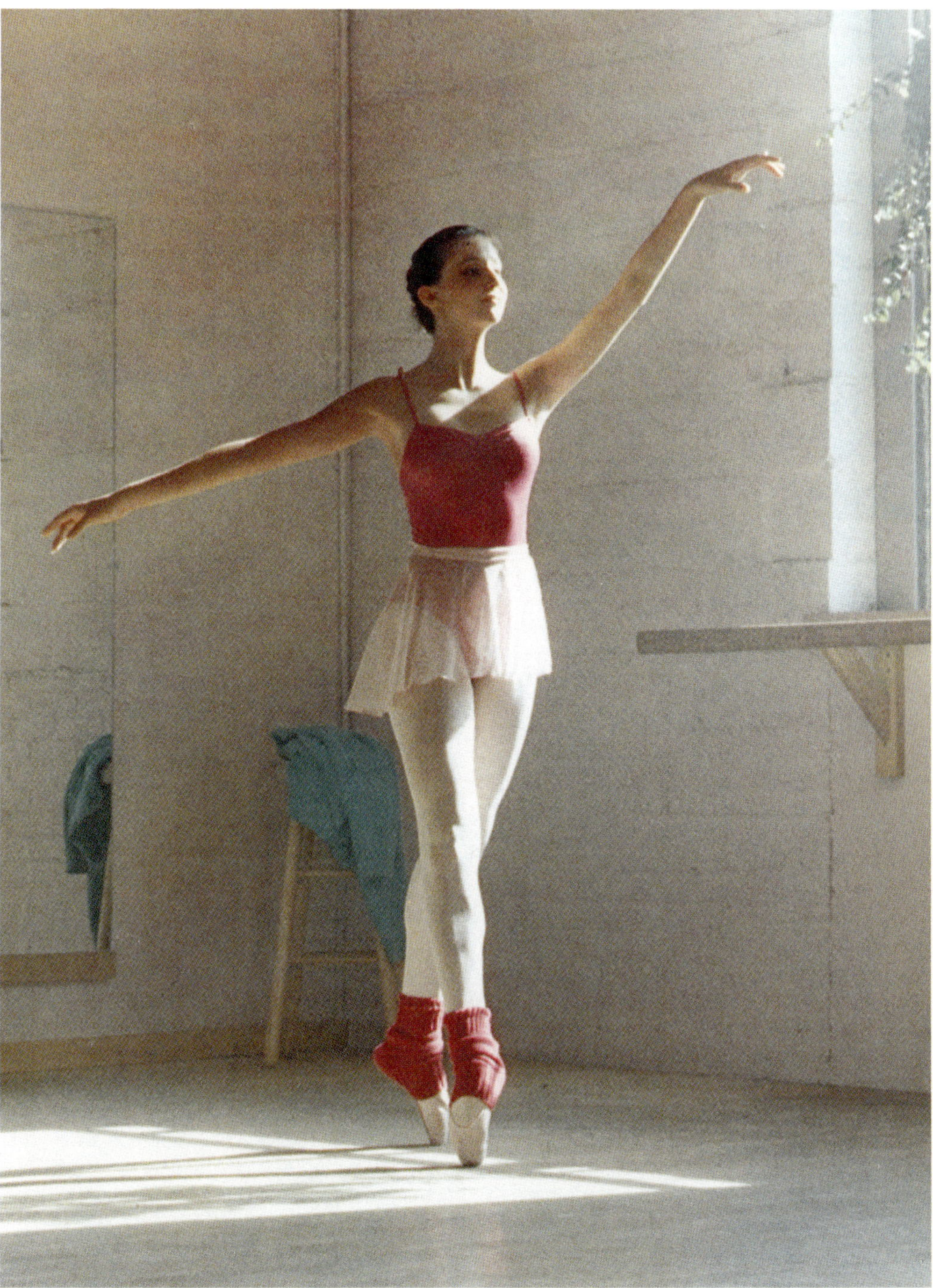

KODAK EKTAR 1000 Film

STEVE KELLY

KODAK EKTAR 1000 Film is an excellent choice for existing-light pictures when you want color prints. This film is designed for exposure with daylight or electronic flash, but its improved sensitivity to tungsten light will provide pleasing results in situations where the lighting is difficult to meter.

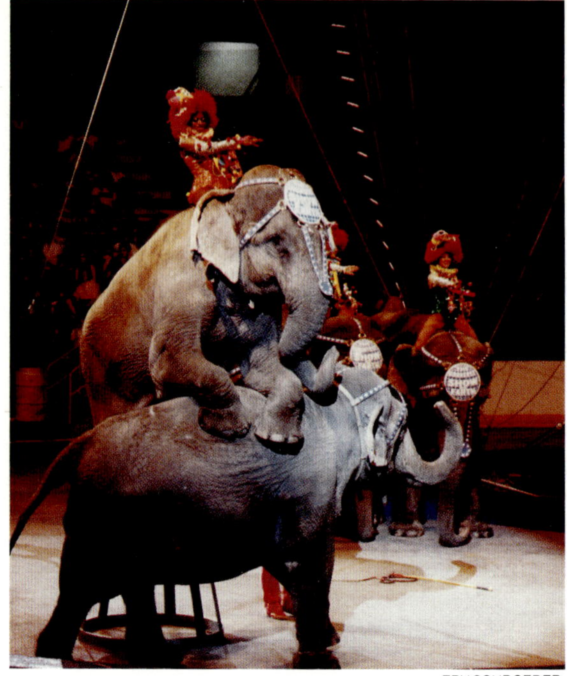

ERV SCHROEDER

KODACOLOR GOLD 1600 Film has special sensitization that produces pleasing results under various kinds of existing light without filters. You can take advantage of its high speed by taking candid pictures with a hand-held camera. Ringling Bros. and Barnum & Bailey Circus

light photography outdoors at night, too. Your photos will be warmer, or more yellow-red, than pictures made on tungsten film. With mercury-vapor lamps, which are used at some sports stadiums and for some street lighting, you'll get best results on daylight film. However, your pictures will have a blue-green appearance because mercury-vapor lamps are deficient in red. You can usually identify mercury-vapor lighting by its slightly blue-green appearance in comparison with tungsten light.

Multi-vapor lamps illuminate the playing area in some large sports stadiums. These lamps provide improved color quality suitable for color television and photography. Pictures taken on daylight film without filters under this illumination will have good color rendition for noncritical purposes. You can identify this lighting at sports stadiums by its more neutral appearance compared with the slightly blue-green color of mercury-vapor lamps.

Another type of lighting commonly used for street lighting is sodium-vapor lamps. These lights are easy to identify by their strong amber color. Pictures on daylight film will look similar to the way the lighting appears, i.e., yellow-amber. Tungsten film will produce photos with a more neutral appearance.

The various types of vapor lamps are also referred to as high-intensity discharge lamps. If the light provided by the vapor lamps is bright enough, you can use filters over the camera lens to improve the color rendition in your photos. See the recommendations in the table "Filters for High-Intensity Discharge Lamps" on page 47.

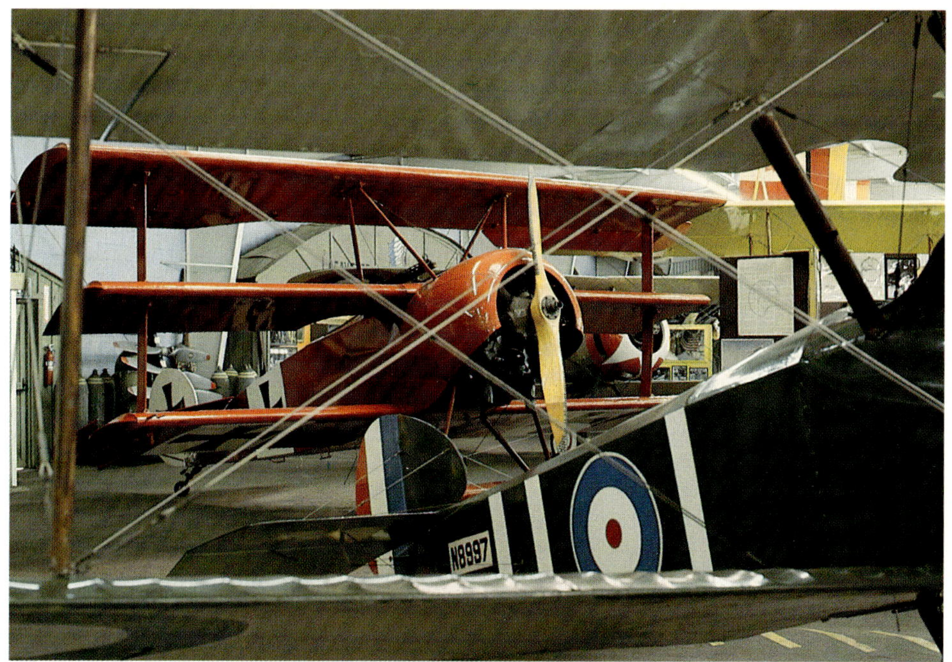


CAROLINE GRIMES

KODAK EKTACHROME 400 Film (Daylight) was used to record these antique airplanes illuminated mainly by existing daylight with some fluorescent illumination from the overhead lights. Movieland of the Air, Santa Ana, California

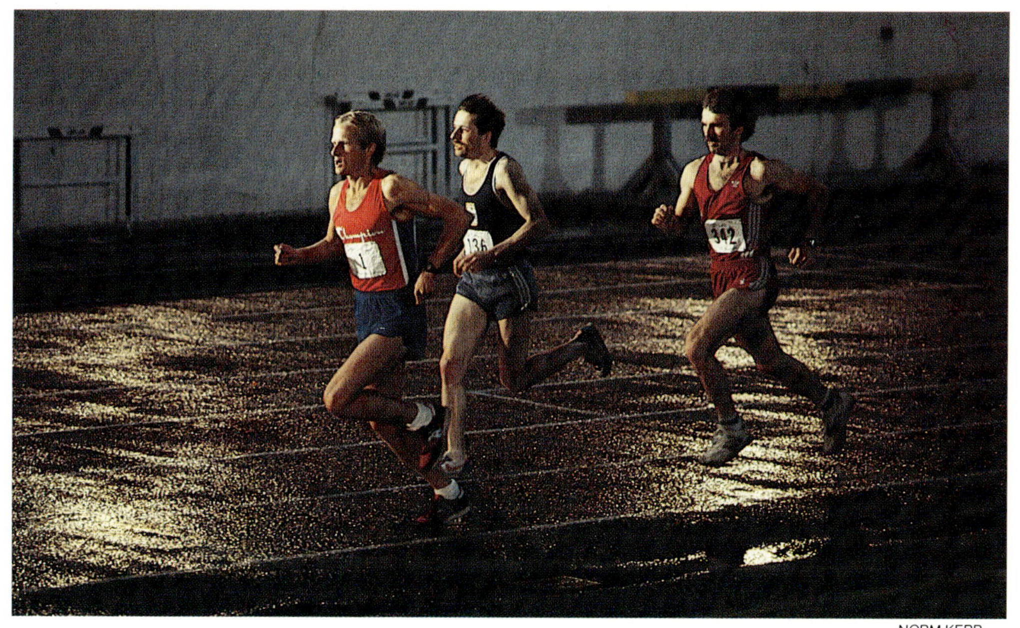

NORM KERR

When you want to stop action in color slides, you can choose KODAK EKTACHROME P800/1600 Professional Film (Daylight) for exposure and processing to EI 1600. 1/1000 second *f*/2.8

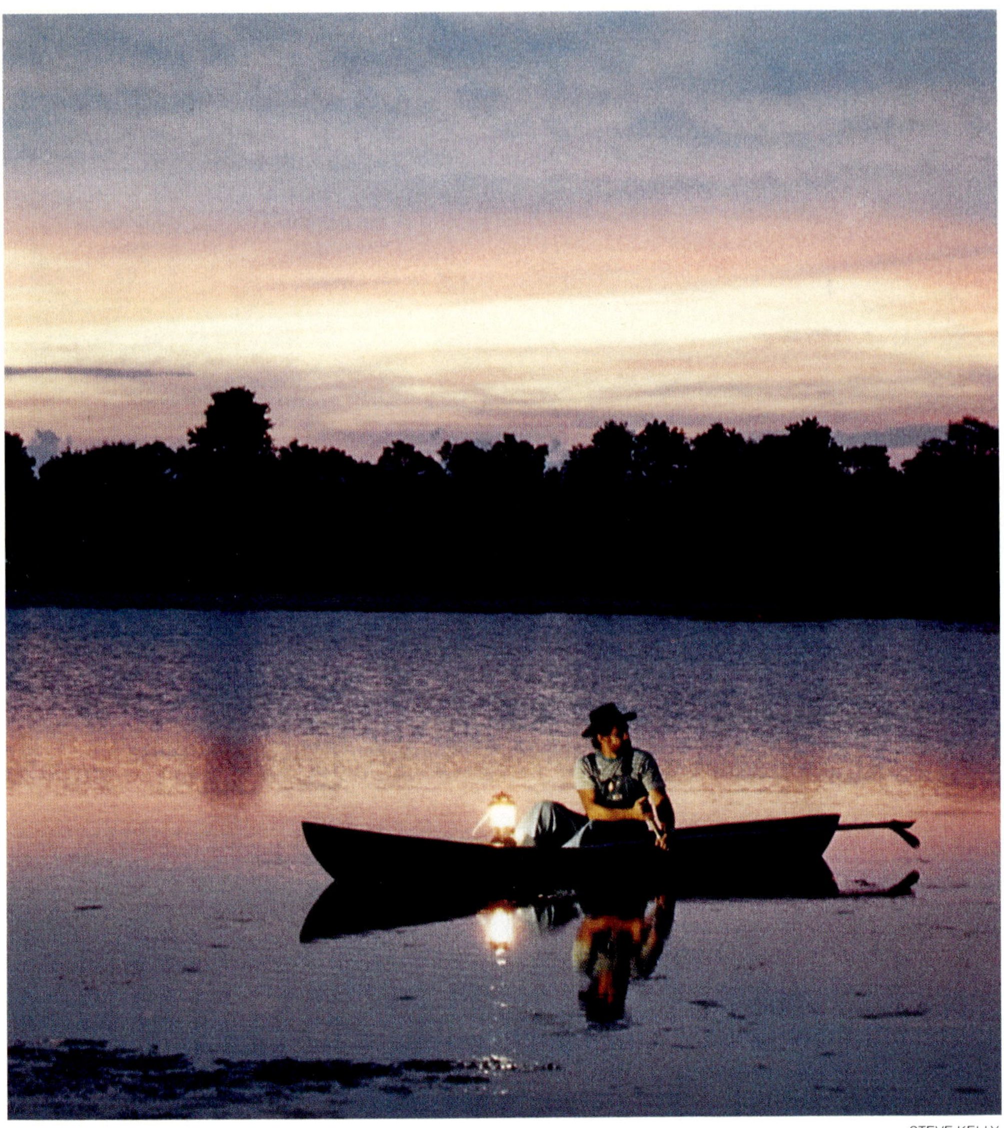

Kodak Ektar 1000 Film

STEVE KELLY

With its very high speed and very fine grain, Kodak Ektar 1000 Film lets you make high-quality photos in dimly lighted scenes. It also lets you use high shutter speeds for hand-holding telephoto lenses or small apertures for increased depth of field.

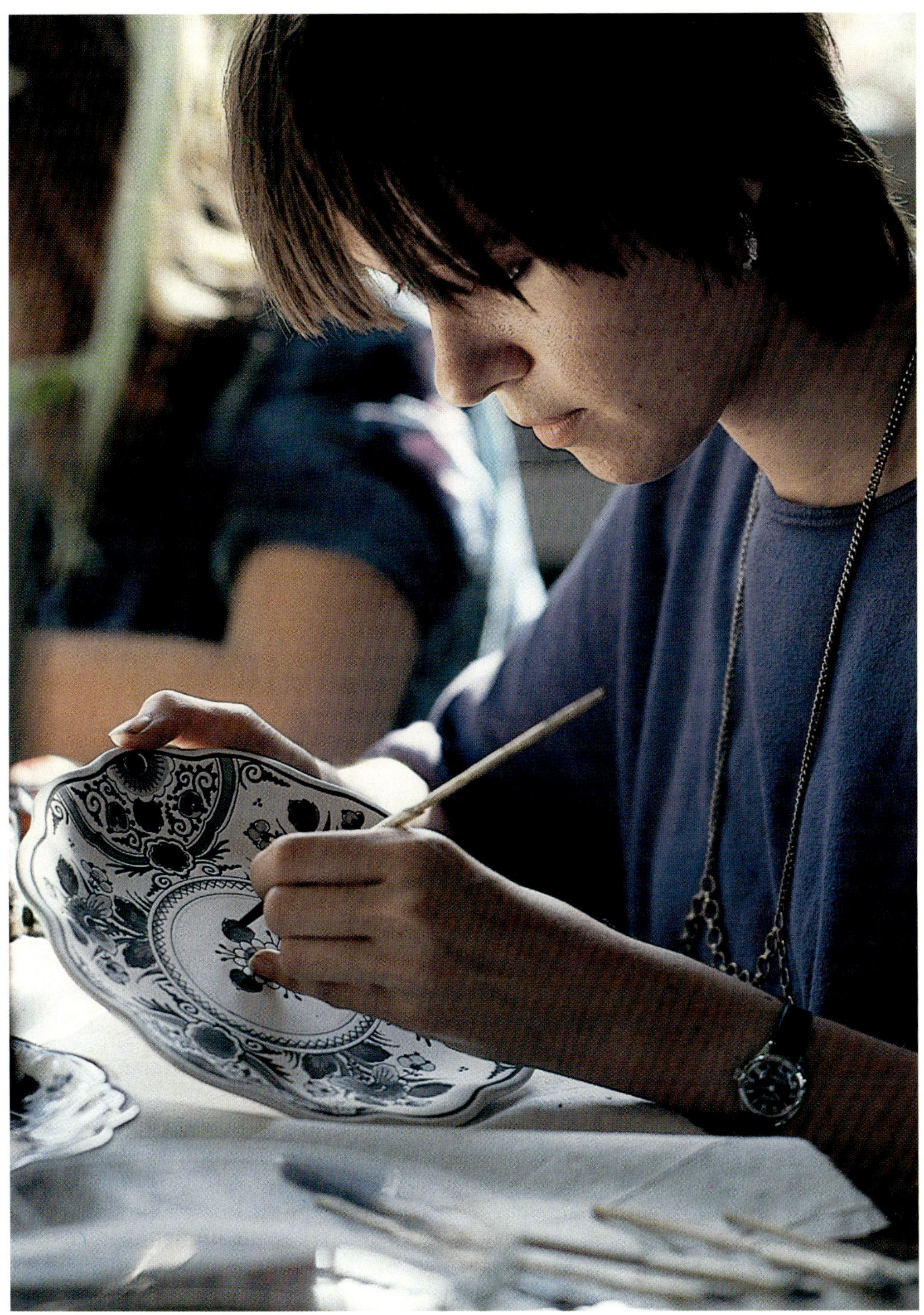

KODACHROME 64 Film (Daylight) STEVE KELLY

You can sometimes use a medium-speed film, such as KODACHROME 64 Film (Daylight), in existing daylight, depending on the capabilities of your camera.

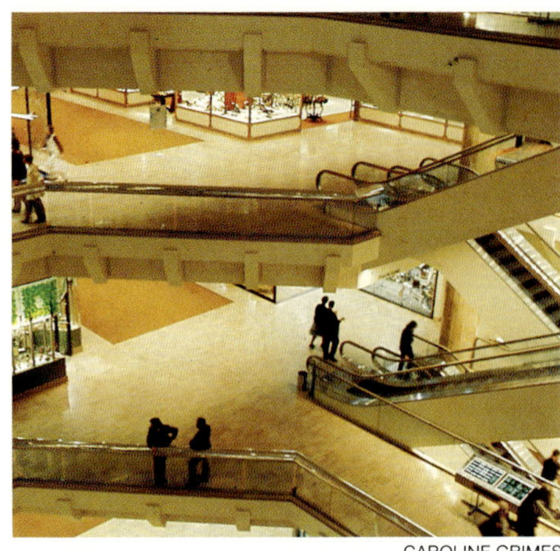

CAROLINE GRIMES

When the existing lighting is provided predominantly by tungsten lamps, you'll get more natural-looking color slides by using film balanced for tungsten light. KODAK EKTACHROME 160 Film (Tungsten) at Water Tower Place, Chicago, Illinois

KODAK EKTACHROME 160 Film (Tungsten) is an excellent film for making slides in existing tungsten light, such as the light from household lamps and other general-purpose tungsten lamps. Outdoors at night, you can use tungsten film for pictures of illuminated buildings, fountains, statues, signs, street scenes, and similar subjects. Slides of such subjects taken on tungsten film may look more natural than those taken on daylight film. Your choice of a color-slide film for making outdoor pictures at night is a matter of personal taste. Both types produce pleasing results. If you need higher speed with tungsten film, you can expose EKTACHROME 160 Film at twice the speed (EI 320) and push-process it.

Sometimes you'll find more than one kind of illumination in a scene. If one type of light source is predominant, use color-slide film balanced for that light source. For example, in an indoor scene

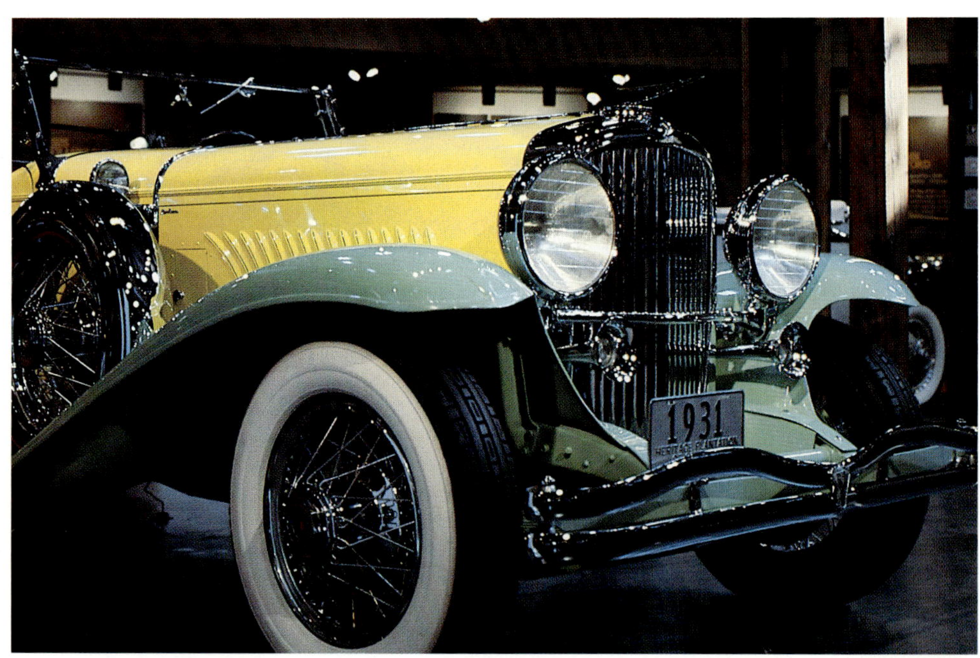


CAROLINE GRIMES

For photographing scenes illuminated by existing tungsten light on color slide film, it's often helpful to have a film with high speed. An excellent film to choose is KODAK EKTACHROME 160 Film (Tungsten) with push processing, ISO 320. Heritage Plantation of Sandwich, Massachusetts

that includes both daylight and tungsten light, daylight is usually the predominant light source and daylight film would give more pleasing results. If the kinds of illumination in the scene are about equal in intensity and distribution, the choice of color-slide film is a matter of personal taste. If you like warmer-looking pictures, use daylight film; if you prefer colder-looking pictures, use tungsten film.

Because most existing light is dim, you'll often need all the film speed you can get. KODACOLOR GOLD 1600 and EKTACHROME P800/1600 Films offer very high film speeds of ISO 1600 and EI 800 or 1600, respectively. When you are using other EKTACHROME Films and you need more speed, you can expose the film at twice the rated speed and then push-process it. See pages 32 and 51 for more information on special processing.

## Filters for Fluorescent Illumination

Pictures made on daylight-type film in fluorescent light without a filter may be acceptable, although they will often have a greenish cast. Tungsten film without filters usually produces pictures that are much too blue. It's often not practical to use filters in existing-light photography, because they absorb too much light and reduce the effective speed of the film. However, when the reduced film speed is acceptable for the type of pictures you want to take, you can improve the color quality of pictures taken under fluorescent light by using filters over your camera lens.

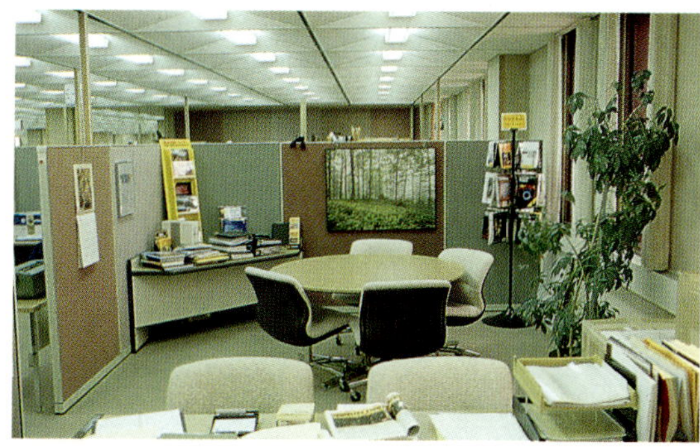

For taking color pictures under fluorescent illumination without a filter, you'll get the best results on daylight film. Although the pictures are usually acceptable, they will often have a greenish cast.

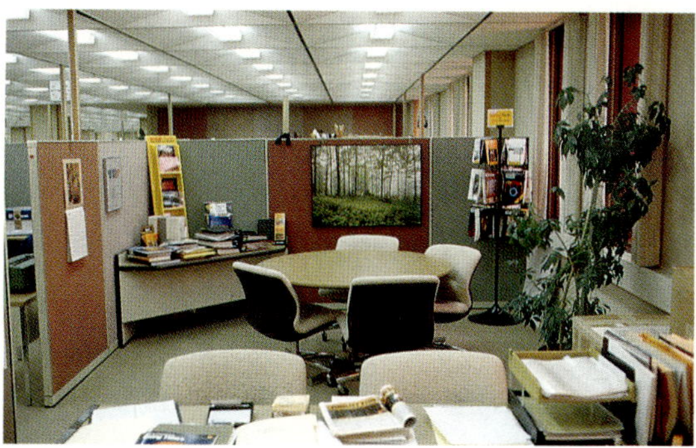

KODAK EKTACHROME 100 Film (Daylight)

KEITH BOAS

You can improve the color quality of pictures taken under fluorescent light by using filters over your camera lens. For general color correction, use a screw-on FLD (fluorescent-daylight) filter. For even better color correction, use KODAK WRATTEN Filters matched to the film and bulb types. See the table on the next page.

If you do not know the type of fluorescent lamp in use, use an FLD or 30M filter.

| Filters for Fluorescent Light | | | | | | |
|---|---|---|---|---|---|---|
| | KODAK Color Film | | | | | |
| Fluorescent Lamp | KODACOLOR GOLD; EKTAR | KODACHROME 64 (Daylight) | KODACHROME 200 (Daylight) | KODACHROME 25; EKTACHROME (Daylight) | EKTACHROME 160 (Tungsten) | KODACHROME 40 (Type A) |
| Daylight | 40R +⅔ stop | 45R + 10M +1⅓ stops | 30R +⅔ stop | 50R +1 stop | No. 85B + 40M +30Y +1⅔ stops | No. 85 + 40R +1⅓ stops |
| White | 20C + 30M +1 stop | 05C + 40M +1 stop | 15B + 05M +1 stop | 40M +⅔ stop | 50R + 10M +1⅓ stops | 40M + 30Y +1 stop |
| Warm White | 40B +1 stop | 25B + 20M +1⅓ stops | 35B + 05C +1⅓ stops | 20C + 40M +1 stop | 50M + 40Y +1 stop | 20R + 10M +⅔ stop |
| Warm White Deluxe | 30B + 30C +1⅓ stops | 40B + 05C +1⅓ stops | 10B + 45C +1⅓ stops | 30B + 30C +1⅓ stops | 10R +⅓ stop | No Filter None |
| Cool White | 30M +⅔ stop | 15R + 30M +1⅓ stops | 20M +½ stop | 40M + 10Y +1 stop | 60R +1⅓ stops | 50R +1 stop |
| Cool White Deluxe | 20C + 10M +⅔ stop | 05B + 10M +⅔ stop | 05B + 20C +⅔ stop | 20C + 10M +⅔ stop | 20M + 40Y +⅔ stop | 10M + 30Y +⅔ stop |
| Unknown Fluorescent* | 10C + 20M +⅔ stop | 05C + 30M +1 stop | 10B + 05C +⅔ stop | 30M +⅔ stop | 50R +1 stop | 40R +⅔ stop |

**Note:** Except for the KODAK WRATTEN Gelatin Filters No. 85 and No. 85B, all filters are KODAK Color Compensating Filters (CC). Increase exposure by the amount shown in the table. Red filters have been substituted for equivalent values in magenta and yellow, and blue filters have been substituted for equivalent values in cyan and magenta. These substitutions were made to reduce the number of filters or to keep the exposure adjustment to a minimum (or both).

*These filters are for emergency use only, when it's not possible to determine the type of fluorescent lamp. Color rendition will be less than optimum.

Selecting filters for fluorescent illumination is sometimes difficult because the lamps are often inaccessible and hard to identify. There are several kinds of fluorescent lamps, and each kind produces light of a slightly different color. If optimum color rendition is important and you can find out the kind of lamps in use, you can improve the color in your pictures by using the filters recommended in the table below. These filters are available from photo dealers.

If you can't find out what kind of fluorescent lamps are in use, you can use the compromise filtration given in the table for unknown, or average, fluorescent light.

For critical work with color-slide film, you should make test pictures by exposing your film with the filters recommended in the table and with filters that vary by at least plus and minus CC10M and CC10Y from the filters listed. Color-negative films, such as KODACOLOR GOLD Films, are a good choice for taking pictures under fluorescent illumination because the color rendition can usually be improved when the negatives are printed.

With fluorescent lamps, use a shutter speed of 1/60 second or longer to avoid uneven exposure or underexposure due to the variations in brightness of the lamps caused by the alternating current.

## Filters for High-Intensity Discharge Lamps

Daylight film is the best choice for mercury-vapor and multi-vapor lighting. The bluish-green cast in pictures taken under mercury-vapor illumination without filters is often acceptable for noncritical photos, and the reasonably good color rendition in pictures exposed with multi-vapor lighting without filters is acceptable to most people. However, for more demanding color quality, use the filters suggested in the table below.

With high-intensity discharge lamps, as with fluorescent lamps, it's often difficult to find out what kind of lamps are in use. If possible, make test pictures with the suggested filters and with filters that vary by at least plus and minus CC10. If you use a color-negative film, color rendition can usually be improved in printing.

Taking pictures under high-intensity discharge lamps with high shutter speeds may give uneven exposure or under-exposure. This is caused by the lamps pulsating with 60-cycle current. These exposure problems are most evident when you use shutter speeds higher than 1/125 second. The effects, however, are unpredictable and depend on the lighting installation. Photographs made in an area illuminated by a large number of lamps may not show any adverse effects.

For more information on taking pictures by existing light, see KODAK Publication No. KW-17, *Existing-Light Photography,* available from your photo dealer or bookstore.

**Filters for High-Intensity Discharge Lamps**

| High-Intensity Discharge Lamp | KODAK Color Film | | | | | |
|---|---|---|---|---|---|---|
| | KODACOLOR GOLD; EKTAR | KODACHROME 64 (Daylight) | KODACHROME 200 (Daylight) | KODACHROME 25; EKTACHROME (Daylight) | EKTACHROME 160 (Tungsten) | KODACHROME 40 (Type A) |
| General Electric Lucalox* | 70B + 50C +3 stops | 70B + 30C +2⅔ stops | 50B + 70C +2⅔ stops | 80B + 20C +2⅓ stops | 50M + 20C +1 stop | 50B +1⅓ stops |
| General Electric Multi-Vapor | 10R + 20M +⅔ stop | 30R + 15M +1⅓ stops | 20R + 15M +1 stop | 20R + 20M +⅔ stop | 60R + 20Y +1⅔ stops | 50R + 10Y +1⅓ stops |
| Deluxe White Mercury | 20R + 20M +⅔ stop | 30R + 30M +1⅓ stops | 10R + 25M +1 stop | 30R + 30M +1⅓ stops | 70R + 10Y +1⅔ stops | 50R + 10Y +1⅓ stops |
| Clear Mercury | 80R +1⅔ stops | 120R + 20M‡ +3 stops | 110R + 10M‡ +2⅔ stops | 70R† +1⅓ stops | 90R + 40Y +2 stops | 90R + 40Y +2 stops |

**Note:** The filters in the table are KODAK Color Compensating Filters (CC). Increase exposure by the amount shown in the table. Do not use sodium-vapor lamps for critical applications. Red filters have been substituted for equivalent values in magenta and yellow, and blue filters have been substituted for equivalent values in cyan and magenta. These substitutions were made to reduce the number of filters or to keep the exposure adjustment to a minimum (or both).

*This is a high-pressure sodium-vapor lamp. The information in the table may not apply to other manufacturers' high-pressure sodium-vapor lamps because of differences in spectral characteristics.

†For EKTACHROME 400 Film (Daylight) and EKTACHROME P800/1600 Professional Film (Daylight), use 25M + 40Y and increase exposure by 1 stop.

‡This combination includes 4 filters; it is an exception to our recommendation of using a maximum of 3 filters.

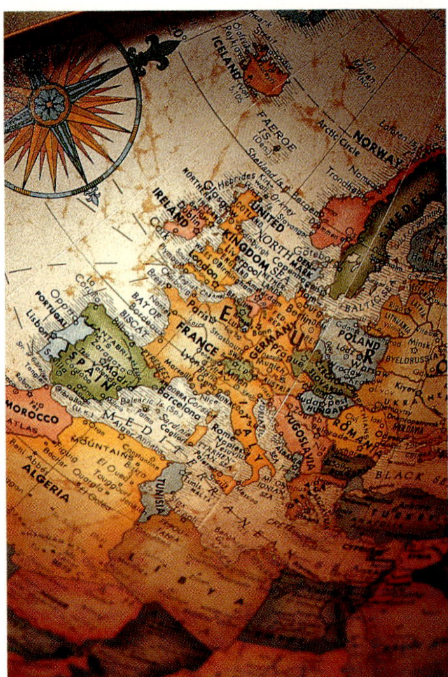


KODACHROME 40 Film (Type A) SAM CAMPANARO

Photolamps let you see and adjust the lighting before you take the picture.

## USING PHOTOLAMP ILLUMINATION

You may want to make some indoor portraits of your family or friends, photograph small objects close up, or make title slides for your slide shows. Photolamps sold by photo dealers are excellent light sources for these subjects. Lamps are generally available in two color temperatures designated 3400 K and 3200 K. The advantage of using photolamps is that it's so easy to control the light. You can see the effect of light placement and make corrections before you take the picture, and you can use your exposure meter to determine the exposure accurately.

When you want the highest quality and you don't need much film speed, KODACHROME 40 Film 5070 (Type A) is the best choice for color slides. You can use this slide film with 3400 K photolamps without a filter. To use it with 3200 K tungsten lamps, see the table on the next page for the recommended filter and film speed.

If you need a color-slide film with more speed, an excellent choice is KODAK EKTACHROME 160 Film (Tungsten), which requires no filter when you expose it with 3200 K illumination. You can also use it with 3400 K lamps if you use the proper filter. See the table.

You can take pictures on daylight color-slide film under photolamp illumination, but the conversion filters absorb a lot of light and reduce the speed of the film considerably, as shown by the table. So when you want color slides, it's better to use Type A or tungsten film.

If you want color prints of subjects lighted by photolamps, KODACOLOR GOLD and KODAK EKTAR Films exposed with the filter recommended in the table will give you excellent results. Even though you can use KODACOLOR GOLD and EKTAR Films under many existing-light sources without filters, you should use the recommended filter to expose these films with photolamps. The 3400 K and 3200 K lamps used for photography are brighter than normal household tungsten lamps, so you can use filters and still have plenty of light for proper exposure. Also, people expect accurate color rendition in photos made with photolamp illumination because of their professional appearance and because accurate color is more important for subjects such as portraits.

| Filters and Film Speeds for Exposing Daylight Films with Photolamp Illumination | | | | |
|---|---|---|---|---|
| KODAK Color Film | Photolamps (3400 K) | | Tungsten Lamps (3200 K) | |
| | Filter | Speed | Filter | Speed |
| KODACHROME 40 (Type A) | None | 40/17° | No. 82A | 32/16° |
| EKTACHROME 160 (Tungsten) | No. 81A | 125/22° | None | 160/23° |
| KODACHROME 25 (Daylight) | No. 80B | 8/10° | No. 80A | 6/9° |
| KODACHROME 64 (Daylight) | No. 80B | 20/14° | No. 80A | 16/13° |
| KODACHROME 200 (Daylight) | No. 80B | 64/19° | No. 80A | 50/18° |
| EKTACHROME 64 (Daylight) | No. 80B | 20/14° | No. 80A | 16/13° |
| EKTACHROME 100 HC | No. 80B | 32/16° | No. 80A | 25/15° |
| EKTACHROME 200 (Daylight) | No. 80B | 64/19° | No. 80A | 50/18° |
| EKTACHROME 400 (Daylight) | No. 80B | 125/22° | No. 80A | 100/21° |
| KODACOLOR GOLD 100 | No. 80B | 32/16° | No. 80A | 25/15° |
| KODACOLOR GOLD 200 | No. 80B | 64/19° | No. 80A | 50/18° |
| KODACOLOR GOLD 400 | No. 80B | 125/22° | No. 80A | 100/21° |
| KODACOLOR GOLD 1600 | No. 80B | 500/28° | No. 80A | 400/27° |
| EKTAR 25 | No. 80B | 8/10° | No. 80A | 6/9° |
| EKTAR 125 | No. 80B | 40/17° | No. 80A | 32/16° |
| EKTAR 1000 | No. 80B | 320/26° | No. 80A | 250/25° |

**Note:** If your camera has a built-in exposure meter that makes the reading through a filter used over the lens, see your camera manual for instructions on exposure with filters. Also, see page 94.

## DEFINITION

Definition is the clarity of detail that you see when you view a photograph. Several elements of image structure combine to give you the impression of definition. The degree of graininess, resolving power, and sharpness are usually used to describe the definition of a film. Classifications for each of these factors have been assigned to Kodak films for general use. (See the Data Sheets for the films.) For a more thorough discussion of definition, see page 67.

Because the "Degree of Enlargement" classification described on page 70 applies to prints, this classification isn't included in the Data Sheets for color-slide films. When color prints are made from color slides, the degree of enlargement depends on the method used to make the prints, i.e., through internegatives or directly on color-reversal paper.

## PROCESSING

Have your film processed promptly after exposure. You can return Kodak color film to your photo dealer for processing, or you can process KODACOLOR GOLD, KODAK EKTAR, and KODAK EKTACHROME Films yourself by using processing kits sold by photo dealers. All the required chemicals and instructions for processing are included in the kits.

When you have taken some unusually important pictures, and you're concerned that they could be misplaced or lost when sent to a processing lab, you may want to take special precautions in identifying your film. You can photograph a piece of paper or cardboard with your name and address printed on it on one frame of the film to identify you as the owner. For extra assurance in the mail, it's also a good idea to attach a name-and-address sticker or band directly to the film magazine in case the film

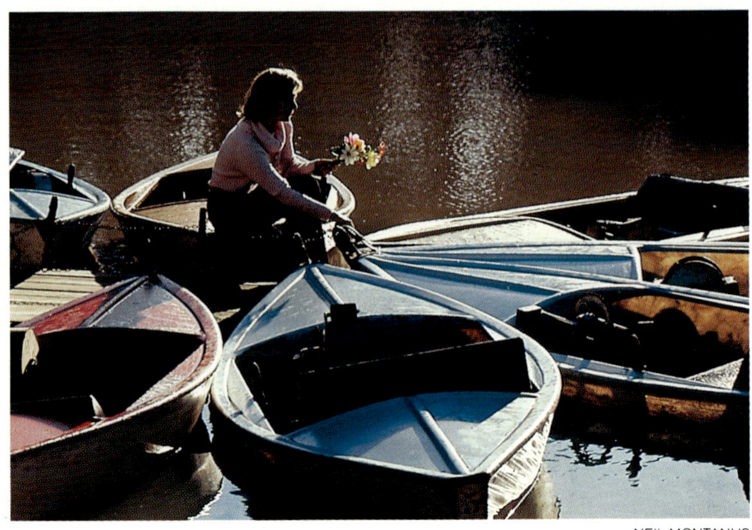

NEIL MONTANUS

KODACHROME Films are well known for their outstanding definition characteristics. KODACHROME 64 Film (Daylight), 1/125 second *f*/8

becomes separated from the mailing package.

See pages 73 through 75 for information on film tanks and procedures for film processing. For more information on processing and printing Kodak color films, see your photo dealer or write to Kodak Information Center, Eastman Kodak Company, Rochester, New York 14650-0811, and request *Introduction to Processing and Printing KODAK Color Films,* KODAK Publication No. AE-12.

### Processing KODACOLOR GOLD and KODAK EKTAR Films

To process these films, you can use the KODAK HOBBY-PAC™ Color-Negative Film Kit or KODAK FLEXICOLOR Chemicals for Process C-41. The HOBBY-PAC Kit features foil packets of concentrated chemicals that make 500 mL (16.9 fluidounces) of each of the four solutions.

The process requires 7 steps that take 24¼ minutes, not including the time it takes for the film to dry. The temperature of the developer for the first step must be 100°F ±0.25° (37.8°C ±0.15°). The other solutions and the wash water should be within the range 75 to 105°F (24 to 41°C). The processing steps are as follows:

| Step/Solution | Time (min:sec) |
|---|---|
| Developer | 3:15* |
| Bleach | 6:30 |
| Wash (running water) | 3:15 |
| Fixer | 6:30 |
| Wash (running water) | 3:15 |
| Stabilizer | 1:30 |
| Dry | 10 to 20 min |

*See the chemical instructions for development-time increases for subsequent processes.

After your film is processed, you can have prints made through your photo dealer or you can make them yourself in your own darkroom. If you have questions about making your own color prints, write to Kodak at the address given above. You can purchase Kodak books on film processing and making color prints, such as KODAK Publication No. R-19, *KODAK Color Darkroom DATAGUIDE,* from your photo dealer or bookstore.

### Processing KODAK EKTACHROME Films

To process these films, you can use the KODAK HOBBY-PAC Color Slide Kit. The process for the HOBBY-PAC Kit has 8 steps and takes approximately 30 minutes at 100°F (38°C), not including the time it takes for the film to dry. You can use processing temperatures between 70 and 110°F (21 and 43.5°C) if you adjust the solution times, but you'll obtain best results with solution temperatures between 96 and 110°F (35.5 and 43.5°C). The higher process temperatures require a recirculating water bath to keep the containers of solutions at the proper temperature.

Complete instructions are provided in the processing kit. The steps in the process and the time in each solution at 100°F (38°C) are as follows:

| Step/Solution | Time (min:sec) |
|---|---|
| First Developer | 6:30* |
| Wash | 1 to 3 min |
| Color Developer | 6:00 |
| Wash | 1 to 3 min |
| Bleach-Fix | 10:00 |
| Final Wash | 4:00 |
| Stabilizer | 1:00 |
| Dry | As needed |

*See the chemical instructions for development-time increases for subsequent processes. Different processing times in the first developer are required for processing EKTACHROME P800/1600 Film. See the discussion below.

To process EKTACHROME P800/1600 Professional Film, extend the time in the first developer at 100°F (38°C) to 10½ minutes for a speed of EI 800 (Push 1), or to 13 minutes for a speed of EI 1600 (Push 2). The times for the other steps in the process remain the same. For other temperatures and film speeds, see the kit instructions.

You can also process EKTACHROME Films in the KODAK EKTACHROME Film Processing Kit, Process E-6 (1 gallon). This process has 11 steps and requires 37 minutes (not including the drying time). Instructions are provided in the processing kit.

With both of these kits, you can increase the effective speed of EKTACHROME Films by as much as three stops by push-processing, or decrease the speed of the films by as much as two stops by pull-processing. To push-process, you increase the time in the first developer; to pull-process, you decrease the time in the first developer. See "Special Processing for Increased Speed," below, the table on page 52, and the processing-kit instructions.

Handling color film during processing is similar to handling black-and-white film (see page 73). The main differences are that different processing chemicals are required, color processes include more steps, and solution times and temperatures are more critical. Color processing has to be precise and consistent for satisfactory results, so carefully follow the instructions that come with the chemicals. KODAK Publication No. R-19, *KODAK Color Darkroom DATAGUIDE*, provides information on processing Kodak color films.

**Special Processing for Increased Speed**—When lighting conditions are dim, as they are in many existing-light scenes, you may need higher film speed for hand-holding your camera, stopping action, using a telephoto lens, or using a small lens opening to gain depth of field. You can increase the speed of KODAK EKTACHROME Films by obtaining special processing from a processing lab, or by extending the first-developer time if you process the film yourself.

KODAK EKTACHROME P800/1600 Professional Film is designed for push processing to attain its very high speeds. If you want to process the film yourself to obtain increased speed, simply increase the normal first-development time by the amount given in the table on page 52. For all the other steps, follow the normal processing times given in the instructions

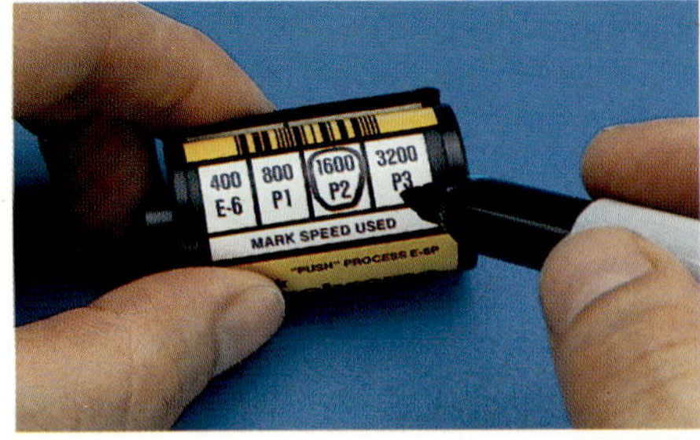


DON BUCK

For KODAK EKTACHROME P800/1600 Professional Film (Daylight), circle the speed you used to expose the film.

that come with the chemicals. When you process your own films, you can change their effective speeds over a wide range, as shown in the table. Exposing and processing the film at speeds other than the normal EI 800 or 1600 will result in some loss of photographic quality. The more you vary the speed from normal, the greater the reduction in quality.

**Process Adjustments for KODAK EKTACHROME Films**

| KODAK EKTACHROME Film | | | | | KODAK EKTACHROME Film Processing Kit | | KODAK HOBBY-PAC Color Slide Kit |
|---|---|---|---|---|---|---|---|
| 800/1600 Professional | 400 | 200 | 160 | 100 HC | Change First-Developer Time by (min:sec) | OR Change Temperature by | Change First-Developer Time by (min:sec) at 100°F/38°C |
| Film Speed (ISO or EI) | | | | | | | |
| 200 | 200 | 100 | 80 | 50 | −2:00 | −6°F (3.3°C) | −1:15 |
| 400 | 200 | 160 | 100 | 100 | No change | No change | No change |
| 800 | 800 | 400 | 320 | 200 | +2:00 | +8°F (4.4°C) | +4:30 |
| 1600 | 1600 | 800 | 640 | 400 | +5:00 | +12°F (6.7°C) | +6:30 |
| 3200 | — | — | — | — | +7:30 | +16°F (8.9°C) | +9:30 |

### Prints or Slides from Your Negatives, Prints, or Slides

After your color negatives or slides are processed, you can have prints made through your photo dealer, or you can make them yourself in your own darkroom.

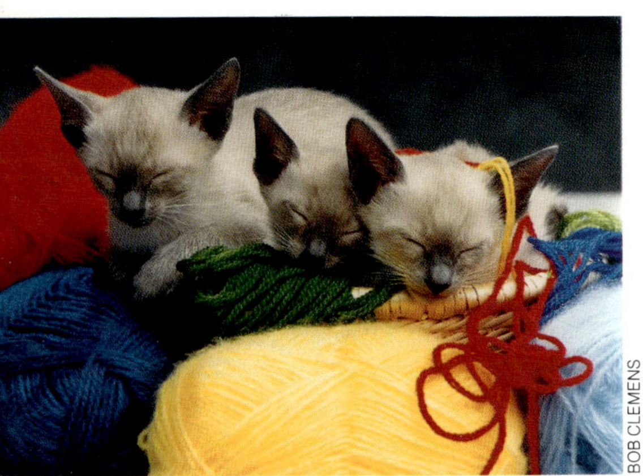

BOB CLEMENS

You can make black-and-white prints from color negatives by printing them on KODAK PANALURE Paper (see next page).

You can have duplicates made of your slides or transparencies, or have color slides made from your color negatives or color prints. It's also possible to have color negatives made from color prints or slides.

If you want black-and-white prints from color negatives, you can make them on KODAK PANALURE Papers, which are specially designed for printing color negatives. Instructions are included with the paper. To make black-and-white prints from color slides, you'll need to make a black-and-white negative from each slide first. Some processing labs also make black-and-white prints from color negatives or slides.

If you are interested in making your own prints or duplicate slides, see KODAK Publication No. R-19, *KODAK Color Darkroom DATAGUIDE*, available from your photo dealer or bookstore.

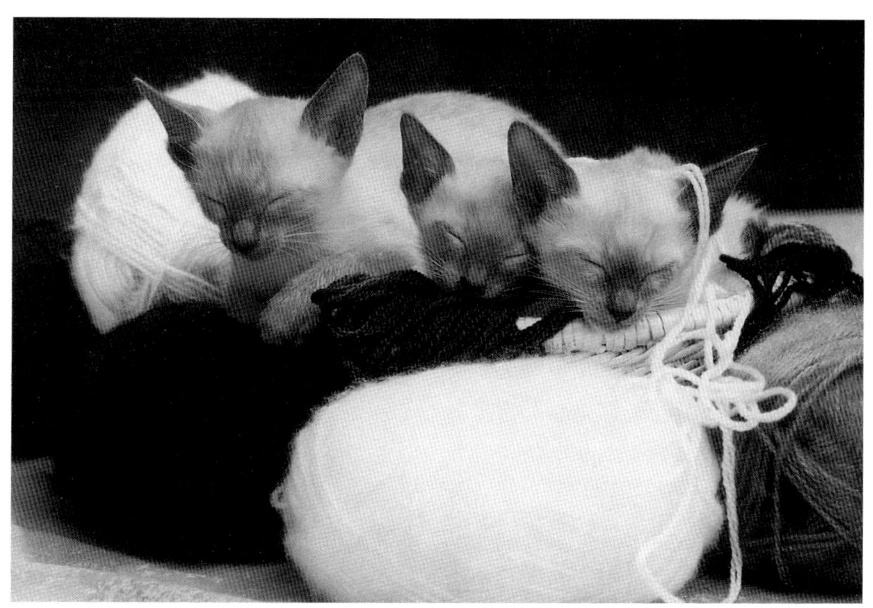

Color negative printed on KODAK PANALURE Paper—no filter.

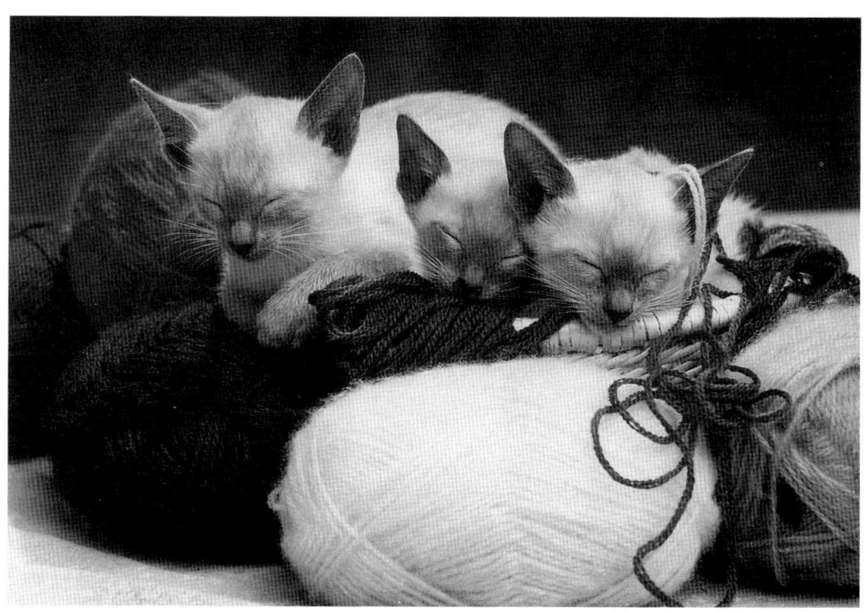

Although PANALURE Paper is intended for exposure without filters, you can use KODAK Color Compensating Filters or KODAK WRATTEN Gelatin Filters in the enlarger to obtain results other than the usual panchromatic rendering. KODAK WRATTEN Gelatin Filter No. 25.

# *KODAK* BLACK-AND-WHITE FILMS

The most important considerations in selecting a black-and-white film for conventional photography are film speed and definition. A few films are designed for special purposes, such as recording infrared radiation and copying printed material. See the table of Kodak black-and-white films on page 118.

## FILMS FOR GENERAL USE

**KODAK T-MAX 100 Professional Film**, which incorporates KODAK T-GRAIN Emulsions, is a medium-speed (EI 100) general-purpose film that is especially well suited for photographing detailed subjects when you need maximum image quality. It has extremely high sharpness, extremely fine grain, and very high resolving power, which allow a very high degree of enlargement. You can also expose this film at EI 200 and process it normally; at EI 400 or EI 800, you should push-process the film (see page 78).

You can also use T-MAX 100 Film with the KODAK T-MAX 100 Direct Positive Film Developing Outfit to produce high-quality black-and-white slides of continuous-tone photographs, duplicate black-and-white slides, black-and-white slides from color slides, or copy negatives from black-and-white or color negatives. Expose the film at EI 50 when you use it for these applications.

This film is also available in 120-size rolls and in sheets.

**KODAK T-MAX 400 Professional Film** also incorporates T-GRAIN Emulsions to combine high speed with extremely fine grain. It is especially useful for dimly lighted subjects or fast action, for extending the flash range, and for subjects that require good depth of field and fast shutter speeds with maximum image quality for the film speed. This film has high speed (EI 400), very high sharpness, extremely fine grain, and high

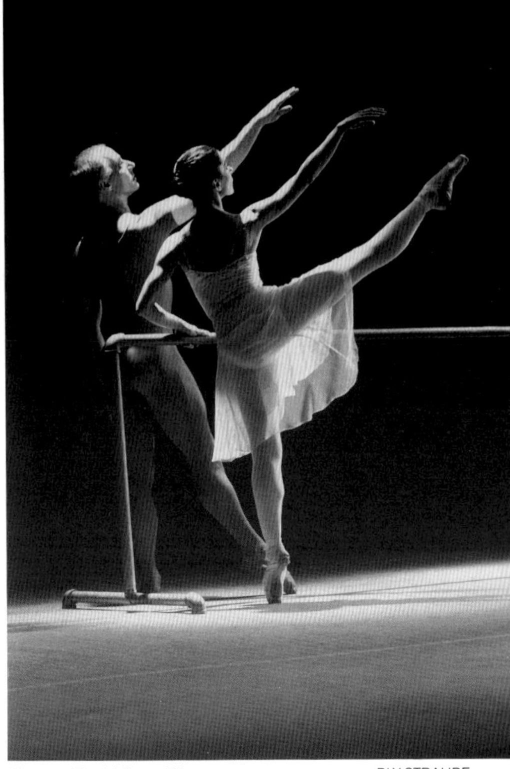

KODAK TRI-X Pan Film BLY STRAUBE

resolving power; it allows a high degree of enlargement. You can also expose it at a speed of EI 800 with normal processing, or at EI 1600 with push processing to obtain excellent results with many types of scenes and subjects. This film is also available in 120-size rolls and in sheets.

**KODAK T-MAX P3200 Professional Film** is a multi-speed film that combines high to ultra-high film speed with finer grain than that of other fast black-and-white films. It also has T-GRAIN Emulsions. T-MAX P3200 Film is especially useful for very fast action; for dimly lighted scenes where you can't use flash; for subjects that require good depth of field combined with fast shutter speeds; and for hand-holding telephoto lenses for fast action or in dim light. It is an excellent choice for indoor or nighttime sports

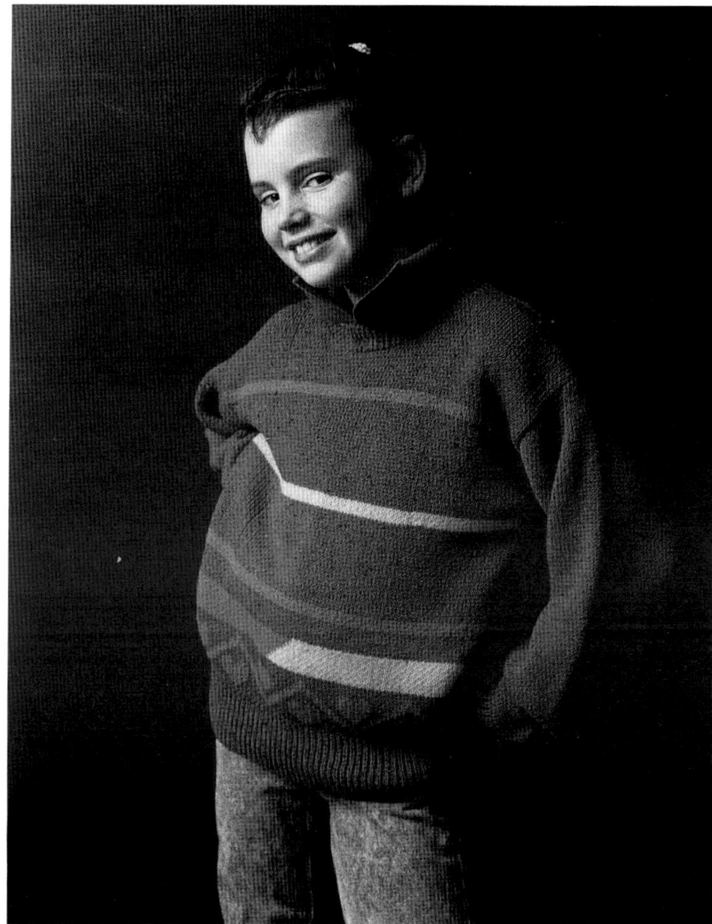

KODAK T-MAX 100 Professional Film KEITH BOAS

KODAK T-MAX 100 Professional Film, a medium-speed general-purpose film, has extremely high sharpness and very high resolving power, which allow a very high degree of enlargement.

events and available-light press photography, as well as law-enforcement and general surveillance applications that require exposure indexes of 3200 to 25,000.

The nominal speed is EI 1000 when the film is processed in KODAK T-MAX Developer, or EI 800 when it is processed in other Kodak continuous-tone black-and-white developers. For ease in calculating exposure, the nominal speed has been rounded to EI 800.

Because of its great latitude, you can expose this film at EI 1600 and yield negatives of high quality. When you need a higher speed, you can expose this film at EI 3200 or 6400 with an increase in development time. At these higher speeds, there will be a slight increase in contrast and granularity with a loss of shadow detail.

For general use, it's best to expose this film at EI 3200 or 6400. These speeds allow you to take photographs in many situations where photography was previously impossible. To expose film at speeds higher than EI 6400, run tests to determine if the results are satisfactory for your needs.

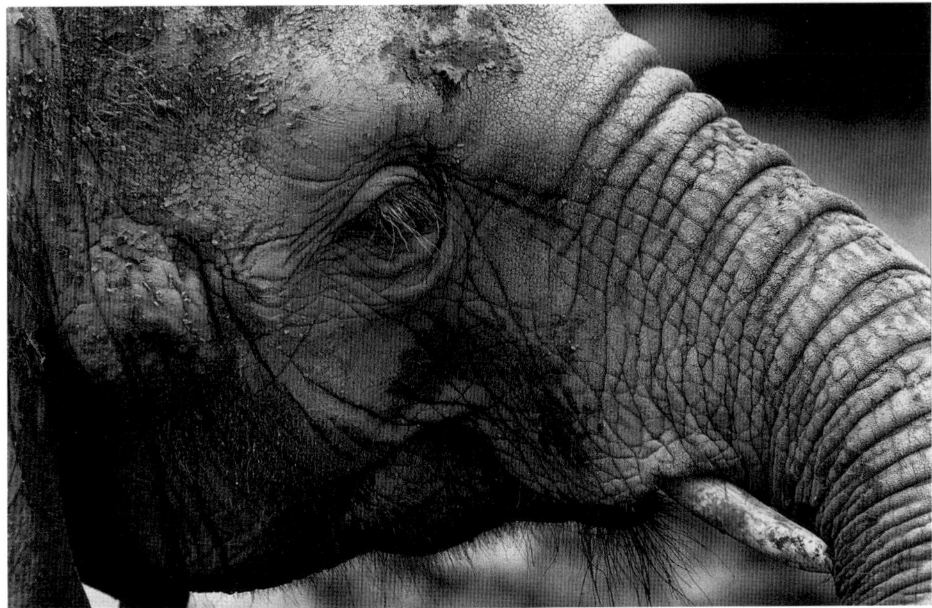

Kodak T-Max 400 Professional Film — KEVIN HIGLY

Kodak T-Max 400 Professional Film combines high speed with extremely fine grain. It is especially good for dimly lighted subjects or fast action, and for extending flash range.

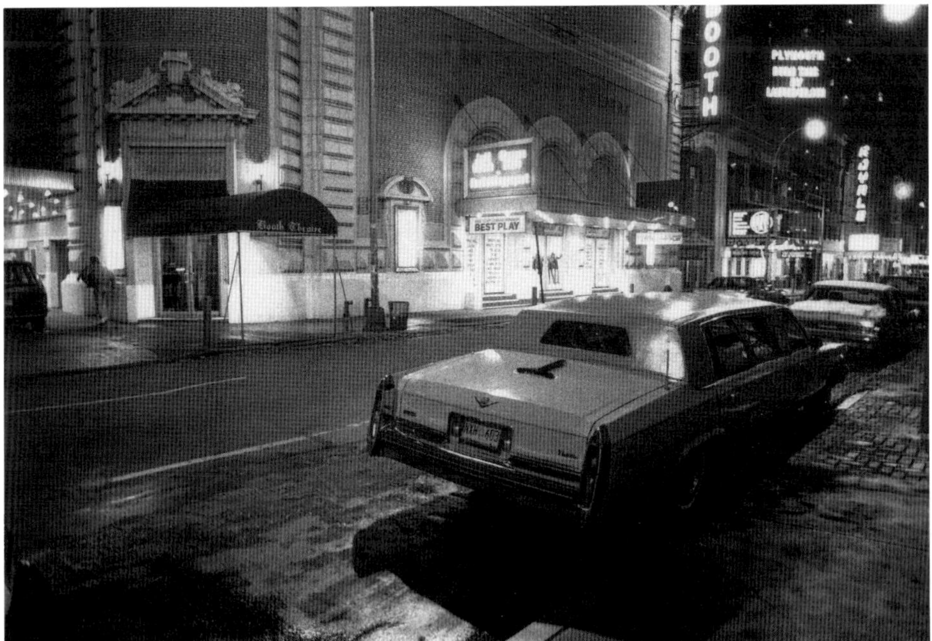


Kodak T-Max P3200 Professional Film — BOB CLEMENS

Kodak T-Max P3200 Professional Film is a multi-speed film that is especially useful in dim light and for very fast action. It is an excellent choice for indoor or nighttime sports events and available-light press photography.

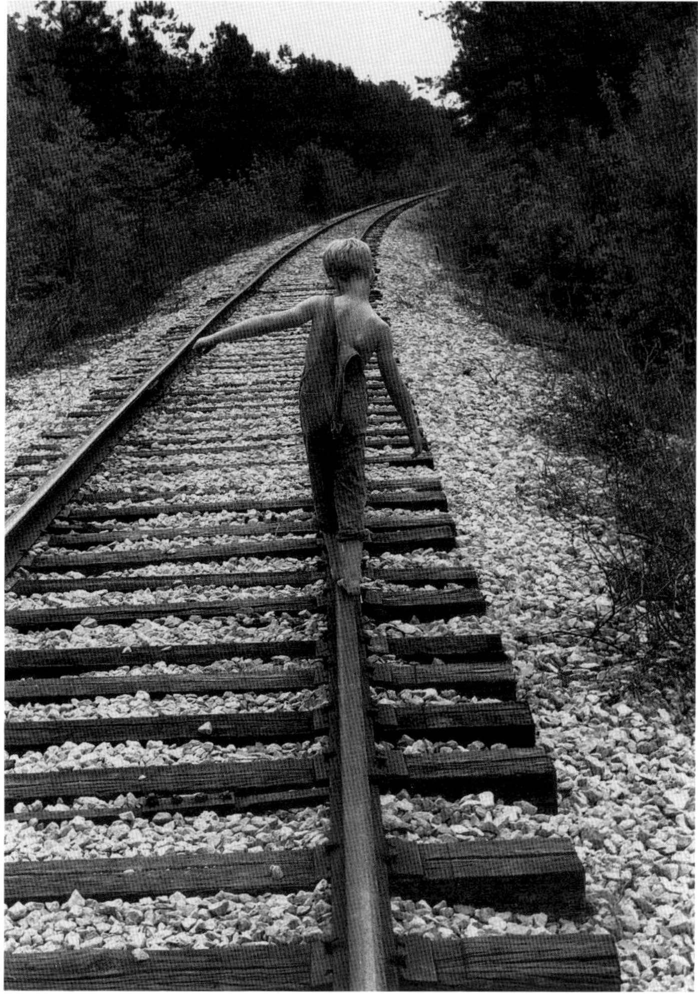

KODAK PLUS-X Pan Film ELAINE WALKER

KODAK PLUS-X Pan Film is a medium-speed film with excellent definition, wide exposure latitude, and beautiful tonal qualities that make it a good choice for all-around picture-taking.

**KODAK PLUS-X Pan Film** is a general-purpose panchromatic film that features extremely fine grain, very high sharpness, and high resolving power, which allow a high degree of enlargement. PLUS-X Pan Film has medium speed—ISO 125—which makes it suitable for use under most average lighting conditions. Its combination of medium speed, excellent definition, wide exposure latitude, and beautiful tonal qualities makes it a good choice for all-around picture-taking.

You can also expose PLUS-X Pan Film at EI 250 with normal processing, or at EI 500 with push processing. A professional version of this film is available in 120 and 220 sizes.

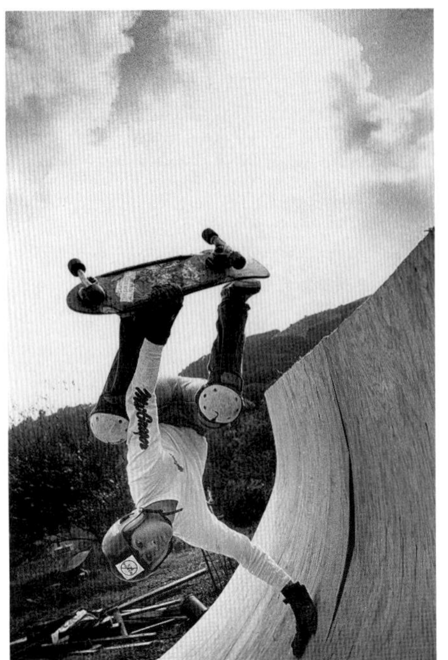

KODAK TRI-X Pan Film BRENTON GREGORY

KODAK TRI-X Pan Film is a great film for sports photography. Its film speed of 400 captured this skateboader in midair.

**KODAK TRI-X Pan Film** is a high-speed panchromatic film with fine grain and high sharpness. The combination of high speed—ISO 400—with very good definition characteristics and wide exposure latitude makes TRI-X Pan Film an excellent choice for photographing existing-light subjects, fast action, and subjects that call for good depth of field or high shutter speeds. It also extends the distance range for flash pictures. This film has great flexibility because it lets you take pictures under a wide range of subject and lighting conditions from bright sunlight to relatively low light. You can expose it at EI 800 and process it normally, or expose it at EI 1600 with push processing. TRI-X Pan Film is also sold in 120 size.

**KODAK Technical Pan Film** is a multi-purpose, panchromatic film with extended red sensitivity, micro-fine grain, and extremely high resolving power. You can vary the contrast of the film from normal, for pictorial uses, through moderately high to high by your choice of developer and development time. The speed of the film varies with the type of photographs you make and the development.

This film is superb for making impressive giant-sized pictorial enlargements with extreme sharpness and a minimum of grain. For pictorial uses, you should expose the film at EI 25 and develop it in a special low-contrast developer, such as KODAK TECHNIDOL Liquid Developer or KODAK TECHNIDOL LC Developer, to achieve normal contrast and sufficient exposure latitude. Conventional developers produce negative contrast that's too high for pictorial photographs. See page D 33 for important information on using TECHNIDOL Developers.

Technical Pan Film developed in TECHNIDOL Developer provides the finest grain and highest resolving power of any black-and-white pictorial film ever offered by Kodak. Extremely high sharpness and micro-fine grain provide enlargements of excellent quality at magnifications of 25X or even 50X, which is equivalent to a 4 x 6-foot enlargement from a frame of 35 mm film. The film-and-developer combination produces a full tonal range ideally suited to pictorial photography, exhibition prints, and similar premium-quality applications of black-and-white photography.

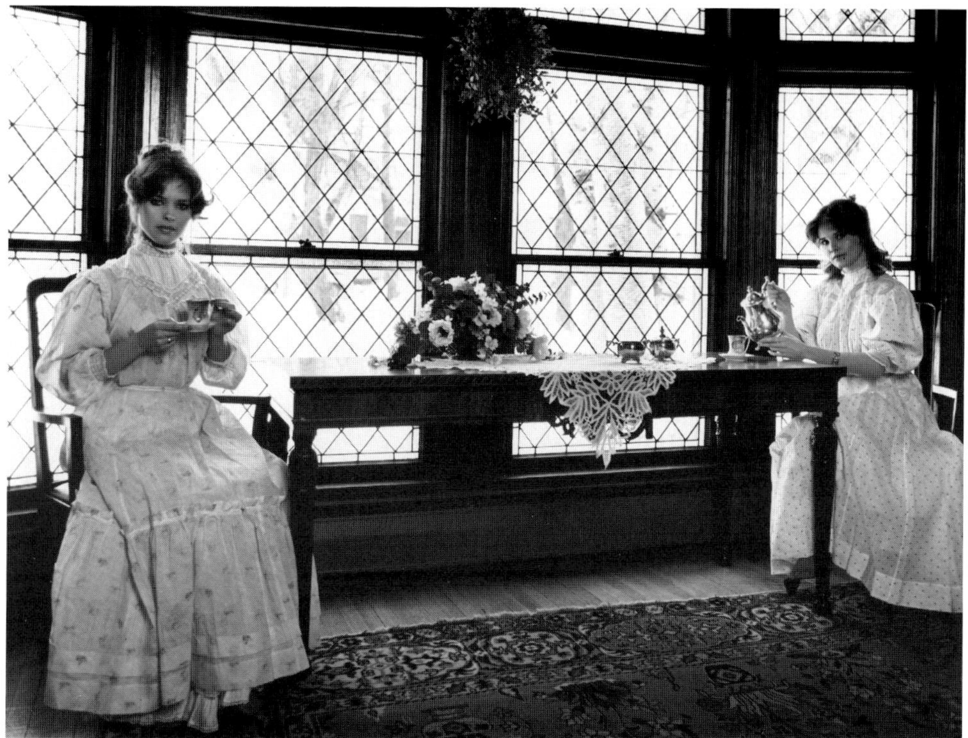

KODAK Technical Pan Film — BOB CLEMENS

KODAK Technical Pan Film is superb for making impressive giant-sized pictorial enlargements with extreme sharpness and a minimum of grain.

The variable contrast and excellent definition characteristics of Technical Pan Film make it very useful for copying. You can use it to copy black-and-white or color originals and printed matter that includes both illustrations and type, such as books, magazines, and documents. (See the discussion on photographing copyrighted material on page 61.) This is an excellent film for microfilming and record-keeping. It has a tungsten speed of EI 320 when you use it as a high-contrast material.

You can also use it with the KODAK T-MAX 100 Direct Positive Film Developing Outfit to produce high-contrast black-and-white slides of line art, computer-generated graphics, typography, etc. Expose the film at EI 64 when you use it to make slides.

Technical Pan Film is also available in size 120 and sheets.

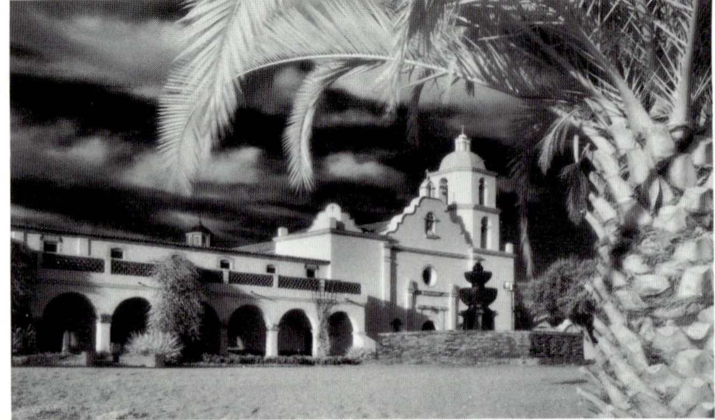

For an eerie, abstract quality in architectural or landscape photographs, take your pictures on KODAK High Speed Infrared Film 2481 with a No. 25 filter. 1/60 second *f*/16

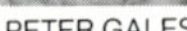

PETER GALES

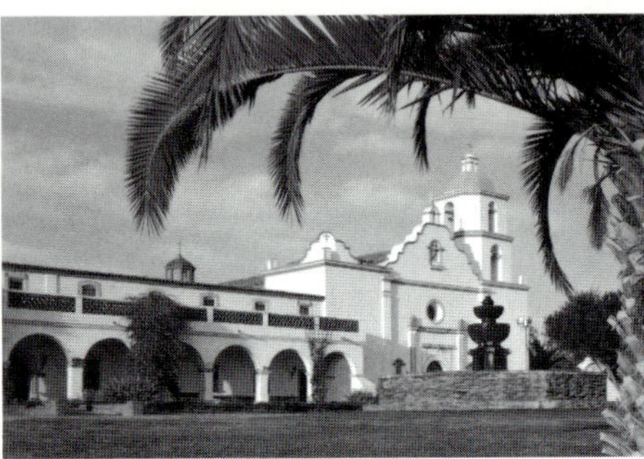

Conventional rendering on KODAK PLUS-X Pan Film, no filter. 1/125 second *f*/16

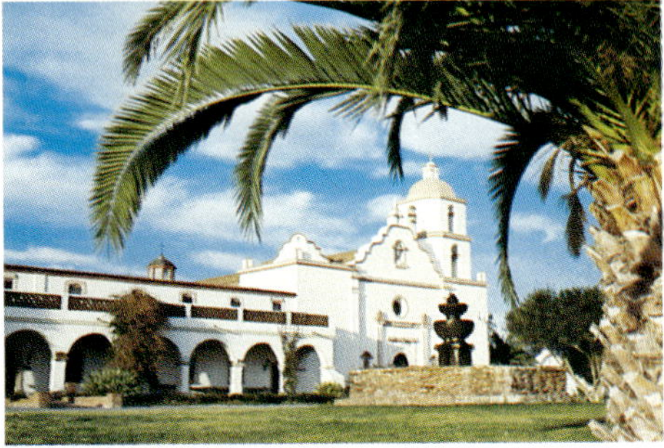

Normal appearance

**KODAK High Speed Infrared Film** is a fast, moderately high contrast film that's sensitive to infrared radiation. When you use the recommended filter with this film, you can create striking and unusual photographs of subjects such as landscapes and architecture. In infrared photographs, the sky appears almost black; shadows are dark, but usually show adequate detail; live grass and leaves appear very light, as though covered by snow; and distant details obscured by haze in the original scene show up with remarkable clarity. This film has many applications in technical and scientific photography.

You can take pictures on High Speed Infrared Film with daylight, electronic flash, or photolamps with the recommended filter. See pages D 36 and D 37. The film has an approximate tungsten speed of 125 and an approximate daylight index of 50 with a KODAK WRATTEN Gelatin Filter No. 25 (red). The film has fine grain, but it is not intended for high degrees of enlargement. You can print the negatives on conventional black-and-white photographic papers.

Camera lenses do not focus infrared rays in the same plane as visible light rays. Some camera lenses have index marks for infrared focusing on their focusing scales. If your lens does not have an infrared focusing mark, focus on the near side of the main subject, and use a small lens opening. See page D 36.

Because of the sensitivity of KODAK High Speed Infrared Film, you must load and unload your camera in total darkness; do not use a safelight. (See page D 36.) Store 135 magazines of this film in the tightly closed film cans. Unexposed film requires refrigerated storage at 55°F (13°C) or lower. A sheet film is also available.

## OTHER *KODAK* BLACK-AND-WHITE FILMS

Several Kodak black-and-white 35 mm films are designed for professional or special use. Descriptions of the most popular special films are given below; if you have questions about these films, write to Kodak at the address given on page 33. For complete information on professional black-and-white films, see KODAK Publication No. F-5, *KODAK Professional Black-and-White Films,* available from photo dealers or bookstores.

The following films are sold by photo dealers who sell professional or audio-visual photographic products.

**KODAK EKTAGRAPHIC HC Slide Film** is an extremely high contrast orthochromatic film intended primarily for making reverse-text black-and-white title slides. It produces clear images on a black background when you use it to photograph black text or artwork on a white background. You can then color the clear image areas of the transparency with water-soluble dyes or watercolors, or you can "sandwich" a color filter with the transparency to produce a title slide with colored lettering.

EKTAGRAPHIC HC Slide Film is the 135-size version of KODALITH Ortho Film / 6556, Type 3. The speed of the film varies with the developer used to process it. It has a tungsten speed of EI 8 when developed in KODALITH Developers. Development recommendations are provided in the instructions packaged with the film.

**EASTMAN Fine Grain Release Positive Film / 5302** is a low-speed blue-sensitive film with extremely fine grain and high sharpness for making black-and-white slides from continuous-tone or line negatives. This film is not intended for picture-taking. It's sold in 35 mm x 100-foot rolls.

### Films for Copying

To photograph continuous-tone originals—photographs, paintings, or pictures in magazines or books, for example—you can use one of the films recommended for general picture-taking, such as KODAK T-MAX 100 Professional Film or PLUS-X Pan Film. The speed of these films is adequate for originals lighted by photo-lamps. If the lighting is dim, such as existing light in an art gallery (ask permission to take pictures first), a better choice would be T-MAX 400 Professional Film or TRI-X Pan Film.

If you want to copy printed matter, such as the text in documents, magazines, or newspapers, you'll get better results with a high-contrast film. For example, if you copy printed material with KODAK Technical Pan Film and develop it to a high contrast, your photos will have a cleaner, whiter background and will look more like the originals than photos made on conventional, general-purpose films.

**Copyrighted Material**—Although this is not legal advice, here's a note of caution. By law, the exclusive right to reproduce a copyrighted work belongs to the copyright owner. Limited copying for "fair use," such as criticism, news reporting, teaching, or research, is permitted. However, to avoid copyright problems, it's a good idea to get written permission from the copyright owner before making a copy. Responsibility for complying with copyright laws remains with the person making the photographic copy; Eastman Kodak Company can take no responsibility for copyright matters.

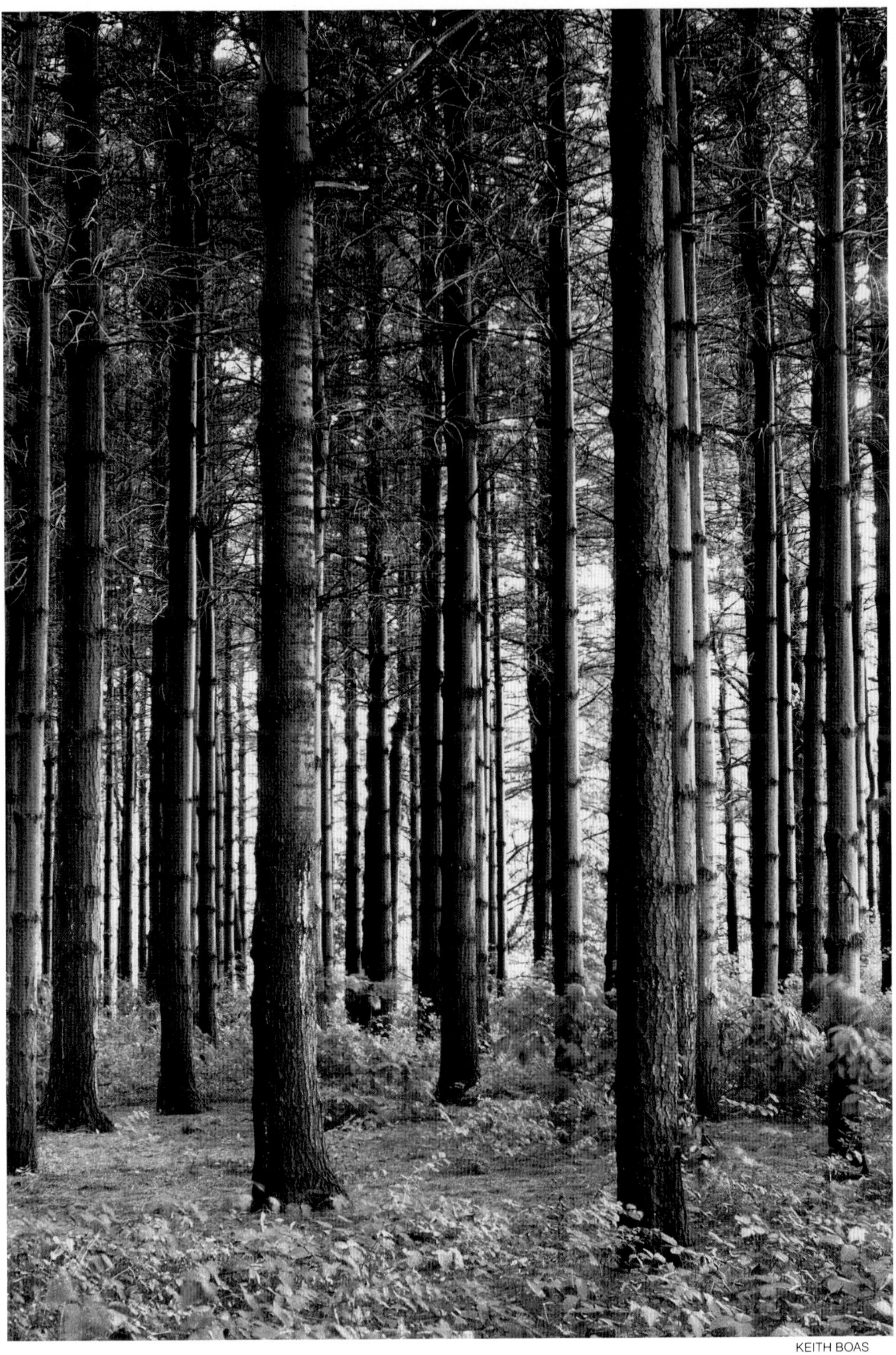

KEITH BOAS

## COLOR SENSITIVITY

The color sensitivity, or spectral sensitivity, of a film describes its response to light of different wavelengths or colors. While the normal eye is sensitive to all colors, the same is not necessarily true of films. Silver bromide, the basic light-sensitive element in all emulsions, is sensitive only to blue and ultraviolet light. Sensitizing dyes in the emulsions of panchromatic, orthochromatic, and infrared films make these classes of films sensitive to certain other colors or wavelengths of light or other radiation. The type of sensitizing is one of the most important photographic characteristics of a black-and-white film, because it affects both the monochomatic rendition of colors and the handling of the film in the darkroom.

Kodak black-and-white films are divided into several spectral-sensitivity classes. Except for certain special sensitizations, there are four general classes. Professional films are available in all four classes; films for general use are available in only two of them—panchromatic and infrared. The spectral sensitivity of each black-and-white film is given in the Data Sheets in this book. The four spectral-sensitivity classes are as follows:

**Non-color-sensitized or blue-sensitive** films are sensitive only to ultraviolet and blue-violet; this sensitivity is inherent in silver halides—the light-sensitive element in the emulsion.

**Orthochromatic** films are sensitive to green light in addition to ultraviolet and blue-violet.

**Panchromatic** films are sensitive to all visible colors, including red, as well as to invisible ultraviolet radiation. Some panchromatic films have extended red sensitivity.

**Infrared** films are sensitive to ultraviolet and all visible colors, including deep red, as well as to invisible infrared radiation.

The color sensitivity of a black-and-white film determines the following:

### Gray-Tone Rendition of Colored Objects

A film that's not sensitized to green or red light will reproduce these colors as very dark tones of gray in the print. Panchromatic films for general use will record colors as gray tones in the print with approximately the same relative brightnesses that your eye sees in the original scene. For critical work, you can use filters to control gray-tone rendition. See the filter recommendations in the Data Sheets.

A few panchromatic films, such as KODAK Technical Pan Film, have extended, or increased, red sensitivity. These films reproduce red objects as tones of gray that appear lighter than they appear to the eye and lighter than the tones produced by conventional panchromatic films. Caucasian flesh tones in photographs made with films that have extended red sensitivity may look lighter than normal. This characteristic may help mask the appearance of some types of skin blemishes.

You can reduce the effects of extended red sensitivity by using a color-compensating filter, such as KODAK Color Compensating Filter CC40C or CC50C (cyan) over the camera lens. Increase exposure by 1 stop with tungsten light or by 2 stops with daylight or electronic flash to compensate for the light absorbed by the filter. Because of variations between films, experiment to find the effect you like best.

### Filters and Filter Factors

The filters that you can use depend on the color sensitivity of your film. For example, you'd use a red filter only with a film sensitive to red light, such as a panchromatic film. Because filters absorb light, you must increase your camera exposure. This exposure increase is specified by the filter factor, which depends on the color sensitivity of the film and the color quality of the light source. For example, a film with a large portion of its sensitivity in the blue-violet region requires a much greater relative exposure through a yellow filter, which eliminates most of the blue light, than a panchromatic film requires. Panchromatic film is sensitive to all colors and therefore can record the red and green light transmitted by the yellow filter. Applying the filter factors for proper exposure is explained on page 94.

If you want to make an object appear darker in the print than it appears to the eye, use a filter of a color that is complementary to the color of the object. For example, a yellow filter darkens a blue sky. To lighten the gray-tone rendering of an object, use a filter similar in color to the object. You can also use filters to increase the contrast between colored objects that would normally photograph as nearly the same shade of gray.

**Filter Designations—**The following list shows current filter designations, colors, and the effects produced by filters for use with black-and-white films:

Recommended filters and filter factors for each black-and-white film are given in the Data Sheets. For more information on filters, see KODAK Publication No. KW-13, *Using Filters*, available from photo dealers or bookstores.

### Safelight Filters

The function of a safelight filter is to provide maximum visibility in the darkroom without fogging film or paper. With some films, you can use a filter that transmits light in the region to which the film is least sensitive. For example, an orthochromatic film is sensitive only to blue-violet, blue, and green light. You can safely handle this kind of film under a safelight filter that transmits only red light, such as the KODAK 1A Safelight Filter (light red).

Because panchromatic films are sensitive to all colors of visible light, you must normally handle them in total darkness. With some films, you can use a KODAK 3 Safelight Filter (dark-green) for orientation in the darkroom or for inspecting the film for a few seconds during development.

Safelight recommendations for each Kodak black-and-white film are given in the film Data Sheets.

| Filter | Color | Effect |
|---|---|---|
| No. 8 | Yellow | Natural tone rendition. Darkens blue skies and slightly lightens foliage to improve landscapes, water, snow scenes, buildings, and other outdoor subjects. |
| No. 11 | Yellowish-Green | Retains natural skin tones while darkening the sky in outdoor portraits. Lightens foliage to improve rendering of texture in sunlight. |
| No. 15 | Deep Yellow | Makes blue skies darker than No. 8. Penetrates distant bluish haze in mountain scenes, aerial photos, outdoor telephoto shots. |
| No. 25 | Red | Darkens blue skies dramatically. Also good for scenes with light-colored buildings, trees, or snow against a blue sky. Underexposure gives a moonlight effect. |
| No. 29 | Deep Red | Makes blue skies almost black. Lightens skin tones dramatically. |
| No. 47 | Blue | Gives increased haze effects. Darkens skin tones, lips, and hair. |
| No. 58 | Green | Lightens foliage. Darkens lips dramatically. Increases contrast to add dimension to faces. |

## Graphical Representation of Typical Black-and-White Photographic Tone Reproduction

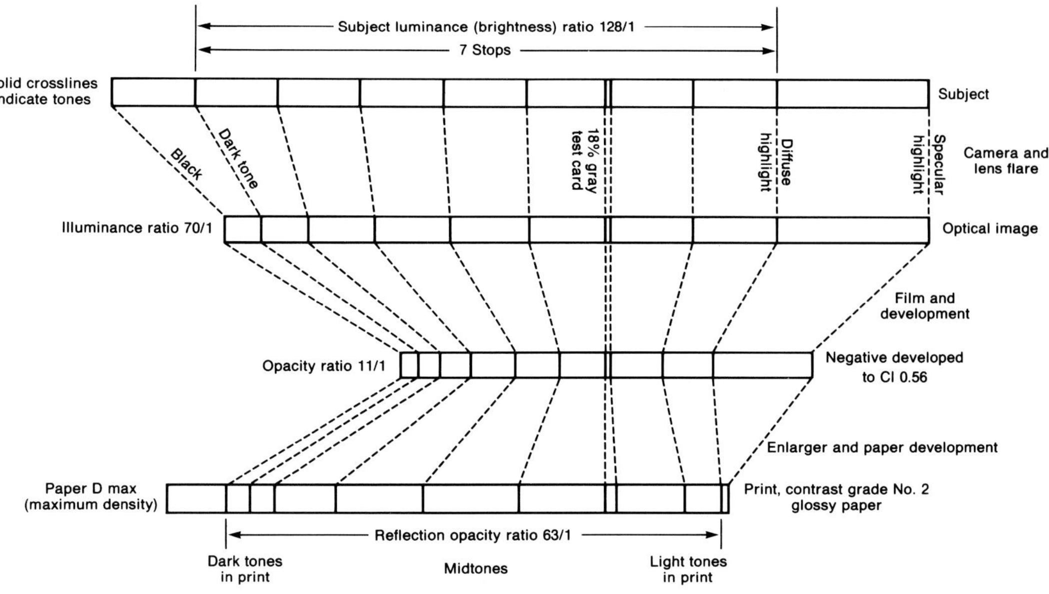


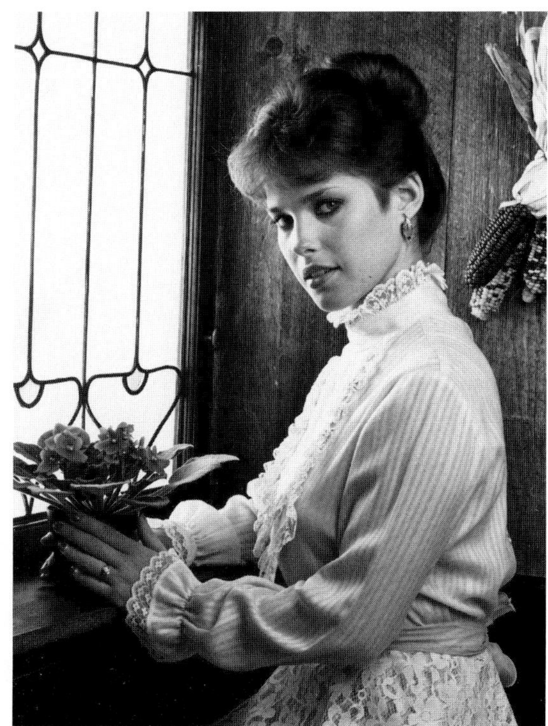

BOB CLEMENS

Excellent tone reproduction means: delicate gradation in the highlights, with diffuse highlights separated tonally from specular highlights, which are reproduced as white paper; good separation throughout the middle tones; and a range of shadow tones that provide enough detail but still have some areas of deepest black to provide a tonal foundation reference. The contrast and overall brightness should be appropriate for the subject. KODAK Technical Pan Film 2415 developed in KODAK TECHNIDOL LC Developer.

## TONE REPRODUCTION

In photography, the variations in brightness of the subject and the image on film or paper are called *tones*. Tone reproduction is the means by which the elements of the scene are reproduced to form an image. In color photographs, variations in brightness, hue, and saturation are all evident. Tone reproduction for color materials is determined by the manufacturer to produce optimum color rendition. The ability to alter tone reproduction in color photographs is more limited than in black-and-white unless you use complex or exotic methods; the objective in color photography is usually producing accurate color reproduction.

In black-and-white photographs, only the brightness is involved in tone reproduction. The neutral and colored tones of the subject are converted to tones of gray and black in the print. How well these tones are reproduced is an important criterion of photographic quality.

The overall brightness range of the typical outdoor frontlighted subject, with the sun at a 45-degree angle to the camera axis, exceeds 1000:1 when the deepest shadows and specular highlights are included. Typical black-and-white photographic paper can reproduce a brightness range of about 60:1. The brightness range of paper varies with the type of paper. Photographic paper with a glossy surface usually has the greatest brightness range, and is therefore capable of reproducing the greatest range of tones. Because the tonal range of the paper is less than the brightness range of the scene, the tonal scale of the image has to be compressed or selectively printed on the paper. We don't expect to see detail in the brilliant, specular highlights or in deep, black shadows, so we can eliminate these tones from the brightness scale of the subject when we consider tone reproduction. This leaves a subject brightness range of about 125:1, extending from the diffuse highlight areas to dark shadow areas. These dark shadows should appear slightly lighter than black in a print.

When you photograph a subject, the camera lens system introduces some flare into the optical image; this flare compresses the tonal scale, mainly in the shadows. The optical image is recorded on the film, and the film further compresses all the tones; the dark tones are compressed more than the midtones and highlights.

When the negative is finally printed on photographic paper, the paper expands the midtones of the negative while compressing both highlight and shadow areas. The paper compresses the highlight tones more than the shadows. This means that the overall tone reproduction has about the same amount of compression at both ends of the tonal scale. The dark tones of the subject are compressed by camera flare and film characteristics, and highlight tones in the subject are compressed by the paper. The greater compression of highlights by the paper balances the compression of shadows by flare and the film.

A basic understanding of tone reproduction helps photographers obtain high-quality results. Under most conditions, exposing Kodak black-and-white film at its rated speed and processing it as recommended in the film instructions or in the Data Sheets will provide high-quality negatives that will produce a high-quality print on normal-contrast paper. You may need to alter the developing time of your film slightly to adjust the contrast of your negatives for your printing equipment. See "Degree of Development" on page 75.

### Characteristics of a Good Negative

**Sharpness**—The areas of the negative that are intended to be sharp should be sharp and well-defined when you view the negative through a magnifier.

**Density**—The overall density (degree of blackness) of the negative should allow reasonably short printing times, such as

10 to 20 seconds for an 8X enlargement. See the center negative in the negative ringaround on page 77.

**Density Range (Tonal Scale)**—The tonal scale of the negative should give good highlight and shadow reproduction with good separation of midtones when it is printed on grade 2 (normal-contrast) photographic paper with your enlarger.

**Shadows**—Deepest shadows and black areas should be clear in the negative. Medium shadows should show detail and have varying light densities.

**Highlights**—Diffuse highlights should show gradation and detail, and have noticeably less density than brilliant white areas and specular highlights.

**Graininess**—The print image should not show excessive graininess for the kind of film and degree of enlargement that you used.

**Uniformity**—The negative should be free from mottle or unevenness caused by improper agitation during development or a short developing time. Development times shorter than 5 minutes in a small film tank may produce poor uniformity.

**Physical Defects**—The negative should not have physical imperfections, scratches, static markings, scum, water spots or marks, pinholes caused by dust or improper development, or dried-on dust particles or contaminants from the processing solutions or wash water.

## DEFINITION

The terms definition and sharpness are often used interchangeably, but such usage is only partly correct. Definition refers to the overall appearance of detail. Sharpness is one factor that affects definition; it describes the appearance of edge sharpness between details in a photograph.

Definition is the composite effect of several factors, including sharpness, resolving power, and graininess. Usually resolving power and sharpness increase as graininess decreases, but there are exceptions.

Descriptive terms for sharpness, resolving power, and graininess are given in the Data Sheet for each film. However, do not use these descriptions to compare films in one group, such as black-and-white negative films, with films in another, such as color-negative or color-slide films. Use them only to compare films within a single group. These terms are determined by instrument measurements and by critical observation. Instrument measurements and images are affected by factors such as diffusion, spectral sensitivity, halation, and contrast. These effects are less of a factor among films in a class, so comparison of definition terms within a class of films is valid. However, comparison of definition terms between different classes of films is not valid.

### Graininess

This refers to the sand-like or granular appearance in a film, slide, or print that results from the apparent clumping of silver grains in black-and-white film or prints or dye particles in color film or prints. Graininess is caused by the irregular distribution of the silver grains rather than by the individual grains themselves. Individual grains are not visible under the magnifications used for ordinary enlargements.

In films of a general type, graininess tends to increase with film speed. When a black-and-white film is developed in different developers to the same contrast index (see page 77), graininess will vary somewhat with the type of developer. Some fine-grain developers produce less graininess, but at the expense of film speed. The Data Sheets in this book normally offer a choice of several Kodak developers. For descriptions of black-and-white developers, see page D 38.

Graininess increases with overexposure or overdevelopment of black-and-white negatives, underexposure or over-

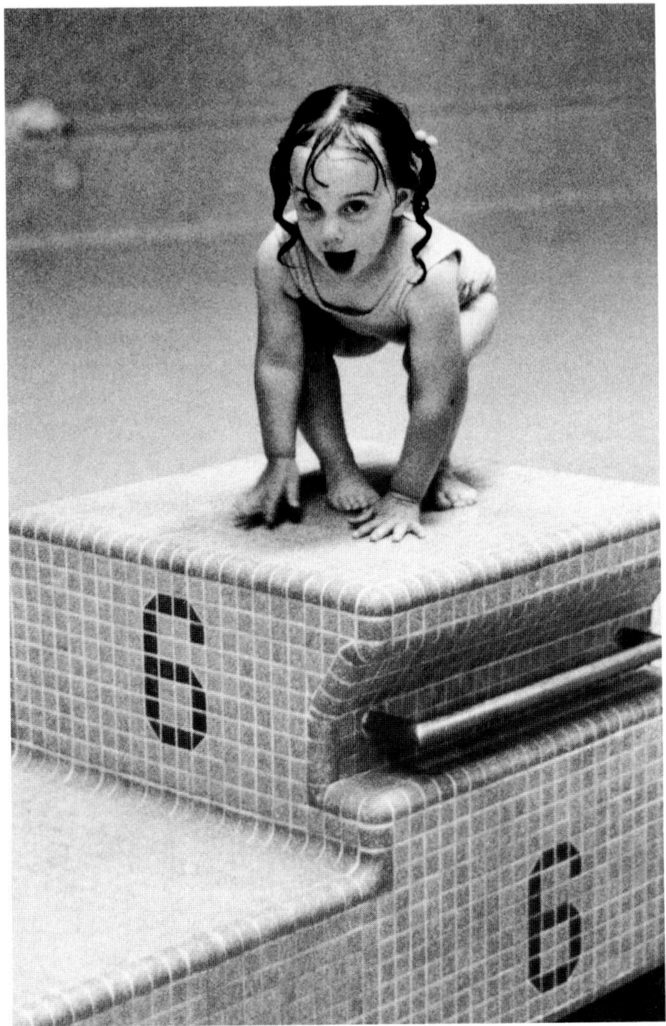

MARYE HORSMAN

The print image should not show excessive graininess and detail for the kind of film and degree of enlargement that you used.

development of color negatives, and overdevelopment of color-slide films in the first developer. Overdevelopment occurs when the temperature of the developer is too high, the development time is too long, or the film receives excessive agitation during development.

The graininess in a print is most apparent in the lighter midtones, especially in large, uniform areas such as the sky. You can make graininess less apparent by softening the focus of your enlarger or by printing on a paper with a rough-textured surface, but this also sacrifices sharpness. The type of enlarger you use affects the apparent graininess of black-and-white prints and slightly affects the sharpness. An enlarger with a diffuse light source produces slightly softer images and tends to minimize graininess. A condenser enlarger, which has a more specular light source, produces images that appear slightly sharper, but makes graininess more apparent.

The graininess of both negatives and prints increases with increasing contrast. Use the recommended development for your film, and use paper of the contrast grade that's suitable for the contrast of the negative. Printing paper that's too low in contrast for the negative reduces apparent sharpness; paper too high in contrast increases the appearance of graininess.

Graininess classifications, such as *micro fine, extremely fine, very fine, fine, medium, moderately coarse, coarse,* and *very coarse,* are given in the Data Sheets.

**Resolving Power**

The ability of a film or print material to record fine detail is referred to as resolving power. In resolving-power measurements, a parallel-line test chart is photographed at a great reduction in size (see the illustration). The lines of the test chart are separated by spaces of the same width as the lines. The image is examined under a microscope at a specific magnification, and the number of lines per millimetre that can be seen as separate lines is determined. Lines closer together than this number (more lines per millimetre) are indistinct from each other on the film and appear as a gray mass.

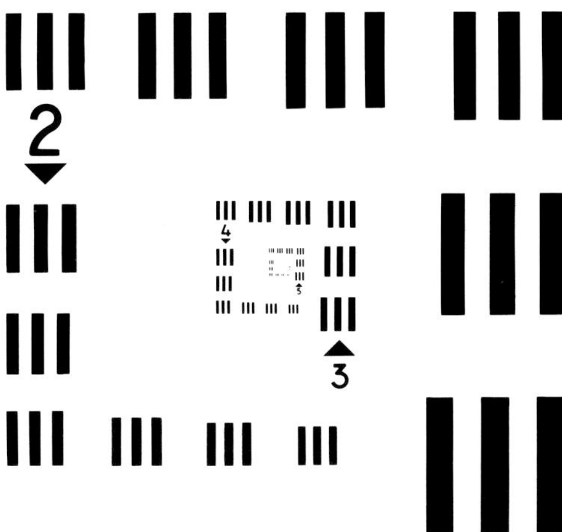


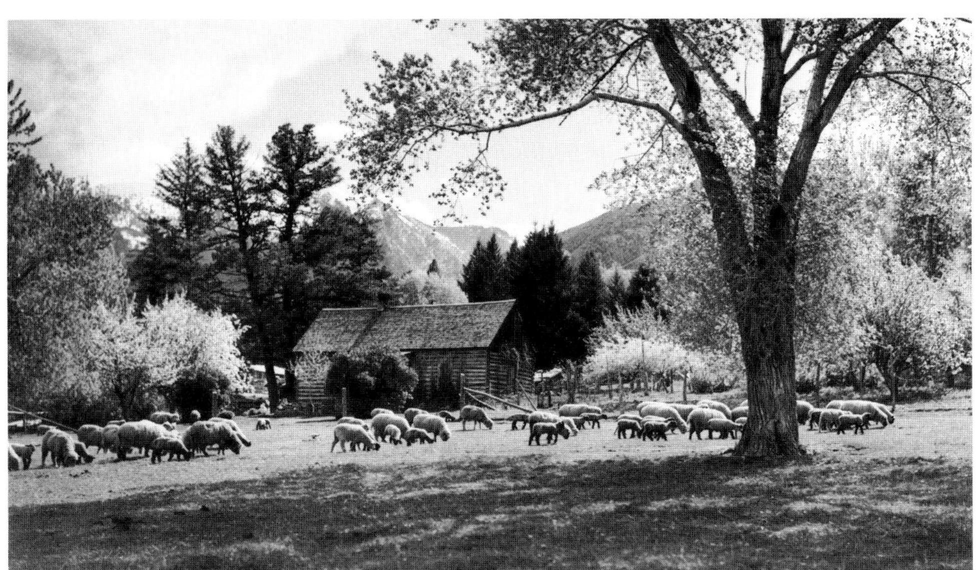

JOHN C. HABERSTROH

This picture shows excellent definition.

The resolving power of a film depends only slightly on the degree of development, but resolution falls off considerably with both overexposure and underexposure. This is one important reason for exposing negatives correctly. The resolving-power classifications given in the Data Sheets are based on the maximum values determined with recommended exposure and processing of the film.

The maximum resolution that you can obtain in your negatives is limited by your camera lens as well as by the film, and it will be lower than the resolution of either the film or the lens alone. To obtain the maximum resolution of which a film is capable, the resolving power of the lens would have to be at least three times the resolving power of the film.

**Resolving-Power Classifications**

| Resolving Power | Lines per mm |
|---|---|
| Ultra High | 630 or Above |
| Extremely High | 250 to 500 |
| Very High | 160 to 200 |
| High | 100 to 125 |
| Medium | 63 to 80 |
| Low | 50 or Below |

## Sharpness

The sharpness of a film is the subjective impression of good edge distinction between details in a photograph. However, the boundary between detail that is dark and detail that is light is not a perfectly sharp line. The dark area in the negative tends to bleed over into the light area because of light scattering or diffusion in the emulsion. This effect varies with different types of emulsions, the thickness of the emulsion, and the thickness of the film base, as well as with the antihalation properties of the base and its backing. Kodak films have thin emulsion coatings and very efficient antihalation properties.

Sharpness measurements are made by film manufacturers. The procedure is complex and beyond the scope of this book; but briefly, a sine-wave test pattern of varying frequencies is photographed. The test pattern recorded on the film is scanned by sensitive measuring equipment. Then the data is plotted graphically as modulation transfer function, and is analyzed to determine the sharpness classification. The films in the Data Sheets are assigned one of the following sharpness classifications: *extremely high, very high, high, medium, moderately low, low.*

The sharpness of some films is enhanced when you develop them in certain dilute developers to produce edge effects that make boundaries between objects appear sharper. Development recommendations for increasing sharpness are given in the Data Sheets for the appropriate films.

## Degree of Enlargement

Graininess, resolving power, and sharpness have a combined effect on definition. However, under certain conditions, any one of these may be more important than the others in determining the definition of a photograph.

When a negative made on a coarse-grained film is enlarged, graininess usually increases to an objectionable level before the loss of resolution or sharpness becomes unacceptable. In this situation, graininess is the limiting factor in definition.

Although the resolving power and the sharpness of a film are related, resolving power alone does not determine sharpness. In some cases, resolving power may be misleading. When you view a picture at a normal reading distance under the best viewing conditions, your eyes can resolve about 10 lines per millimetre. If the resolving power of the film is too low to reproduce details about twice as fine as this in the print, definition will be limited by the resolving power. However, when resolving power is adequate and graininess is not noticeable, the sharpness of the image is the most important factor that affects definition. All these factors were taken into consideration in assigning the "Degree of Enlargement" potential for each negative film in the Data Sheets.

## Tips for Good Definition

When a photographer takes pictures, processes the film, and makes prints, the definition may be limited not by the film characteristics but by the way the photographer handles the equipment and materials. To obtain the maximum definition from your film, follow these tips:

### Picture-Taking Tips

1. Use a high-quality camera lens that's clean and free of dust and fingerprints.
2. Use a lens hood to block the light source from illuminating the front of the lens. This will reduce flare to increase contrast and detail in the image.
3. If you aren't using an autofocus camera, focus carefully with an accurate rangefinder or ground glass. If your camera doesn't have either of these, estimate the distance as accurately as you can; for close-up pictures, use a tape measure to measure the subject distance.
4. When you want sharp images of both near and distant objects in a scene, check the depth-of-field scale on your camera lens or a depth-of-field table in your camera manual for the best focus setting and lens opening to use. Most lenses produce best definition at a lens opening about midway on the lens-opening scale. *KODAK Pocket Photoguide*, KODAK Publication No. AR-21, includes a dial for calculating depth of field for close-up lenses.
5. Hold your camera steady and squeeze the shutter release slowly. When you can, use a shutter speed of 1/125 second or higher to minimize the effects of camera movement. Hand-held telephoto lenses, including zoom lenses at a telephoto setting, require higher shutter speeds than normal or wide-angle lenses. For maximum steadiness, place your camera on a tripod or other firm support and use a cable release or a self-timer to trip the shutter. A tripod will usually increase sharpness at all but the very highest shutter speeds. For shutter speeds slower than 1/30 second, using a tripod or other support is a must.

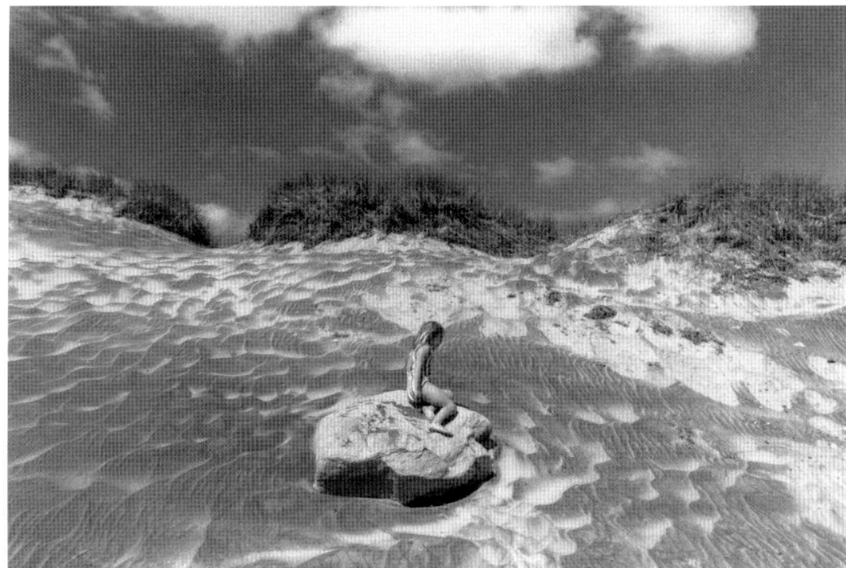

KODAK T-MAX 100 Professional Film — DEREK DOEFFINGER

In addition to sharp camera focus, one of the most important factors in obtaining high definition is to hold your camera steady while you press the shutter release slowly.

6. With a single-lens-reflex camera, locking the camera mirror up or using the self-timer will reduce vibration and increase sharpness. These techniques are especially helpful when you're using slow shutter speeds with long telephoto lenses or close-up equipment.
7. Expose the film correctly; avoid overexposure and overdevelopment, either of which will produce negatives that are too dense (dark). Excess density causes a loss of definition and increased graininess. Use the minimum exposure that will produce an excellent print with good shadow detail. Develop your film by using the recommended developer, time, temperature, and agitation.

### Printmaking Tips

1. Use a clean, high-quality enlarger lens. The bottom lens surface is especially prone to fingerprints and the top lens surface to dust.
2. If definition is very important, use a smooth-surface printing paper, such as a glossy or smooth-lustre paper.
3. Print your negative on the grade of black-and-white printing paper that will give you a print with good tone rendition without too much or too little contrast.
4. When you make enlargements, focus the image accurately, and be sure that your enlarger is free of vibration.
5. Use the recommended safelight filter and bulb at the proper distance.

## FLASH PICTURES

Electronic-flash guide numbers for black-and-white films are given in the Data Sheets. If you use flashbulbs, see the bulb carton for guide numbers.

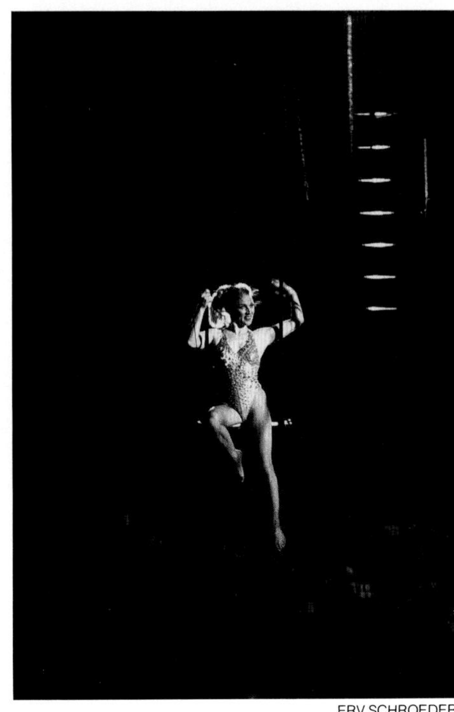

ERV SCHROEDER

KODAK T-MAX P3200 Professional Film is excellent when you want to hand-hold telephoto lenses for fast action or in dim light. Ringling Bros. and Barnum & Bailey Circus

## EXISTING-LIGHT PHOTOGRAPHY

The primary requirements in choosing a black-and-white film for existing-light photos are high speed and good quality. KODAK T-MAX 400 Professional Film is a superb film for existing-light subjects. If you're photographing subjects in relatively bright existing light, such as existing daylight indoors, or if you don't mind putting your camera on a tripod for subjects in dim light, you can use a film with a lower speed, such as KODAK PLUS-X Pan Film or KODAK T-MAX 100 Professional Film.

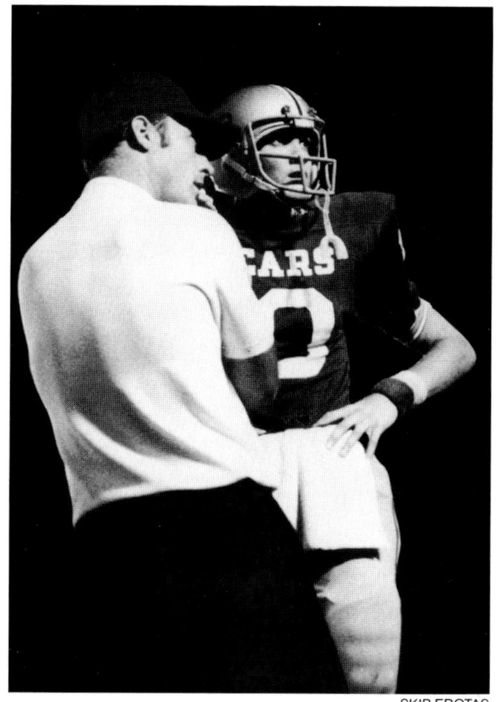


SKIP EROTAS

Since the light levels are often low in existing-light photography, you have much more versatility with a high-speed film such as KODAK TRI-X Pan Film. 1/125 second *f*/1.4

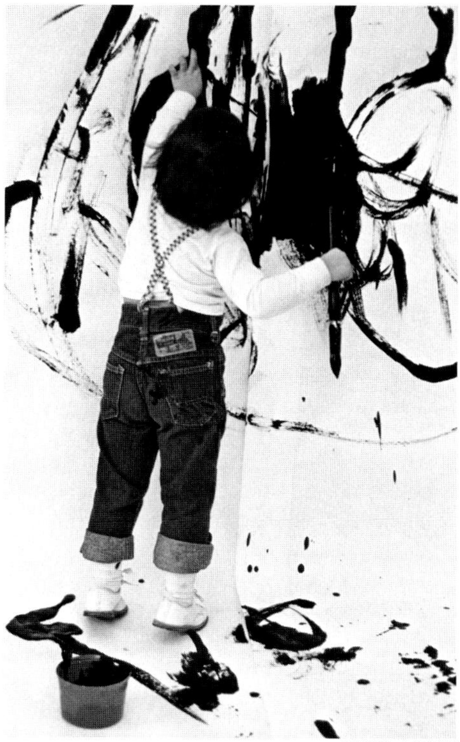

MARIE L. LARKIN

Existing daylight. 1/60 second *f*/5.6

If the lighting is extremely poor, or if you want to stop fast action or use telephoto lenses, you may need an even faster film, such as KODAK T-MAX P3200 Professional Film. It is a multi-speed film that combines high to ultra-high speed with finer grain than that of other fast black-and-white films.

You can also push the speed of many Kodak black-and-white films to a higher exposure index when necessary. See "Push Processing" on page 78.

## PROCESSING

After you have exposed a roll of film, you should have it processed promptly for best results. You can take your film to your photo dealer for developing and printing by a processing lab, or you can process it yourself.

Doing your own darkroom work is a lot of fun; it's a rewarding and interesting extension of your photo hobby. You'll also have much more control over the results when you process the film and make your own prints.

You can process Kodak black-and-white films with processing chemicals sold by photo dealers. Follow the instructions given below and in the Data Sheets, or the instructions packaged with the film and chemicals. If you have questions, write to Kodak at the address given on page 33.

We recommend that you use a light-tight invertible film tank to process your film. Several different kinds are available from your photo dealer. Be sure that the one you select is for 35 mm film.

Open the film magazine and load your film into the developing tank in TOTAL DARKNESS. To open the magazine, hold it with the long end of the spool down, and use a lid lifter or a hook-type bottle opener to remove the upper end cap from the magazine. Pull the film spool out of the magazine, taking care not to let the film unwind. The inner end of the film is attached to the spool with a strip of tape. Load the film-tank reel according to the film-tank instructions.

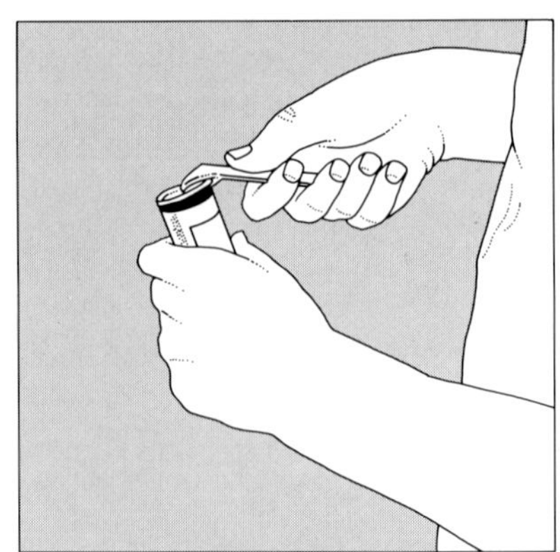

Open the magazine in **total darkness;** use a lid lifter or a hook-type bottle opener.

### Processing Steps

**Develop** your film according to the time and temperature recommendations given in the Data Sheet for the film you're using. Be sure to use the recommended agitation procedure. See "Tips on Using Film-Developing Tanks" on the next page. The development times given in the Data Sheets are for processing in a small (1-pint or 1-quart) roll-film tank.

**Bathe** the film in KODAK Indicator Stop Bath at 65 to 75°F (18 to 24°C) for about 30 seconds with agitation. With most films you can use a water rinse if an acid stop bath isn't available. However, an acid stop bath is better because it stops development instantly by neutralizing the developer. See the Data Sheet for your film.

**Note:** You'll obtain the best results when you keep the temperatures of the stop bath, fix, and wash approximately the same as the developer temperature.

**Fix** in KODAK Fixer, KODAK Rapid Fixer, or KODAFIX Solution at 65 to 75°F (18 to 24°C). *Agitate films frequently during fixing.* See the Data Sheet for your film for the recommended fixing time and other processing recommendations. If the information in the Data Sheets differs from the general information given here, follow the Data Sheets.

**Wash** for 20 to 30 minutes in running water at 65 to 75°F (18 to 24°C).

You can use KODAK Hypo Clearing Agent after fixing to reduce washing time and conserve water. First remove excess fixer (also called hypo) by rinsing the film in water at 65 to 75°F (18 to 24°C) for 30 seconds. Then bathe the film in KODAK Hypo Clearing Agent solution for 1 to 2 minutes at 65 to 75°F (18 to 24°C), with moderate agitation. Then wash it for 5 minutes in running water at 65 to 75°F (18 to 24°C) with at least one complete change of water in 5 minutes.

After washing, to minimize drying marks, treat the film in diluted KODAK PHOTO-FLO Solution for 30 seconds, or wipe the film surfaces carefully with a KODAK Photo Chamois or a soft viscose sponge.

**Dry** in a dust-free place. Remove the film from the reel and hang it up with a film clip or a spring-type clothespin at each end of the roll.

See the Data Sheets for precise processing recommendations for the specific film you're using. When the Data Sheets differ from the general guidelines given here, follow the Data Sheets. If the Data Sheets differ from the information in the film instructions, follow the instructions packaged with the film, which are updated frequently.

For information on processing for maximum image stability for long-term storage, see KODAK Publication No. R-20, *KODAK Black-and-White Darkroom DATAGUIDE*.

### Tips on Using Film-Developing Tanks

In TOTAL DARKNESS, load the film onto the reel. Pour the developer into the tank, and be sure that it's at the correct temperature. Start the timer; place the loaded reel in the tank, and put the cover on the tank. Immediately tap the tank on the work surface to dislodge air bubbles. After you replace the cover, you can carry out the remaining steps in room light.

**Agitation**—Proper agitation is as important as the correct temperature and development time. Too little agitation during development will cause underdevelopment, mottle, and uneven development. Too much agitation can cause overdevelopment and streaks on the film. When you follow the recommended agitation procedures, you'll avoid these problems.

*KODAK T-MAX Films:* Immediately after you tap the tank to dislodge air bubbles, provide initial agitation of 5 to 7 inversion cycles in 5 seconds. Extend your arm and vigorously twist your wrist 180 degrees. Repeat this agitation at 30-second intervals throughout development.

*Other Films:* After the film has been immersed in the developer for 30 seconds, agitate the tank for 5 seconds according to the method recommended for your tank. Repeat this agitation at 30-second intervals throughout development.

**Note:** A special method of agitation is required for KODAK Technical Pan Film in KODAK TECHNIDOL Liquid Developer. See the Data Sheet on page D 34.

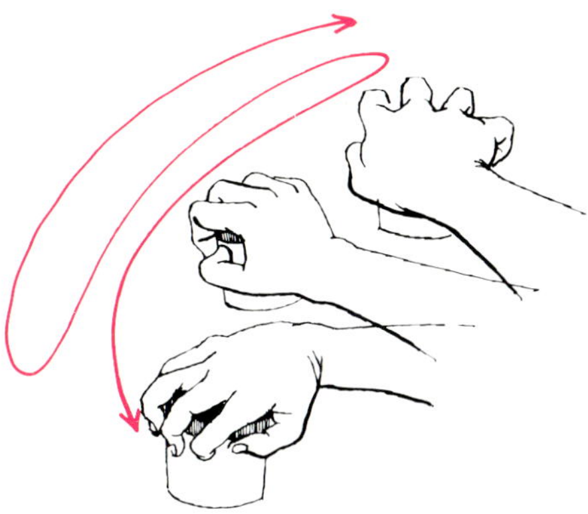

Recommended method of agitation for a film tank that can't be inverted.

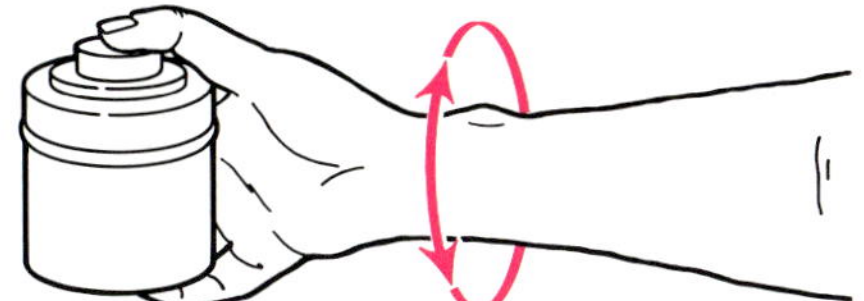

Recommended method of agitation for a film tank that can be inverted.

### Degree of Development

The degree to which you develop your film has an important effect on quality. To a large extent, development determines the contrast grade of photographic paper you'll need to make the best possible prints from your negatives. The degree of development for a film-and-developer combination depends on the developing time, the temperature of the developer, and agitation. Underdevelopment reduces the contrast of the negative and can cause a loss of shadow detail. Overdevelopment increases negative contrast and graininess, reduces sharpness, and blocks up highlights, making the negatives hard to print. Negatives that have received correct exposure and development should print best on contrast grade No. 2 photographic paper. The development recommendations given in the Data Sheets will produce proper contrast in prints made under average printing conditions from properly exposed negatives of average subjects.

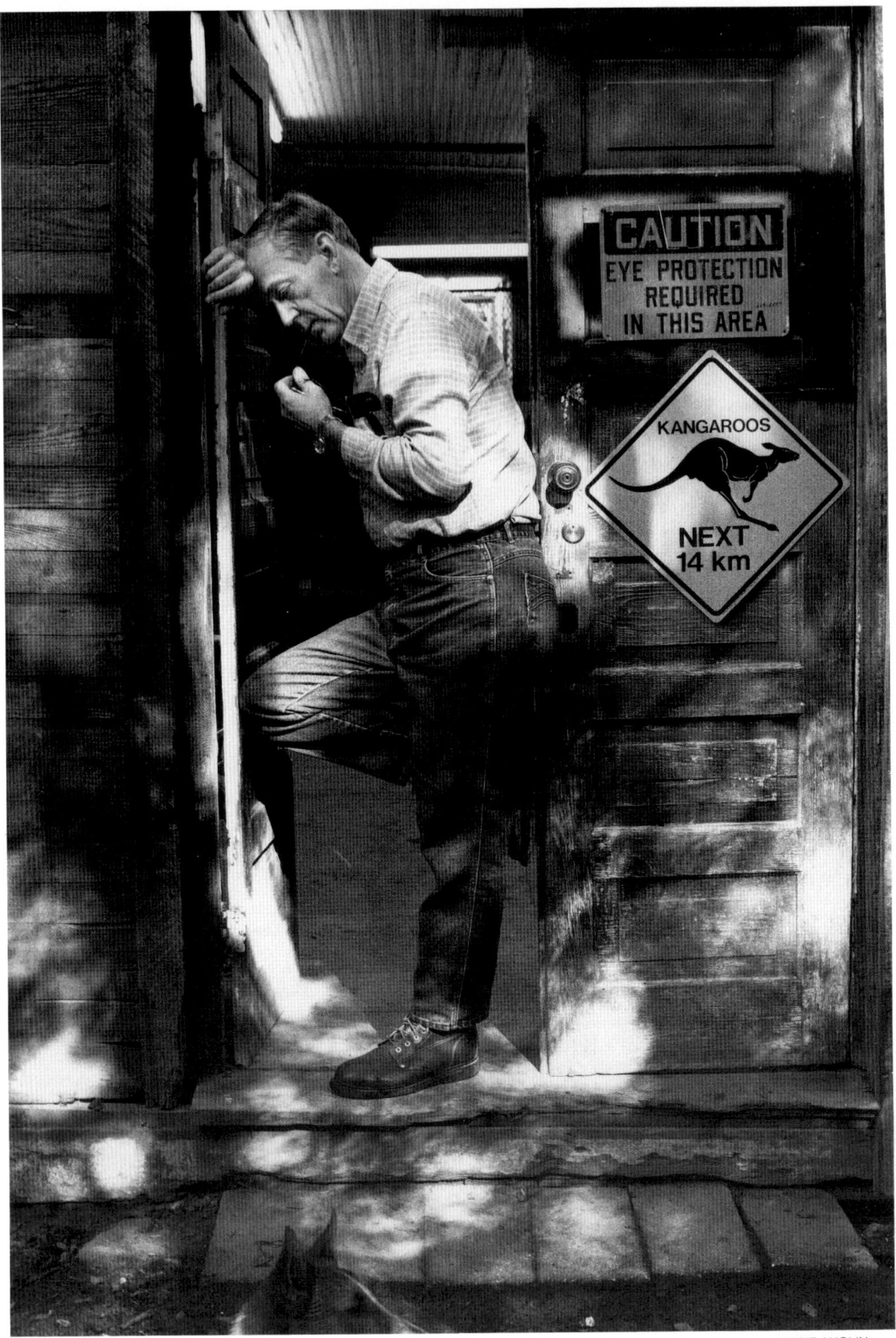


KODAK T-MAX 400 Professional Film

BIRDIE ANGLIN

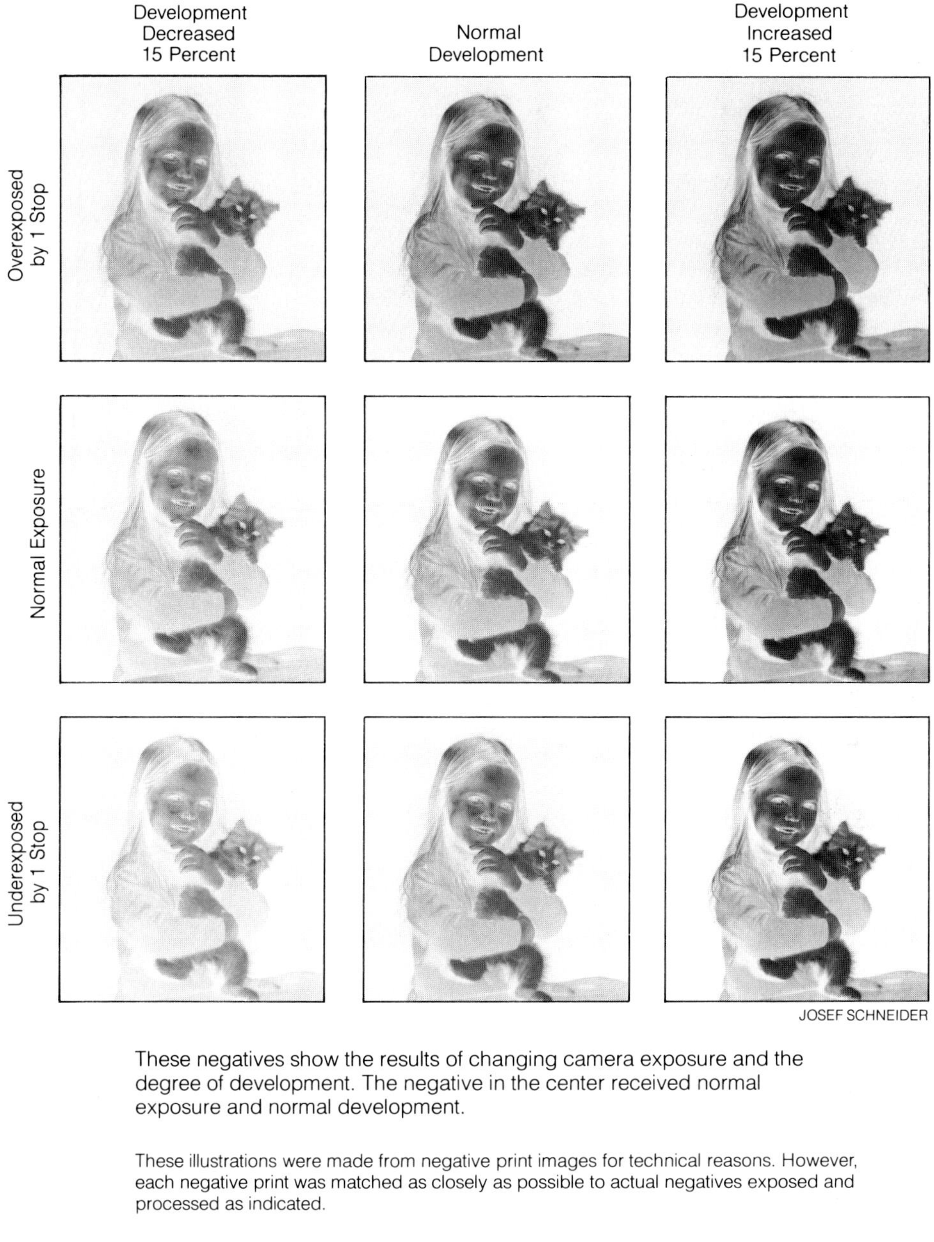

| | Development Decreased 15 Percent | Normal Development | Development Increased 15 Percent |
|---|---|---|---|
| Overexposed by 1 Stop | | | |
| Normal Exposure | | | |
| Underexposed by 1 Stop | | | |

JOSEF SCHNEIDER

These negatives show the results of changing camera exposure and the degree of development. The negative in the center received normal exposure and normal development.

These illustrations were made from negative print images for technical reasons. However, each negative print was matched as closely as possible to actual negatives exposed and processed as indicated.

**Contrast Index**—The degree of development, or development contrast, is specified by contrast-index measurements. Most of the recommended development times given in the Data Sheets are based on a normal contrast index of 0.56. Under average conditions, properly exposed negatives processed to this contrast index should print easily and with good tone reproduction on normal-contrast photographic paper. If your negatives are consistently too contrasty and require low-contrast paper (such as grade No. 1), develop your film to a lower contrast by reducing the development time by about 30 percent. If your negatives are consistently too low in contrast and require a high-contrast paper (such as grade No. 4), develop your film to a higher contrast by increasing the development time by about 40 percent.

To produce negatives consistent in overall density and quality, you should make an exposure compensation when you adjust development times, particularly with shorter development times. When reducing development times, increase exposure by about ⅓ stop. When increasing development times, reduce exposure by about ⅓ stop.

The method you use to make prints determines the effective printing contrast you need in your negatives. A diffusion enlarger produces about the same degree of contrast in the print as a contact printer. A condenser enlarger produces greater contrast. The difference in contrast may be as much as the contrast difference between No. 2 and No. 3 grades of photographic paper. KODAK Publication No. G-1, *Quality Enlarging with KODAK B/W Papers*, contains complete information on papers. If you want to know more about enlarging techniques, a good source is KODAK Publication No. KW-15, *Black-and-White Darkroom Techniques*, available from photo dealers or bookstores.

## Push Processing

The exposure latitude of most Kodak black-and-white films lets you expose your film at a speed higher than the nominal (rated) speed number in situations when you need more film speed. As explained earlier, a higher speed permits you to take pictures in dim existing light, use high shutter speeds to stop action, hand-hold telephoto lenses, or use small lens openings to gain depth of field.

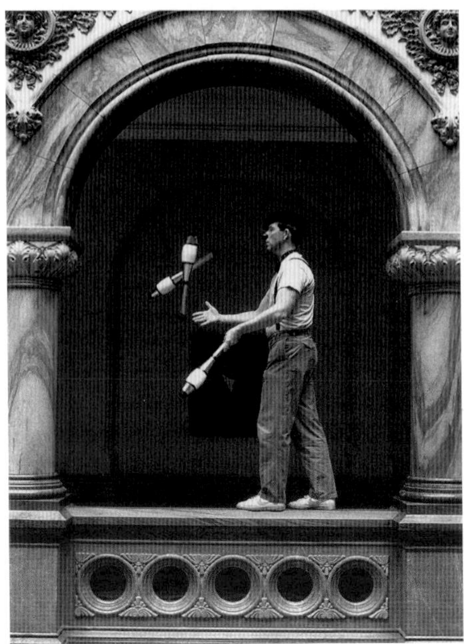

EI 400, 1/30 second, normal exposure, normal processing in KODAK T-MAX Developer

When you underexpose black-and-white film by only 1 stop (expose it at twice the normal speed rating), you can take advantage of the exposure latitude and process the film normally. This works especially well for scenes that have low contrast (a short tonal range). When you underexpose the film by 2 or 3 stops (expose the film at 4 or 8 times the rated speed), you need to push-process the film by increasing the development time. See the table on page 80.

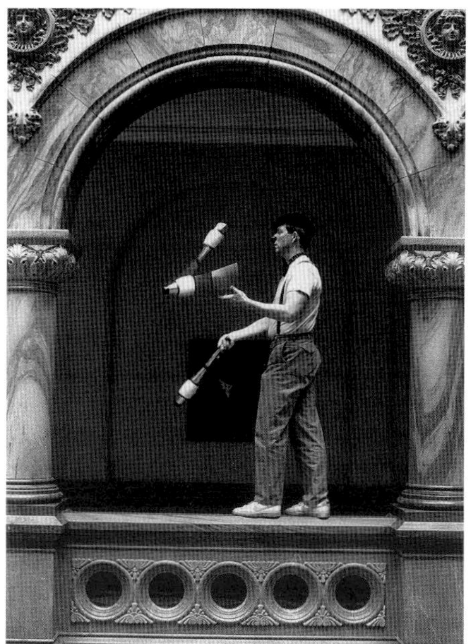

EI 800, 1/60 second, 1 stop less exposure than normal, normal processing in KODAK T-MAX Developer

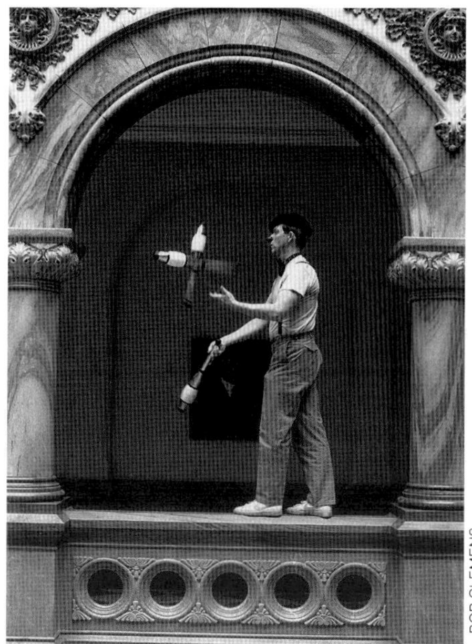

BOB CLEMENS

EI 1600, 1/125 second, two stops less exposure than normal, push-processed in KODAK T-MAX Developer with a ⅓ increase in development time

Push processing black-and-white films works best when scene contrast is low or average. The same lens opening was used for each picture at progressively higher shutter speeds. Scene contrast was average, and all three pictures are acceptable. The photo taken at the normal speed of the film, EI 400, displays the best image quality, while the pushed shots show progressive loss of quality, especially in shadow detail, as the film was exposed at higher exposure indexes. The higher shutter speeds permitted by the higher exposure indexes help eliminate subject motion without sacrificing depth of field. KODAK T-MAX 400 Professional Film processed in KODAK T-MAX Developer

You can use several developers to push-process Kodak black-and-white films, but we suggest that you use KODAK T-MAX Developer or KODAK T-MAX RS Developer and Replenisher. These developers improve tone reproduction by enhancing shadow detail, and minimize graininess.

Push processing is most successful and gives very good results with scenes that have soft, even lighting rather than those with harsh, contrasty illumination. Push-processed negatives of moderately contrasty scenes will also usually produce nearly normal-looking prints, but with some loss of shadow detail.

Generally, with high-contrast scenes, which have harsh lighting that produces brilliant highlights and deep black shadows, you should not underexpose the film by more than 1 stop; that is, don't use more than twice the rated speed. And if detail in the deep-shadow areas is important to the scene, it is better to *over*expose the film by 2 stops and process it normally.

You will probably find that you push-process only higher-speed films. If you need more speed than a lower-speed film can provide at its normal rating, it is easier and better to switch to a faster film. However, you can push-process the slower black-and-white films if it's the only film you have on hand or if you accidentally underexpose the film.

Remember that when the normal speed of the film is adequate for the picture-taking conditions, you'll obtain the highest image quality when you expose and process your film normally. A push-processed black-and-white film will have less shadow detail and more graininess. However, this slight loss in quality is often acceptable when you need the benefits of added speed.

The following table gives development times for films exposed at 2, 4, and 8 times their rated speeds (pushed by 1, 2, and 3 stops).

**Push-Processing KODAK Black-and-White Films in a Small Tank***

| KODAK Developer | Development Time (min:sec)† | | |
|---|---|---|---|
| **T-MAX 400 Professional** | | | |
| | EI 800 | EI 1600 | EI 3200 |
| T-MAX | 6:00 | 8:00 | 9:30 |
| D-76 | 8:00 | 10:30 | NR |
| HC-110 (Dil B) | 6:00 | 8:30 | NR |
| **TRI-X Pan** | | | |
| | EI 800 | EI 1600 | EI 3200 |
| T-MAX | 5:30 | 8:00 | 11:00 |
| D-76 | 8:00 | 13:00 | NR |
| HC-110 (Dil B) | 7:30 | 16:00 | NR |
| **T-MAX 100 Professional** | | | |
| | EI 200 | EI 400 | EI 800 |
| T-MAX | 6:30 | 9:00 | 10:30 |
| D-76 | 9:00 | 11:00 | NR |
| HC-110 (Dil B) | 7:00 | 9:30 | NR |

NR = Not recommended

*Agitation at 30-second intervals

†Times given for T-MAX Developer are for development at 75°F (24°C). All times for other developers are for 68°F (20°C).

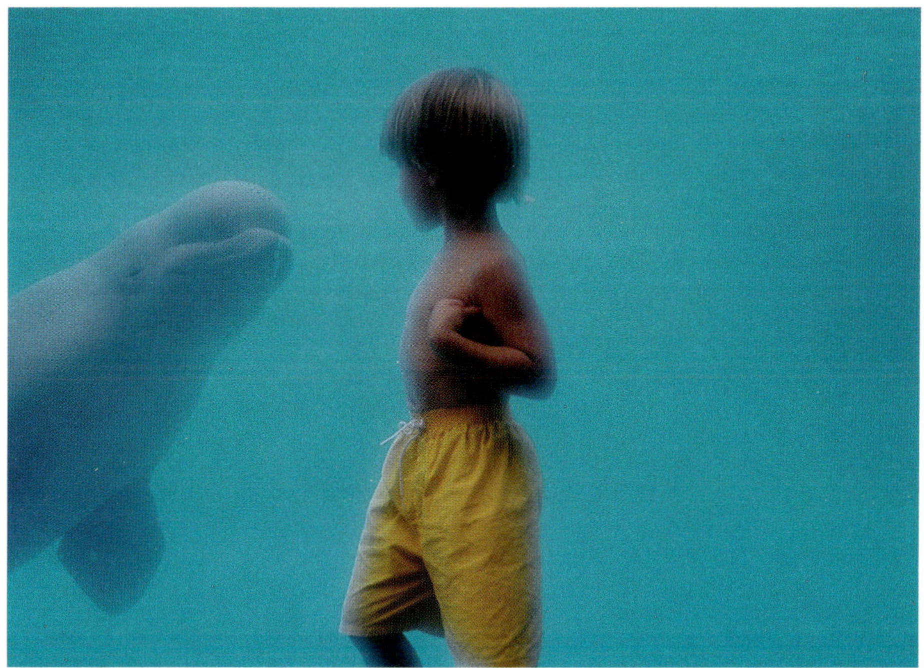

KODACOLOR GOLD 100 Film — CHRISTEN MICHELINI

# EXPOSURE

## FILM SPEED

To take correctly exposed pictures, you need to tell your camera or exposure meter the speed of the film you're using—unless your camera senses the film speed automatically. Understanding film speed also helps you select the best film for the picture-taking conditions in the scenes you're going to photograph. The film speeds discussed in this book are for cameras with built-in exposure meters or for separate exposure meters marked for ISO, ASA, or DIN speeds or Exposure Indexes.

Film speed indicates the relative sensitivity of a film to light. A film with a high speed number is more light-sensitive, or faster, than a film with a low number. For example, a film with a speed of ISO 400 is four times as fast as a film with a speed of ISO 100. Film speeds for Kodak films are given in the Data Sheets in this book, on the outside of film cartons, and in the instructions for the films.

Some cameras automatically sense film speed or are designed for specific kinds of film within a narrow speed range, so you don't have to set the film speed manually. These cameras include those that sense DX encoding on 35 mm magazines. See page 8 and your camera manual.

Film speeds are determined according to international standards and are designated as ISO speeds (formerly ASA speeds). These speed values are arithmetic. ISO *logarithmic* speeds (formerly DIN speeds) are used on some cameras and exposure meters manufactured outside the United States. ISO logarithmic speeds are identified with the degree symbol (°).

ISO designations printed on Kodak film cartons usually look like this: ISO 100/21°. The number after "ISO," 100 in the example, is the ASA equivalent; and the number with the degree symbol (°),

21° in the example, is the DIN equivalent. Since most of the photographic equipment sold in the United States uses ISO arithmetic speeds, this speed system is used throughout this book.

If your in-camera exposure meter or separate hand-held meter is marked with a different scale of film-speed numbers, you can convert ISO arithmetic speeds to the film-speed numbers used on your meter. See the conversion table in the next section for equivalent ISO logarithmic (or DIN) speeds.

### ISO/ASA/DIN Film-Speed Conversions

As mentioned before, the ISO° (DIN) series of speed numbers is different from ISO (ASA) speed numbers. You can use the following table to convert ISO arithmetic speeds to ISO° logarithmic speeds. If your equipment has an ISO°/DIN film-speed dial, set the ISO° logarithmic speed of the film on the dial.

**ISO (ASA)/ISO°(DIN) Film Speeds**

| ISO (ASA) | ISO° (DIN) | ISO (ASA) | ISO° (DIN) |
|---|---|---|---|
| 6 | 9° | 160 | 23° |
| 8 | 10° | 200 | 24° |
| 10 | 11° | 250 | 25° |
| 12 | 12° | 320 | 26° |
| 16 | 13° | 400 | 27° |
| 20 | 14° | 500 | 28° |
| 25 | 15° | 640 | 29° |
| 32 | 16° | 800 | 30° |
| 40 | 17° | 1000 | 31° |
| 50 | 18° | 1250 | 32° |
| 64 | 19° | 1600 | 33° |
| 80 | 20° | 2000 | 34° |
| 100 | 21° | 2500 | 35° |
| 125 | 22° | 3200 | 36° |

## OPTIMUM EXPOSURE

Optimum exposure is the minimum exposure required to produce a photograph of excellent quality. Cameras, exposure meters, and electronic flash units that are operating properly will usually give optimum exposure when you set the equipment for the recommended film speed. Modifying film speeds is discussed on page 99.

Underexposure produces negatives with less density or slides with more density, and both negatives and slides show a loss of shadow detail. Color and black-and-white negatives will be too light, or thin, and color negatives will have increased graininess. Prints from severely underexposed negatives will have milky, gray shadows, flat contrast, and an overall muddy appearance. Underexposed color slides will be too dark.

Overexposure increases negative density or decreases slide density, and produces a loss of highlight detail in both. Overexposure in negatives also increases graininess with conventional black-and-white films, reduces sharpness, increases printing time, and makes focusing the enlarger more difficult. Overexposed color slides will be too light, with desaturated colors and a loss of detail in the highlights.

## EXPOSURE LATITUDE

The exposure latitude of a film is the range of camera exposures from underexposure to overexposure that will produce pictures of acceptable quality. In other words, exposure latitude is the amount of exposure error you can make and still get acceptable pictures. Although exposure latitude is mainly a characteristic of the film you're using, the subject brightness range and your own requirements for picture quality also affect the amount of exposure error you can afford to make.

Continuous-tone negative films have greater exposure latitude than slide films. However, you obtain the best quality with any film when you expose it properly.

Film speeds and exposure guides for Kodak negative films are based on the minimum exposure required to record important shadow detail. Because of the latitude of negative films, slight variations in exposure produce no loss of image quality. In general, color-negative films have greater latitude for overexposure than they do for underexposure. KODACOLOR GOLD Films, for example, produce satisfactory prints from negatives overexposed by up to approximately 3 stops or underexposed by up to 1 stop.

Film speeds and recommended exposures for Kodak slide films are based on the exposure that produces the best picture when highlight detail and shadow detail are equally important. Slide films have higher contrast than most negative films. Also, no corrections can be made after the film is exposed and processed because no printing step is involved. Therefore, camera exposure is more critical with slide films than with continuous-tone negative films. Carefully follow your exposure-meter readings or exposure guides.

Slight underexposure of color-slide films (by ⅓ or ½ stop) can enhance color saturation, an effect that many photographers find pleasing. You may want to experiment by slightly underexposing slide films.

## EXPOSURE GUIDES

Kodak provides exposure tables and exposure calculator dials that are based on many practical picture tests and extensive data on illumination, subject brightness, film speed, and printmaking requirements. The exposure recommendations have been confirmed by years of experience. In any picture-taking situation specifically covered by a Kodak exposure guide, the camera settings indicated by the guide will produce a high percentage of properly exposed photos.

Even if you have an exposure meter, exposure guides are useful for verifying that you're using your meter correctly, for providing a backup in case your meter stops working, and for determining exposure for scenes that are difficult to meter. Exposure guides are helpful for planning; they indicate in advance what camera settings, film speed, and equipment you'll need for the types of scenes you'll be shooting.

The *KODAK Pocket Photoguide*, KODAK Publication No. AR-21, contains exposure calculator dials that cover the use of Kodak films in daylight and with flash, photolamps, and existing light. The text includes information on lighting techniques, filter selection, depth of field, and other essentials. This guide is sold by photo dealers.

Exposure tables are provided in the Data Sheets in this book, in the instructions provided with Kodak films, and in many Kodak publications.

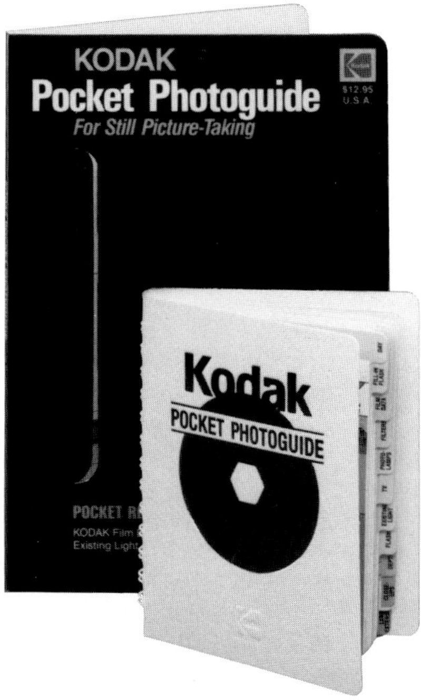


The *KODAK Pocket Photoguide,* KODAK Publication No. AR-21, contains exposure calculator dials that cover the use of Kodak films in daylight and with flash, photolamps, and existing light.

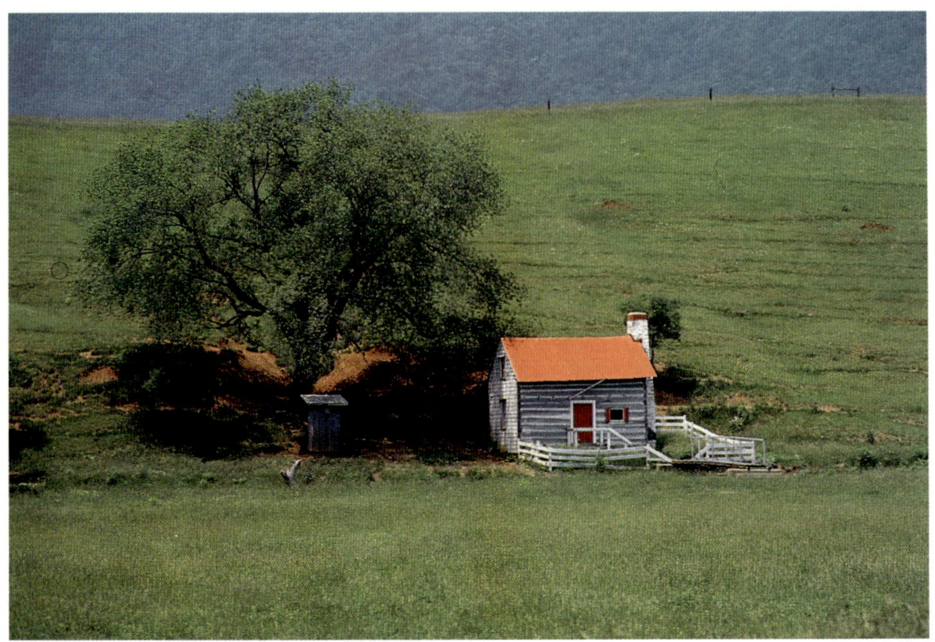

KODACHROME 64 Film WILLIAM LONG

For average scenes such as this, it's a simple matter to determine the correct camera settings. Just make an overall meter reading from the camera position.

## EXPOSURE METERS

Your 35 mm camera probably has a built-in exposure meter. The big plus of owning a camera with a built-in exposure meter or a separate hand-held meter is that you can easily determine the proper exposure for almost any kind of scene and lighting situation. If you use your exposure meter as recommended by the camera or meter manufacturer, you should get a very high percentage of properly exposed pictures.

Many of the newer and more sophisticated autofocus SLRs, and some lens-shutter cameras, offer multipattern metering, or matrix metering systems. Relying on a built-in microcomputer, a multipattern metering system can be extremely accurate. Whatever type of metering system you have, keep in mind how it works. Even "intelligent" meters cannot tell what the subject is and how you want to render it.

Study your camera or exposure-meter instruction book and learn how to use your meter properly; familiarize yourself with the flexibility and limitations of the type of exposure meter you have. Then you can use this knowledge to interpret your meter readings and obtain a larger percentage of correctly exposed pictures.

Basically there are two types of exposure meters: reflected-light and incident-light. The exposure meters built into cameras are reflected-light meters. Some meters have attachments that let you measure either reflected light or incident light. A special kind of reflected-light meter is the spot meter. With this kind of meter, you can selectively read the light reflected from a small area in a scene.

### Reflected-Light Meters

A reflected-light exposure meter measures the light reflected from all the areas included in the meter's field of view. One of the main advantages of a reflected-light meter is that you can make the meter reading from the camera position for most scenes. Because the meter is designed to average the overall light

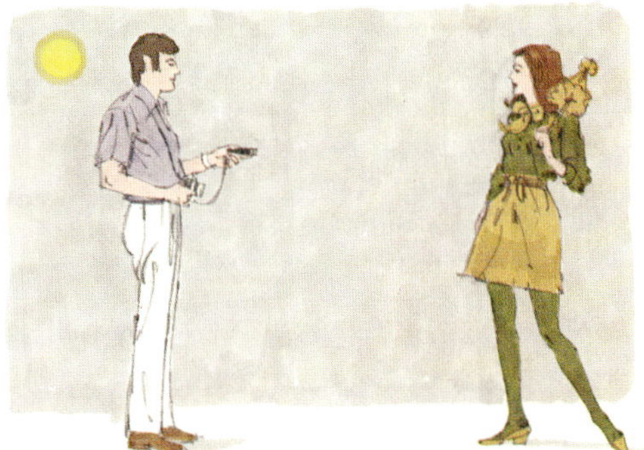

With a reflected-light exposure meter, you point the meter or camera with built-in meter toward the subject to determine the correct exposure.

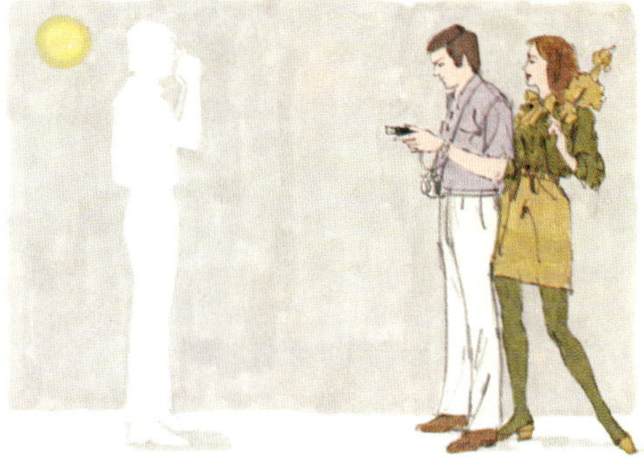

With an incident-light meter, you point the meter toward the camera position to make the reading.

reflected from scenes with normal reflectance characteristics, it gives correct exposure for most pictures.

Because the exposure meters built into cameras are reflected-light meters, you can meter the scene from the camera position when you are ready to take the picture. The information given here for reflected-light exposure meters also applies to in-camera meters. Some cameras are automatic; that is, the camera automatically sets the shutter speed and aperture according to the built-in meter. Built-in exposure meters give very good results for average scenes.

An exposure meter indicates the correct camera settings for reproducing average subjects as a tone equivalent to a medium gray. This works well for average subjects and average conditions. However, with some scenes, an overall exposure-meter reading will indicate an incorrect exposure. When you make an overall meter reading from the camera position, your exposure meter is influenced by any predominant light or dark area in the scene. But the meter has no way of knowing what part of the scene is the most important part of your picture. If the scene has light and dark areas of

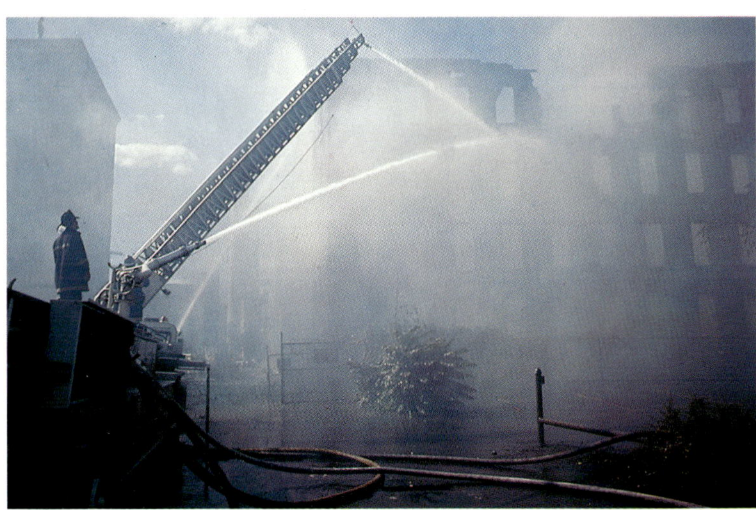

MARTIN TAYLOR

An exposure meter is invaluable when the lighting or atmospheric conditions are unusual. KODACHROME 25 Film (Daylight). 1/125 second *f*/5.6

about equal distribution and importance, your meter will usually indicate the correct exposure. However, if the most important part of the picture is surrounded by a large area that is much lighter or darker, an averaging meter will indicate an exposure that's correct for the large light or dark area, and exposure for the important part of the photograph will be incorrect.

To determine the correct exposure in such situations, you can make a selective meter reading of the principal subject. For example, a close-up reading of the subject will exclude unimportant light or dark surroundings that will mislead your exposure meter. When you make close-up readings, be careful not to measure your shadow or the shadow of the meter or the camera.

Here are some examples of scenes that require selective meter readings:*

1. The most common type of scene that can mislead reflected-light meters is one that includes a large portion of the sky. The sky near the horizon is brighter than the other parts of a scene with average reflectance. Therefore, the meter may be overly influenced by the sky and will indicate too little exposure, causing underexposure of the subject. This effect is even greater on overcast days, when the sky is whitish.

   Some manufacturers of reflected-light meters recommend that you tilt the meter down at a slight angle to avoid reading too much of the sky. Most cameras with built-in meters are designed to make the meter reading mainly from the center and bottom of the scene to reduce the influence of the sky brightness. It's usually not necessary or practical to tilt cameras with built-in meters down to avoid the sky. See your camera manual for the correct use of your built-in exposure meter.

2. Scenes with large light areas of snow, light sand, white concrete, etc, may mislead the exposure meter when the most important part of the scene is much darker than the surroundings. This will cause underexposure of the subject. In these situations, take a close-up meter reading of the principal subject.

*If your camera has matrix metering, refer to your camera manual for scenes that may cause incorrect exposure.

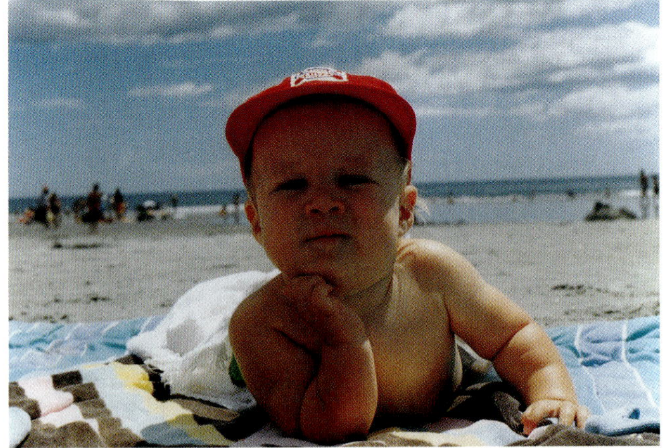

NANCY MALONEY

A close-up meter reading of the subject will exclude unimportant light that can trick your exposure meter. Be careful not to measure your shadow or the shadow of the meter or the camera.

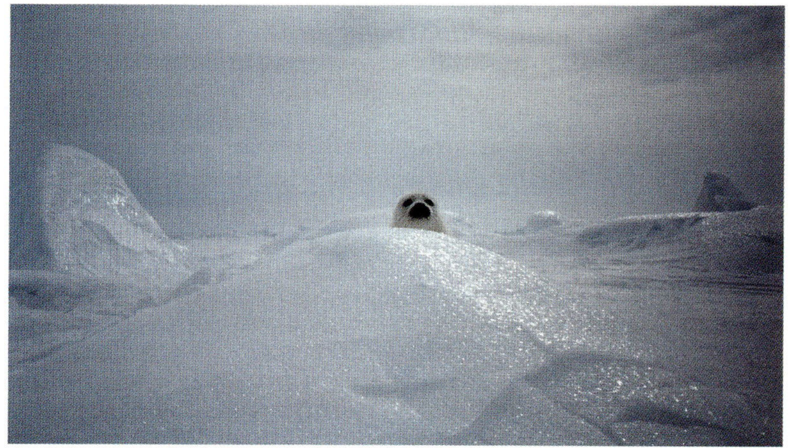

MARILYN JAUCH

A light background, such as bright sand or snow, with an average or dark subject can fool a reflected-light meter; this will cause underexposure. Make a close-up meter reading of the subject for correct exposure.

3. When a large light area is the *important* part of the scene, such as a snowscape, your reflected-light meter may be overly influenced by the bright snow, and the entire picture will be underexposed, with gray-looking snow. In this type of situation, compare your meter reading with a Kodak exposure guide, such as the one in the film instructions. If your meter reading indicates much less than the guide recommends, you'll probably get better results by following the exposure guide. Or you can modify your meter reading made from the camera position by giving 1 stop more exposure than the meter indicates. Conversely, when a large *dark* area is the important part of the picture, use 1 stop less exposure than the overall reflected-light reading indicates.

4. When your subject is much lighter than the surroundings, your exposure meter may indicate too much exposure, causing overexposure of the subject. An example of this is an outdoor scene of a bride in a white wedding dress in front of dark foliage with the camera at a medium distance. Your meter sees the large dark area and indicates too much exposure for the light subject. For proper exposure, take a close-up meter reading of the subject's face.

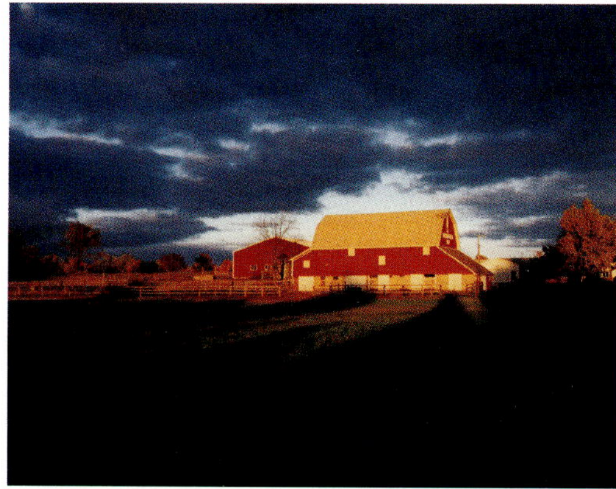

DONALD BARNBROOK

To photograph a light subject in dark surroundings, multiply the speed of your film by 2 and set the number on your film-speed dial; this decreases exposure by 1 stop.

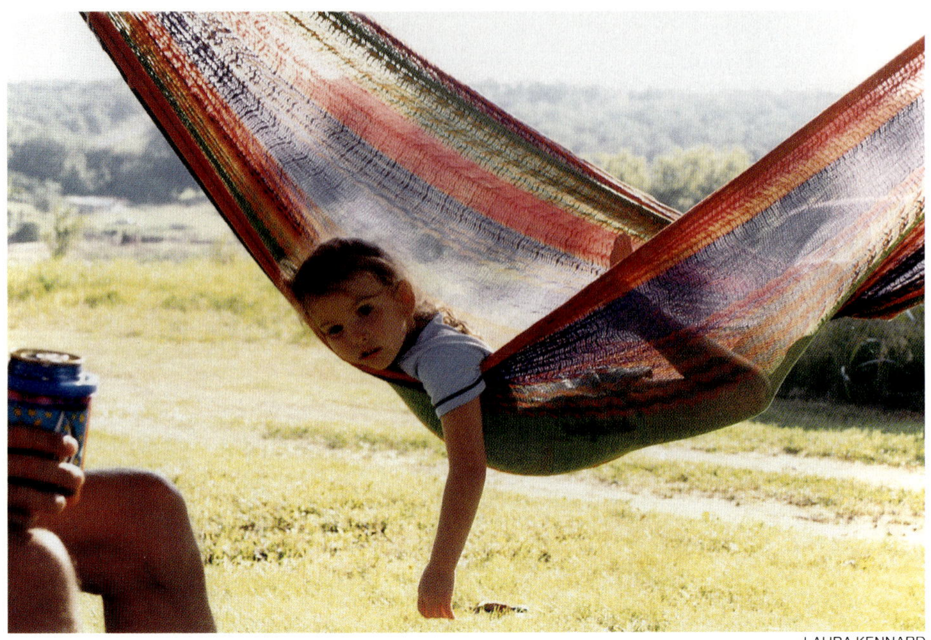

LAURA KENNARD

When the subject is in the shade with a sunlit background, take a close-up meter reading of the subject.

5. In backlighted scenes, the background is often sunlit and brighter than the subject. Also, light can shine directly into the light-sensitive meter cell. Both factors produce a high meter reading that will underexposure the subject. The solution is to take a close-up meter reading while shading the meter with your hand or some other object to keep the sun (or other light) from directly striking the meter cell. Some cameras with built-in exposure meters have a special setting for backlit situations that increases exposure—usually by 1½ to 2 stops. See your camera manual.

   If you're using a zoom lens on a single-lens reflex camera with through-the-lens metering, you can adjust the lens to the telephoto setting. Make the meter reading of the important part of the subject, and then adjust the zoom control for the framing you want.

   As an alternative to selective metering, you can manually adjust exposure for backlighted subjects according to these guidelines: For close-up backlighted subjects illuminated by a large area of open sky, use a lens opening 2 stops larger than for frontlighted subjects. For backlighted subjects at a medium distance, use a lens opening 1 stop larger than normal. For distant scenic views that include no large important shadow areas, use the same exposure as for frontlighting.

If you can't make close-up meter readings with your camera, you may be able to change the film-speed setting to a different number to compensate for unusual lighting or subject brightness. To photograph average or dark subjects in *very light* surroundings, divide the speed of your film by 2 and set the number on the film-speed dial of your camera; this will increase exposure by 1 stop. For example, if you were using KODACHROME 64 Film in this type of situation, you would set 32 on the film-speed dial. To photograph average or light subjects in *very dark* surroundings, multiply the speed of your film by 2, and set the number on your film-speed dial; this decreases exposure by 1 stop. Many automatic cameras have an exposure-compensation dial that lets you increase or decrease exposure by a fixed amount, such as 1, 1½, or 2 stops.

Remember to reset your film-speed dial or exposure-compensation dial to the normal setting after you've photographed the unusual scene.

Because camera controls vary, check your camera instruction manual for the recommended method for making close-up meter readings or for altering the exposure.

**Spot Meters**—You use a spot meter at the camera position to measure the light reflected from a small area in a scene. When you point a spot meter toward the most important part of the scene, it won't be influenced by large light or dark surrounding areas. This type of meter is useful with telephoto lenses, which include only a small portion of the overall scene, and for scenes with uneven lighting or reflectance. However, since a spot meter reads one small area at a time, you must decide which areas in the scene are important. This is especially significant when you're using a normal or wide-angle

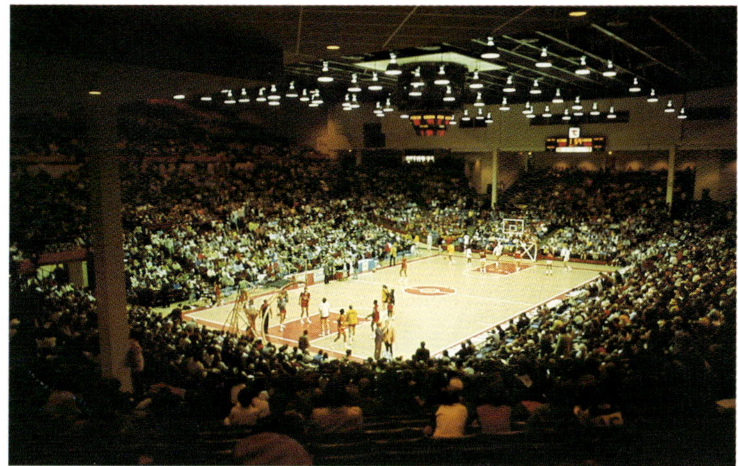

PETE CULROSS

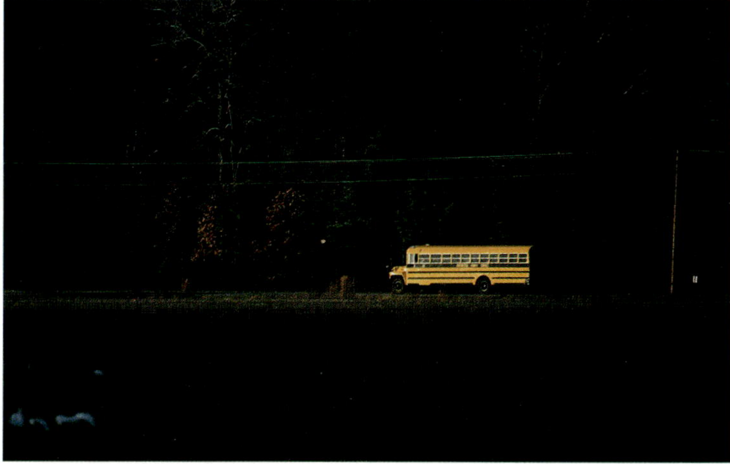

JOHN MENIHAN, JR.

With a spot meter (a special kind of reflected-light meter), you can selectively read the light reflected from a small area in a scene from the camera position.

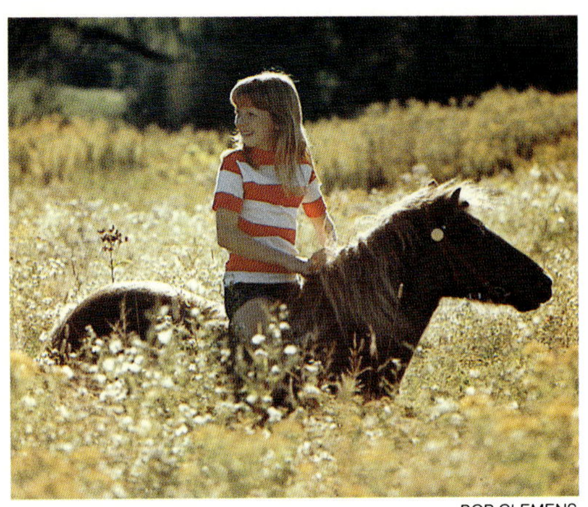

BOB CLEMENS

In backlighted scenes, a reflected-light exposure meter is influenced by the bright background, resulting in underexposure. Make a close-up meter reading of the subject.

lens, which includes a wide field of view.

To determine correct exposure for scenes that include areas of many different brightness levels, make meter readings of the lightest important area and the darkest important area in the scene; then set your exposure halfway between the two. For example, if your exposure meter indicates that 1/250 second at *f*/16 is correct for the light area and 1/250 second at *f*/4 is correct for the dark area, 1/250 second at *f*/8 is the average exposure and the best compromise for the scene.

Because you must often make several exposure-meter readings, using a spot meter is more time-consuming and requires more knowledge of what to measure. Spot meters are used primarily by experienced photographers.

**Reflected-Light Readings of a Gray Card**—When you photograph a subject indoors, the subject is frequently brighter than other parts of the scene, such as the background. A person lighted by photolamp illumination requires the same exposure to produce good flesh tones regardless of background brightness. But if you make reflected-light meter readings of such scenes from the camera position, the readings will be misleading. The meter will be influenced by a background that is much lighter or darker than the subject.

To determine exposure for this type of scene, you can take a close-up reading with a conventional reflected-light meter, or use a spot meter from the camera position. If you make the meter reading of your subject's face, divide the film speed by 2 to compute your exposure. This is necessary because average Caucasian skin has twice as much reflectance as the average indoor scene, and exposure-meter calibration is based on average scene reflectance.

Another way to determine exposure in these situations is to make a reflected-light reading of a test card of known reflectance. Most indoor scenes have an average reflectance of about 18 percent. If you make a reflected-light reading of an 18-percent gray card held close to and in front of your subject, you should obtain accurate exposure for the scene.

*KODAK Gray Cards*, KODAK Publication No. R-27, available from photo dealers, includes two 8 x 10-inch cards and one 4 x 5-inch card. Each gray card has a gray side of 18-percent reflectance and a white side of approximately 90-percent reflectance. You can use the white side to get a higher meter reading in dim lighting. If you use the white side or any other matte white card of about 90-percent reflectance, divide the speed of the film by 5 and set the answer on the film-speed dial of your exposure meter. Reset the film speed to the ISO speed of the film when you're through using the white-card technique.

To make a meter reading of a gray or white card, first turn on all the lights that will illuminate the subject. Position the card facing your camera so that there are no shadows on it, no brightly colored objects reflecting light on it, and no glaring (specular) reflections on the card itself. Position the card close to and in front of your subject, aimed halfway between the main light and the camera.

To be sure you read only the card, hold your meter about 6 inches (15 centimetres) away. Shield your exposure meter from lights that might shine directly into the light-sensitive cell. If you're using a single-lens reflex camera with a built-in meter, or a spot meter, you can see exactly what you are reading. Be careful not to cast a shadow on the card. When you use a 4 x 5-inch card, it's especially important that the card fill the field of view of the meter completely.

You can also use the gray card for meter readings outdoors. This is particularly helpful when distance or a barrier of some sort keeps you from getting an accurate reading of the light reflected from the subject, or when unimportant light or dark areas can mislead your meter. If possible, place the card at or near the principal subject; if you can't, just make sure that the light on the gray card is the same as the light on the subject.

When you use the card outdoors, you must make exposure adjustments if the reflectance of the scene is different from the reflectance of the card (18 percent). Complete instructions are included with the gray cards.

### Incident-Light Meters

An incident-light meter measures the light falling on the subject. To make an incident-light reading, position your meter in the same light that's illuminating the subject and point the meter toward the camera (unless the meter instruction book recommends a different technique). When possible, hold the meter at the subject position. You can make an incident-light reading from the camera position if the light at the camera is the same as the light striking the subject. Point the meter in the same direction that you would if you were making the reading at the subject position.

Exposure determined by an incident-light meter is accurate only if the scene has average reflectance. Fortunately, most scenes have average reflectance, and an incident-light meter will indicate a correct exposure in most situations.

Because an incident-light meter measures the illumination on the subject, scene reflectance does not influence the meter. This means that light or dark areas in the scene will not mislead the meter. If these areas are unimportant in your picture and the principal subject has average reflectance, your picture should be properly exposed. Or if you are photographing an evenly lighted scene that has a large brightness range where detail in the light and dark areas is of equal importance, an incident-light meter will indicate a good compromise exposure.

On the other hand, if either a very light area or a very dark area is the important part of the picture and you want to record detail in this area, you must modify the exposure indicated by an incident-light meter. If a light area is an important part of the picture, use a lens opening ½ to 1 stop smaller than your meter indicates. If a dark area is important, use a lens opening ½ to 1 stop larger than your meter indicates. Note that these exposure corrections are just the opposite of those for reflected-light meters.

When the scene is illuminated by light of varied intensities and you want the best overall exposure, make incident-light readings in the lightest and darkest areas that are important to your picture. Then use the exposure midway between the exposure settings indicated for these areas.

Many scenes, especially those outdoors in daylight, have average reflectance. For these scenes, an incident-light meter and a reflected-light meter will work equally well and yield a high percentage of good exposures. When the lighting remains constant, as it does for most of the day in bright sunlight, you can use the same exposure for similarly lighted scenes with average reflectance without making a separate meter reading of each scene.

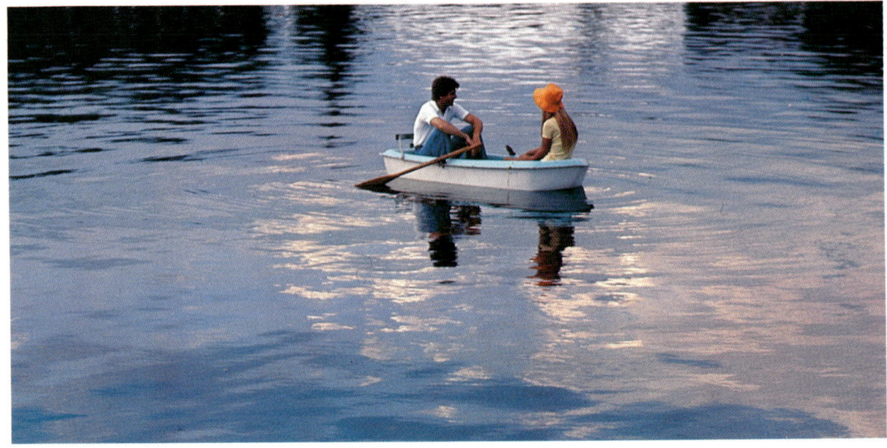

NORM KERR

When you can't get close enough to your subject to make an incident-light meter reading at the subject position, you can make the reading from the camera position if the light falling on the camera is the same as the light falling on the subject.

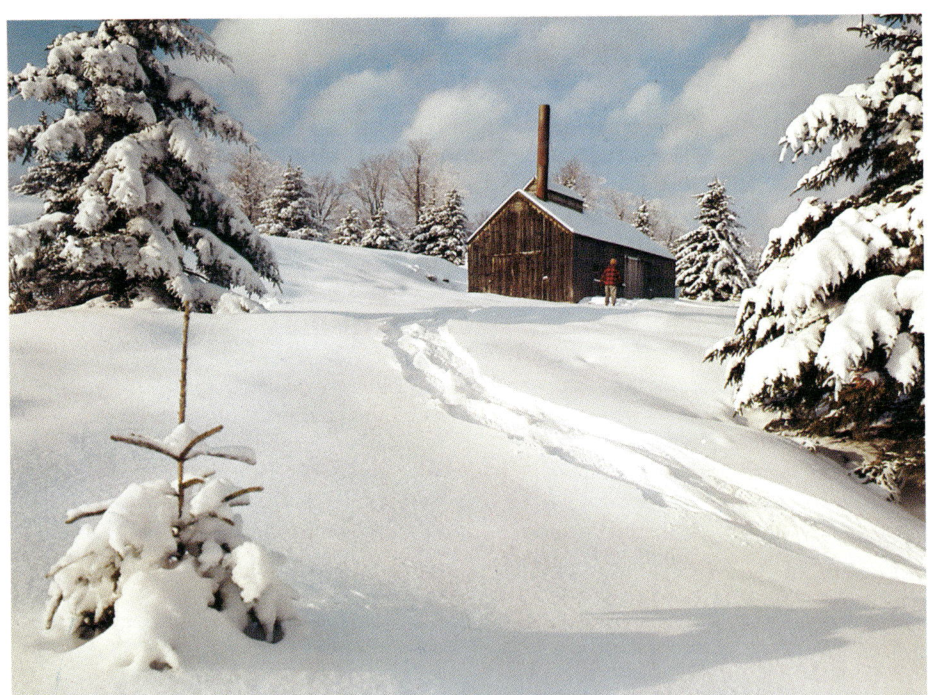

ROBERT HOLLAND

If a bright area, such as snow, is an important part of the picture, use a lens opening 1 stop smaller than your incident-light meter indicates.

## BRACKETING EXPOSURE

When you encounter scenes that are difficult to meter and you're not sure of the proper camera settings, it's a good idea to bracket your exposures. Bracketing gives you more assurance of getting a picture with proper exposure. First determine the exposure as accurately as you can with your exposure meter or an exposure guide, and take a picture at that setting. If you're using a color-negative film, take another picture at 1 stop less exposure and a third picture at 1 stop more exposure. If you want even more assurance of a properly exposed picture, take two *more* pictures—one at 2 stops under and one at 2 stops over the exposure recommended by your meter or the exposure guide.

Because color-slide films have less exposure latitude than negative films, it's better to bracket the estimated exposure by using ½-stop increments rather than full-stop increments.

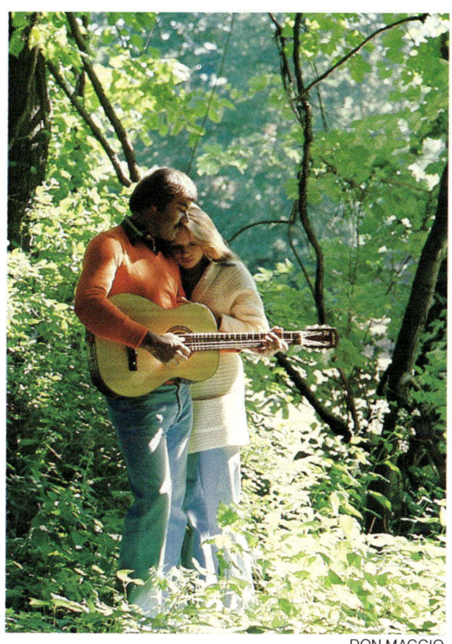

DON MAGGIO

Exposure bracketing gives you more confidence of getting a picture with proper exposure. Normal exposure—1/125 second *f*/5.6, ISO 64, color slide film

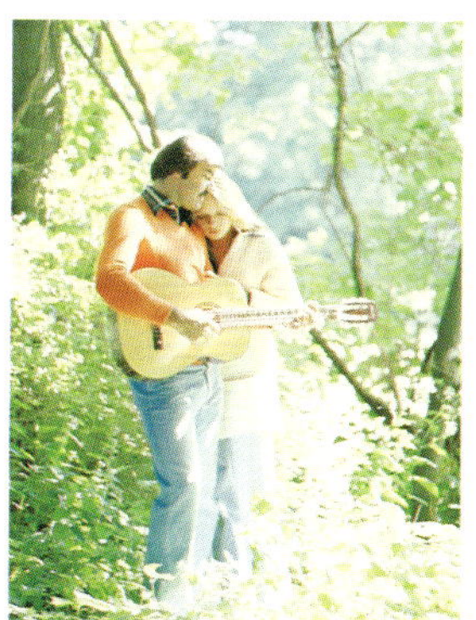

2 stops overexposed—1/125 sec *f*/2.8

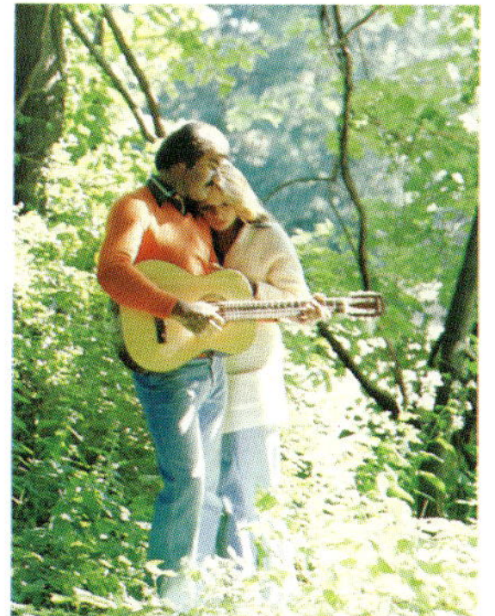

1 stop overexposed—1/125 sec *f*/4

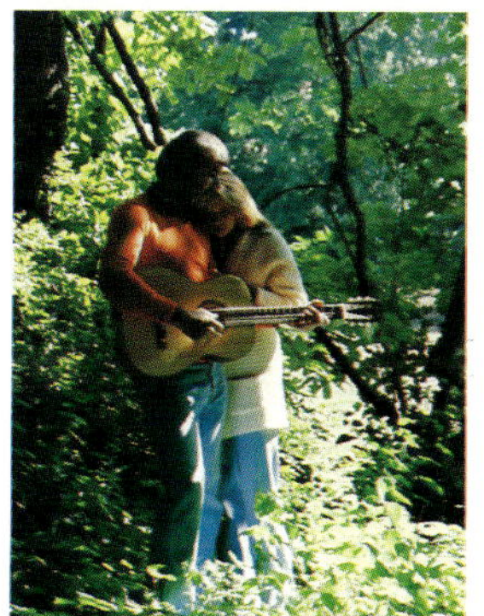

1 stop underexposed—1/125 sec *f*/8

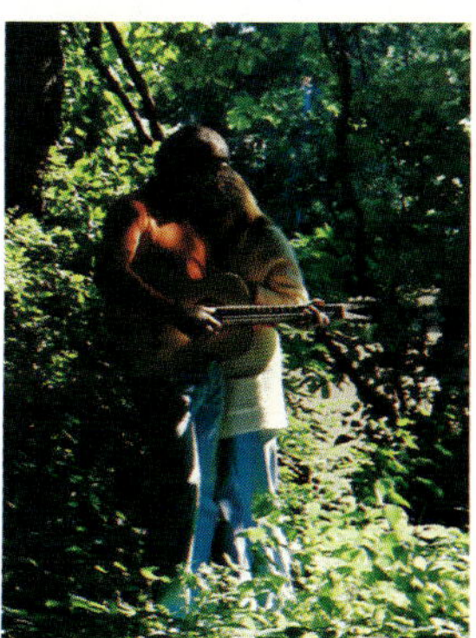

2 stops underexposed—1/125 sec *f*/11

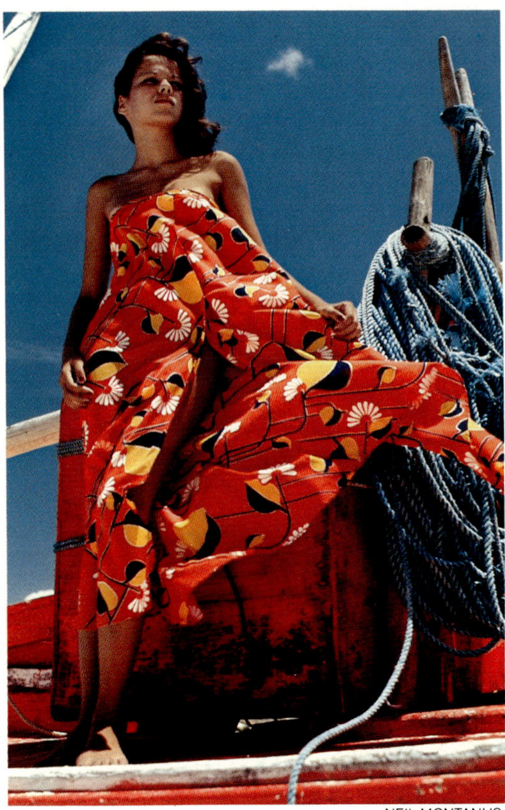

NEIL MONTANUS

Colors often reproduce with more saturation when you use a polarizing screen. KODACHROME 64 Film (Daylight), 1/125 second *f*/5.6

## EXPOSURE WITH FILTERS

Most filters absorb light, so you must increase exposure when you use them. When you use Kodak color films with the conversion filters recommended for various light sources, the compensation is included in the adjusted film speed given for each light-source-and-filter combination. Use the speeds given in the instructions that come with the film or in the Data Sheets in this book.

Filter factors for Kodak black-and-white films are given in some film instructions and in the Data Sheets. Divide the film speed by the filter factor, and set the corrected speed on the film-speed dial of your camera or exposure meter.

Another way you can apply filter factors for black-and-white films is to set your exposure meter at the speed of the film without a filter and then modify the camera settings indicated by the meter. For example, if the filter factor is 2 and the camera setting indicated by the meter is 1/125 second at *f*/11, you can either double the exposure time to 1/60 second or open the lens 1 full stop to *f*/8.

**Equivalent *f*-Stop Corrections for Filter Factors**

| Filter Factor | *f*-Stops | Filter Factor | *f*-Stops |
|---|---|---|---|
| 1.25 | +⅓ | 5 | +2⅓ |
| 1.5 | +⅔ | 6 | +2⅔ |
| 2 | +1 | 8 | +3 |
| 2.5 | +1⅓ | 10 | +3⅓ |
| 3 | +1⅔ | 12 | +3⅔ |
| 4 | +2 | 16 | +4 |

The methods described so far are for use with separate hand-held exposure meters or with built-in meters that *do not* make the meter reading through a filter used over the lens. However, many cameras with built-in meters do measure the light through a filter over the lens. With most cameras of this type, you should set the built-in meter for the speed of the film *without a filter* (although a few filters require a modified film-speed setting because the meter and the film do not respond to the filtered light in the same way). Because camera meters vary, be sure to check your instruction manual for details.

If your camera manual doesn't adequately explain exposure with filters, write to the manufacturer or the American distributor of your camera. Or you can determine your own correction factor for filters by following this procedure:

1. Select an average scene that's typical of the scenes you'll photograph with the filter you're testing. The lighting should remain constant and the subjects should not change position while you're making exposure-meter readings.

2. Put your camera on a tripod. With *color film,* set the film-speed dial on your camera for the speed of the film *with the filter.* For *black-and-white film,* divide the speed of the film by the filter factor for the filter; set the number on the film-speed dial of your camera.
3. Make an exposure-meter reading of the scene *without the filter.* Note the shutter speed and *f*-number indicated by the meter. This tells you what the exposure should be *with* the filter.
4. Without moving the camera, put the filter over the lens, and make a reading through the filter. Do not change the exposure settings; keep the same shutter speed and *f*-number as before. Then adjust the film-speed dial on your camera to obtain the same shutter speed and *f*-number combination.

   Note the new ISO setting on the film-speed dial. This shows you what film speed to set on your camera when you make meter readings through the filter.

   Divide the new ISO setting by the film speed recommended for the film *without a filter.* This is the correction to use for the film, filter, and lighting conditions you used in the test. You can apply the same correction when you use the filter with other films.

   For example, if your film has a speed of ISO 64 *without a filter,* and you find from the test that you should use ISO 50 when you make the meter reading through the filter, divide 50 by 64. The answer, 0.8, is the correction factor you should apply to the speeds of other films for this filter when you make the meter reading through the filter.

Note that some black-and-white films have different basic filter factors for a single filter. For these exceptions, you'll need to make a separate exposure-meter test to find the correction for each film.

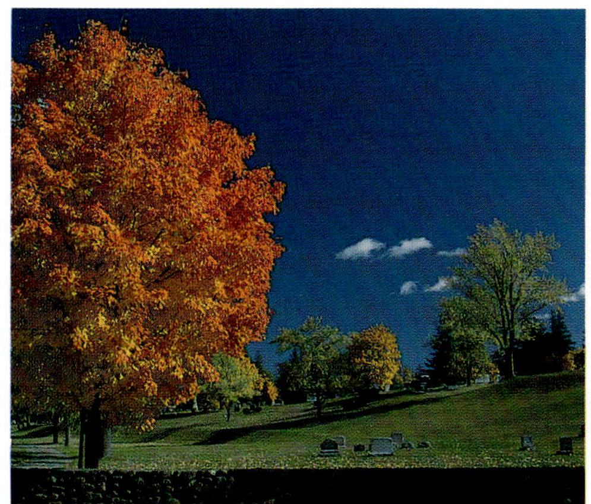

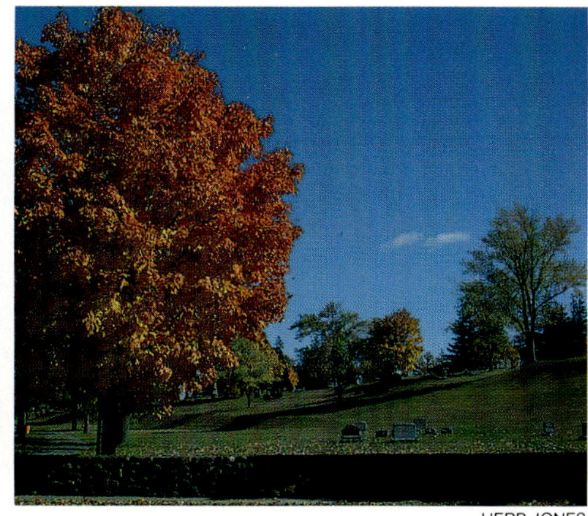

HERB JONES

A polarizing screen with a filter factor of 2.5 was used to produce the dramatic sky in the picture on the top. To determine the correct exposure, divide the film speed by 2.5 or increase exposure by 1⅓ stops. These exposure corrections are for use with meter readings made *without* the polarizing screen; you should not rely on meter readings made through a polarizing screen.

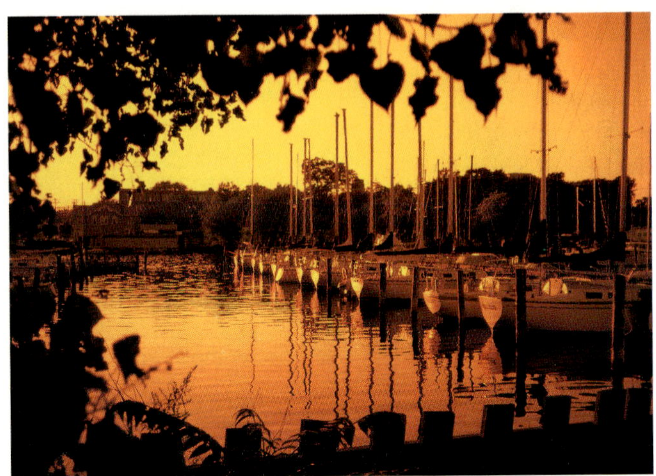

No. 21 orange filter

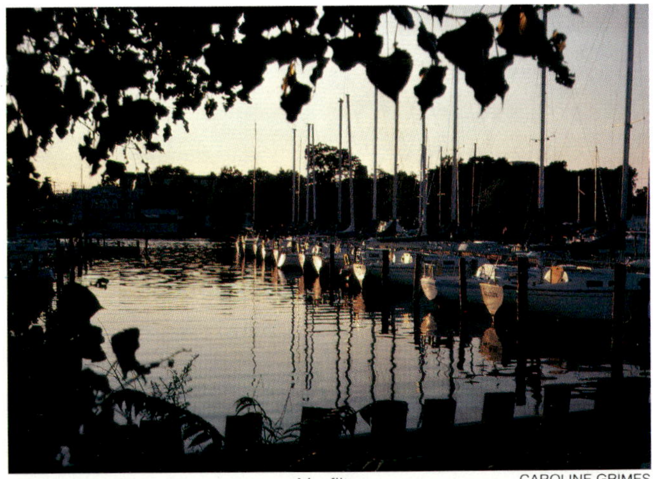

No filter CAROLINE GRIMES

You can often use filters for creative picture-taking. The photographer used a No. 21 orange filter for the top picture taken at sunset in order to create a more colorful photo. Usually with this filter technique, making the meter reading through the filter gives good exposure. KODACHROME 64 Film (Daylight)

## RECIPROCITY CHARACTERISTICS

Most color films are designed for the typical short exposure times used in general picture-taking. At exposure times of 1 second or longer, the speed of most films will begin to decrease and color rendition will shift away from normal. These changes are often referred to as the "reciprocity characteristics" of the film.

You can correct for this effect by using filters and increasing exposure. Recommended corrections for critical work are given in the Data Sheets. In most existing-light situations, it's not practical or essential to use filters, but you can increase exposure to compensate for the decrease in film speed. You can avoid the effect simply by using shutter speeds shorter than 1 second when it's practical. See the recommendations in the Data Sheet section.

When you apply the exposure compensation to correct for this effect, it's better to use a larger lens opening than to use a longer exposure time. Making the exposure time even longer compounds the problem. If you must make large corrections, you can apply part of the exposure compensation to the lens opening and the rest to the exposure time.

The effects of very long exposures are less serious with Kodak black-and-white films than with Kodak color films. You don't have to be concerned with shifts in color balance. However, the speed and contrast of black-and-white films do change when you use very long exposure times.

You can make exposure and development adjustments to compensate for the effect on black-and-white films according to the tables in the Data Sheets. (KODAK T-MAX Professional Films require only an exposure adjustment.) Development-time adjustments are practical only when an entire roll of film was exposed at similar exposure times. When you have exposed a roll with varied exposure times, you should develop the film normally and correct the contrast when you print the negatives.

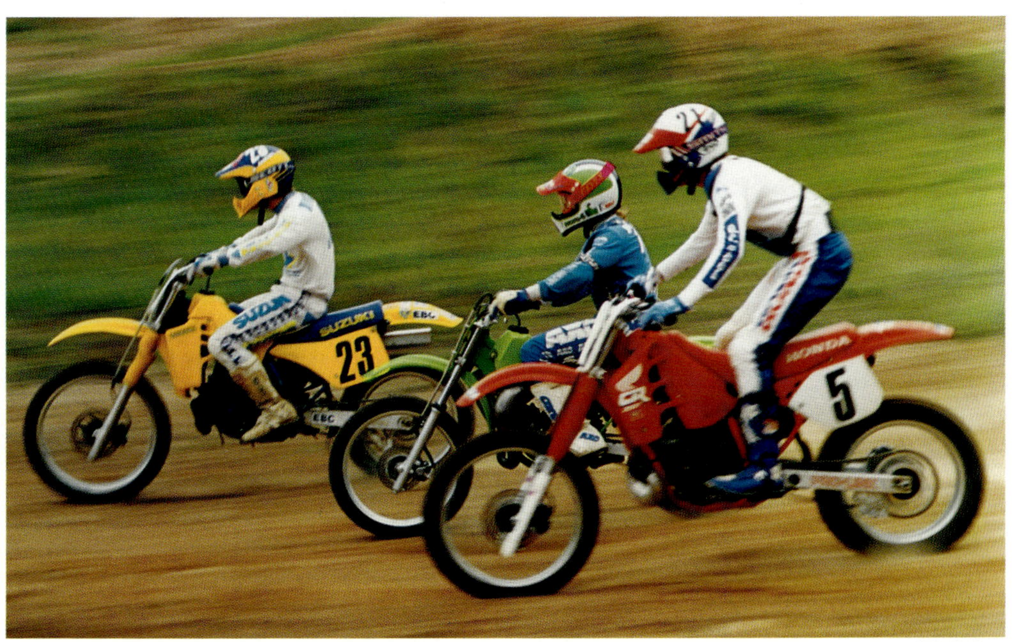


STEVE KELLY

Many scenes, especially those outdoors in daylight, have average reflectance. For these scenes, an incident-light meter and a reflected-light meter will work equally well.

## USING EXPOSURE METERS IN COPYING

Be sure to adjust the lights to provide even illumination over the copy area. To determine exposure for copying, you can hold an incident-light meter in the plane of the original you are copying and point it toward the camera. If you use a reflected-light meter, make a reading of a gray card with 18-percent reflectance (such as a KODAK Gray Card) that you substitute for the original. If you don't have an 18-percent gray card, you can make a reflected-light reading from a matte white surface of 90-percent reflectance, such as the back of a sheet of double-weight white photographic paper, as described on page 90. Remember to compensate for the high reflectance of the white surface by setting the meter calculator or film-speed dial at 1/5 the speed of your film.

The film speeds recommended for copying line copy are intended for trial exposures. Exposure for line copy is affected by the reflectance of the lines or dark areas in the original and by the inherently short exposure latitude of high-contrast films. To obtain the best contrast between the background and the lines, you should use the maximum exposure that you can without causing filling in or graying of the lines on the negative.

## CORRECTION FOR LENS EXTENSION

When you compute exposure for copying or other close-up work for which you extend the camera lens by using extension tubes or bellows, make sure you allow for the decrease in effective aperture, unless your camera does this automatically. Otherwise, your pictures will be underexposed. For example, if you ignore this factor when you take a close-up of an object that will be the same size on the film (a ratio of 1:1), your film will be underexposed by 2 stops. You should make an exposure compensation whenever the subject distance is less than 8 times the focal length of your lens. Close-up lenses require no exposure compensation unless you also use a lens-extension device. The *KODAK Pocket Photoguide*, KODAK Publication No. AR-21, provides a convenient calculator dial for determining the effective aperture quickly and easily.

You can also calculate the effective aperture by using the formula below. The lens-to-film distance is approximately equal to the focal length of your camera lens plus the distance the lens is extended beyond its position at infinity focus.

If your camera has a through-the-lens exposure meter that works with a bellows extension or extension tubes on the camera, the camera makes the exposure compensation automatically. When you're using flash, you usually have to make a manual exposure compensation for lens extension, although some cameras with through-the-lens metering for flash also do this automatically. Check your camera, flash, and close-up equipment instruction manuals.

$$\text{Effective } f\text{-number} = \frac{\text{Indicated } f\text{-number x lens-to-film distance}}{\text{Focal length}}$$

## MODIFYING FILM-SPEED NUMBERS

Film speeds published by film manufacturers provide an excellent basis for obtaining the best exposure. However, to produce the quality you want with your own equipment and procedures, you may sometimes need to modify film-speed numbers. Before you modify a recommended film speed, be sure that you are making exposure-meter readings carefully according to your camera or meter instructions. Then if your pictures are consistently overexposed or underexposed, modify the film-speed setting as follows:

If with normal development, your films are consistently underexposed, increase exposure by using a lower film-speed number; if your films are consistently overexposed, reduce exposure by using a higher film-speed number. Divide the published film speed by 2 to produce 1 stop more exposure. Multiply by 2 to produce 1 stop less exposure.

## FLASH EXPOSURE

The most important factor that affects exposure with a flash unit at a particular power output is the distance from the flash to the subject. Subjects close to the flash receive a lot of light, while subjects farther away receive less light. Many automatic electronic flash units adjust light output for proper exposure, and some cameras automatically adjust the lens opening for proper flash exposure as you focus the lens. Other cameras have through-the-lens exposure meters that automatically adjust the light from the flash. With nonadjustable cameras, flash-to-subject distances of about 5 to 25 feet (1.5 to 7.5 metres) usually produce acceptable exposure, depending on the speed of the film. See your camera manual.

Flash guide numbers provide a convenient means of determining flash exposure for manually adjustable cameras with manual flash units. The guide number you use depends on your film

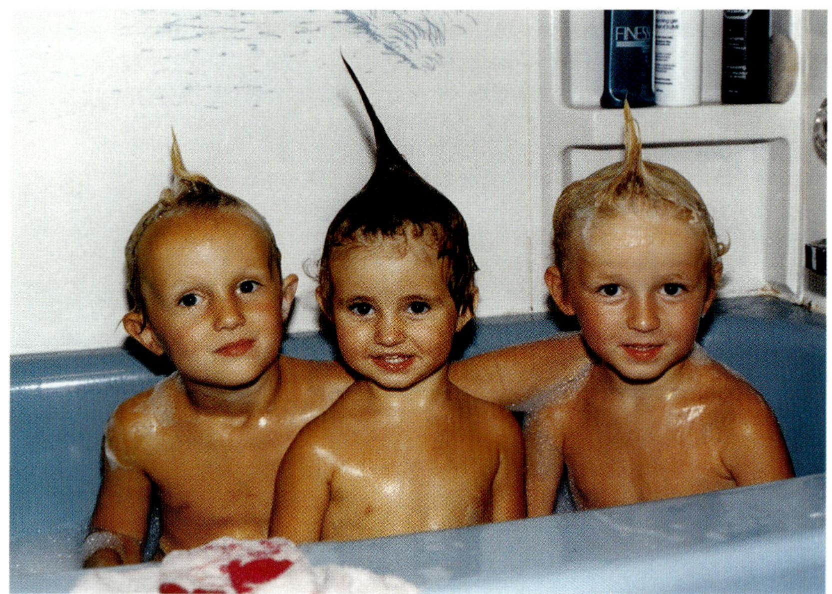

NORMA KOWALSKI

Many automatic electronic-flash units adjust light output for proper exposure, and some cameras automatically adjust the lens opening for proper flash exposure as you focus the lens.

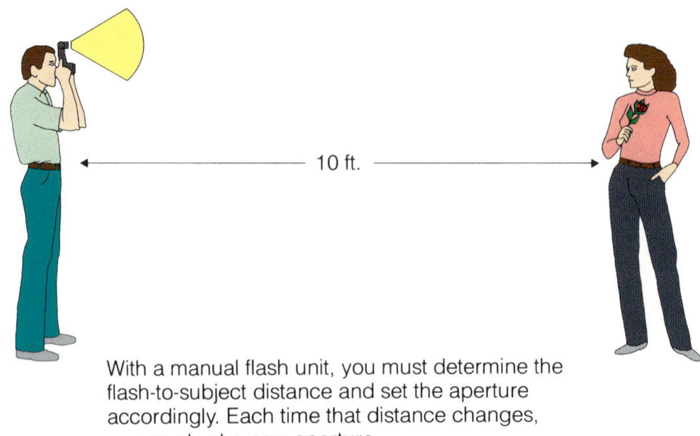


With a manual flash unit, you must determine the flash-to-subject distance and set the aperture accordingly. Each time that distance changes, you must set a new aperture.

and the output of your flash unit. A flash exposure table in the Data Sheet for each film gives guide numbers for different light outputs of electronic flash units. Divide the proper guide number by the flash-to-subject distance in feet (or metres) to find the *f*-number for average subjects. For example, if your guide number is 80 and the subject is 10 feet from the flash, divide 80 by 10. The answer, 8, means that you should set your lens opening at *f*/8. If the answer is between two *f*-numbers marked on your camera lens, set the lens at the nearest *f*-number or halfway between the two, whichever is closer to the answer.

When you use guide numbers, always be sure to use the distance units for which the guide numbers are calculated —feet or metres. You use guide numbers for metres in the same way as those for feet. Just divide the guide number for metres by flash-to-subject distance in metres to obtain the *f*-number.

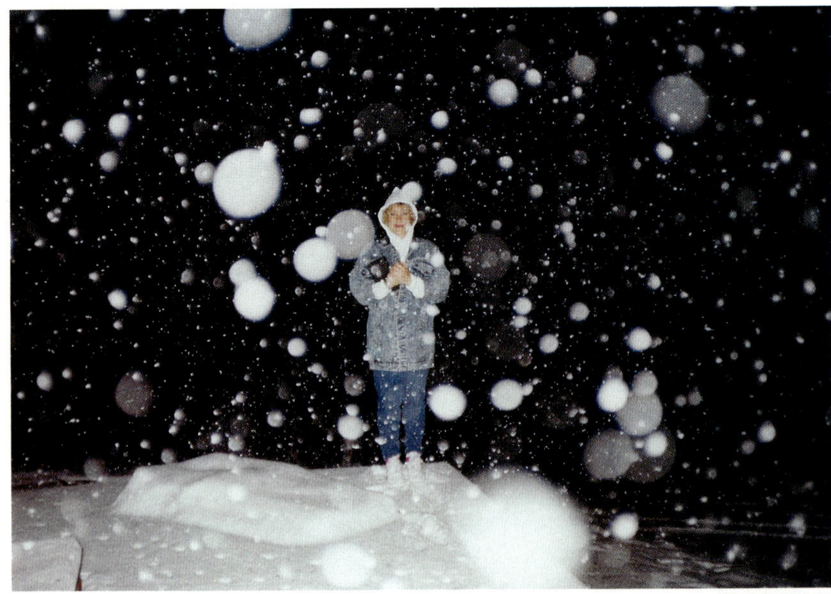

JOANNE KEMLER

Most flash units have easy-to-use calculator dials that tell you the *f*-number setting for the speed of film you are using and the flash-to-subject distance.

Guide numbers are just *guides;* they are for average subjects in average-size rooms. They don't take into account such things as subjects that are much lighter or darker than average or small rooms with light-colored walls that reflect a lot of light. If you're photographing a light subject, use a lens opening ½ stop smaller than the guide number indicates; for a dark subject, use a lens opening ½ stop larger. In small rooms with light-colored walls, use 1 stop less exposure than the guide number indicates.

If *necessary,* you can change the guide numbers to improve your results. If your pictures are consistently underexposed—your negatives are too light or your slides are too dark—use a lower guide number. If your pictures are consistently overexposed—your negatives are too dark or your slides are too light—use a higher guide number.

When you're using an automatic flash unit to photograph subjects with a predominantly light or dark background, the light-sensitive photocell in the flash can be misled by the background, and give incorrect exposure for the subject. In these situations, switch the flash to manual operation and make corrections manually, or use your exposure compensation dial. When you photograph subjects in small rooms with light-colored walls, the walls may fool the flash sensor and underexpose your subject. Use your exposure-compensation dial to increase exposure by ½ to 1 stop.

The *KODAK Pocket Photoguide,* described earlier, takes the arithmetic out of calculating flash exposure. It includes a convenient "Flash Exposure Dial" that indicates the correct *f*-number opposite each subject distance.

Using flash for distant subjects—at sporting or other spectator events—when you are 50 feet (15 metres) or farther from your subject usually doesn't give satisfactory results. The foreground often appears as a large overexposed area that spoils the picture, and the flash just won't carry far enough to expose the subject properly. You can photograph these distant subjects much more effectively by using existing light.

Do *not* use flash to photograph the image on a television screen or projected slide or movie images. The bright light from the flash will overwhelm the image, and your pictures will show a blank screen. Again, you can get good results if you photograph these subjects by existing light. For techniques on photographing television and computer-screen images, see *Existing-Light Photography,* KODAK Publication No. KW-17.

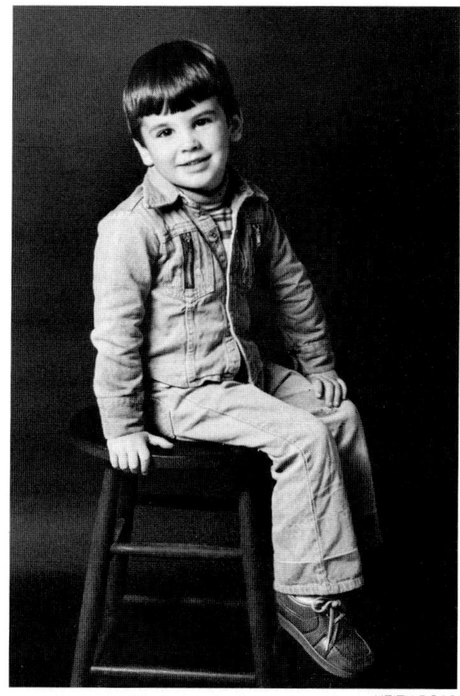

KEITH BOAS

Bouncing the flash off a reflecting umbrella gives this portrait soft, natural lighting. Since some light is lost with bounce flash, use about 1 stop more exposure than you would need for direct flash. KODAK TRI-X Pan Film, 1/60 second *f*/11

# STORAGE AND CARE OF *KODAK* FILMS

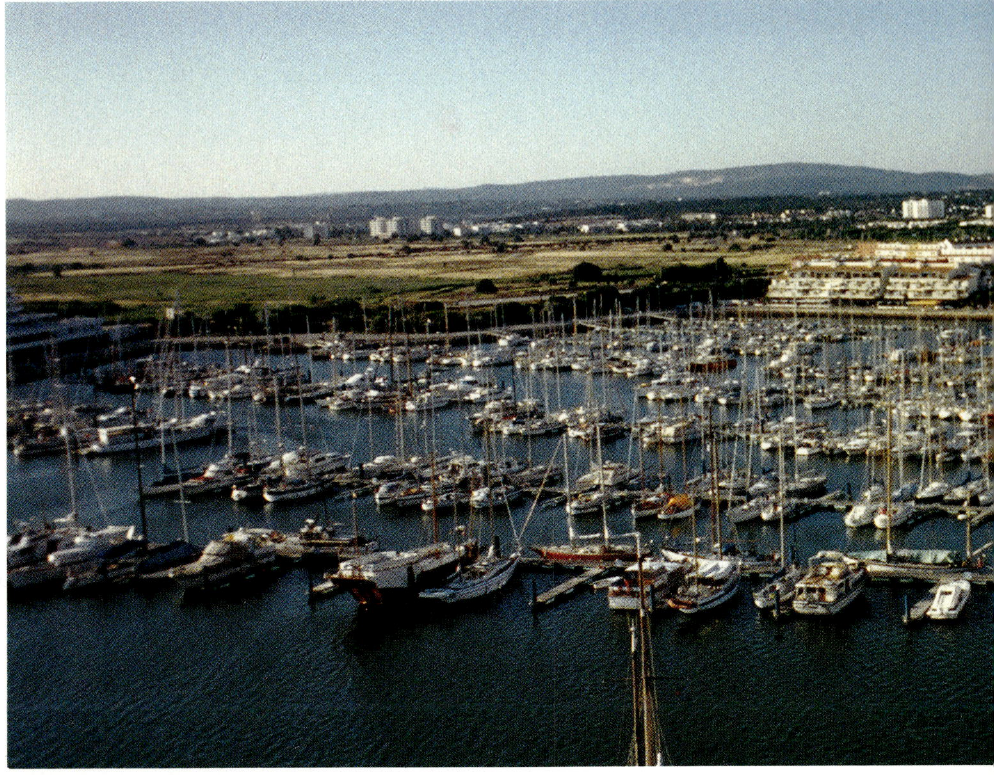

KODACOLOR GOLD 200 Film

Photographic films are perishable, and can be damaged by high temperatures, high relative humidities, and harmful gases. Some photographic characteristics—speed, color balance, and contrast of color films, and speed, contrast, and fog level of black-and-white films—change gradually after manufacture. Adverse storage conditions accelerate these changes. Color films are more seriously affected than black-and-white films because adverse conditions usually affect the three or more emulsion layers of a color film to different degrees. Moisture may also cause physical defects such as mottle.

For best results, handle and store unprocessed films properly both before and after exposure, with adequate protection from heat, moisture, harmful gases, x-rays, and radioactive substances. In moderate climates, storage precautions are few and simple; greater care is necessary under hot and humid conditions. Processed films also require proper storage and care for long-term keeping.

## STORAGE IN THE ORIGINAL PACKAGE

Kodak 135 films are packaged in snap-cover plastic cans. This vapor-tight packaging provides protection from humidity in tropical regions or any other location where high relative humidities (RH) prevail. Kodak 135 films require no additional protection from high humidity until

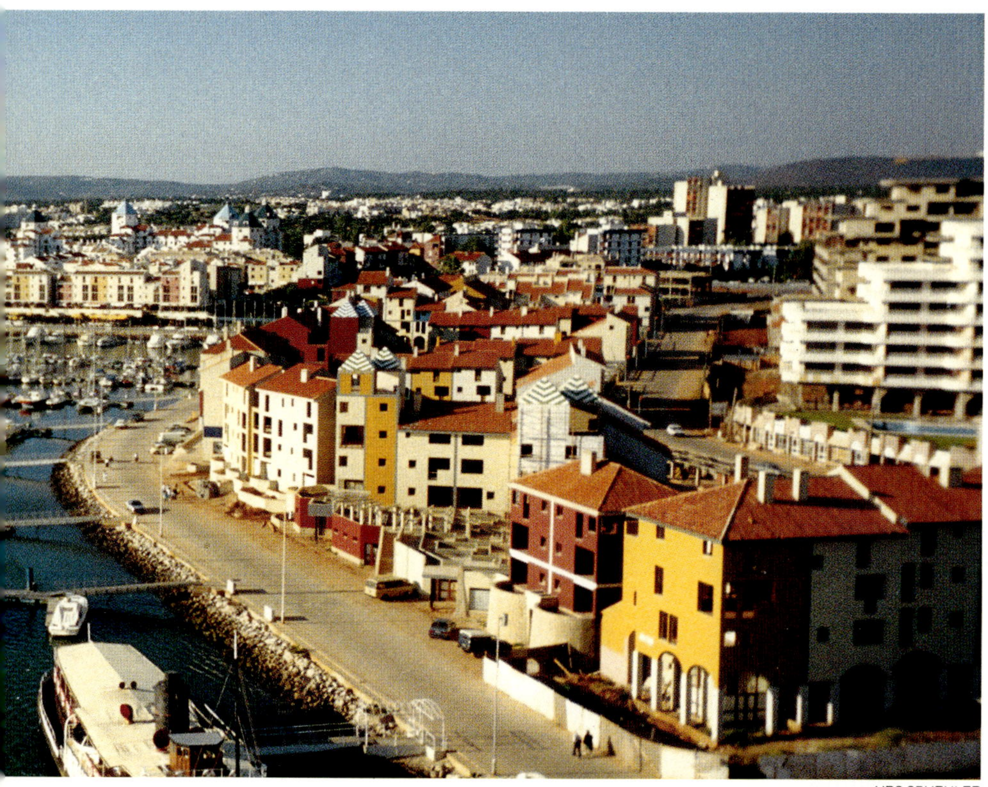

URS SPUEHLER

you open the packaging. *Don't open the vapor-tight packaging until you are ready to use the film.*

### Protection from Heat

*Vapor-tight packaging provides no protection from heat.* Don't leave film near heat registers, steam pipes, or other sources of heat. In warm weather, don't leave film in areas on the top floors of uninsulated buildings or in hot places in a car.

Kodak color-negative and color-slide films are available as films designed for general use and films designed for professional use. The requirements for storing and handling professional color films are more rigid than those for films for general use.

Kodak color films for general (non-professional) use are manufactured with an allowance for room-temperature aging. These films approach optimum color balance during the time over which they are most frequently stored and used by amateur photographers. Although they are designed for room-temperature storage, you must protect them from heat.

Kodak professional color films are manufactured so that they are near optimum color balance at the time of shipment, and will remain at that point if they are refrigerated. Store professional color films at 55°F (13°C) or lower before exposure to maintain optimum color balance and contrast.

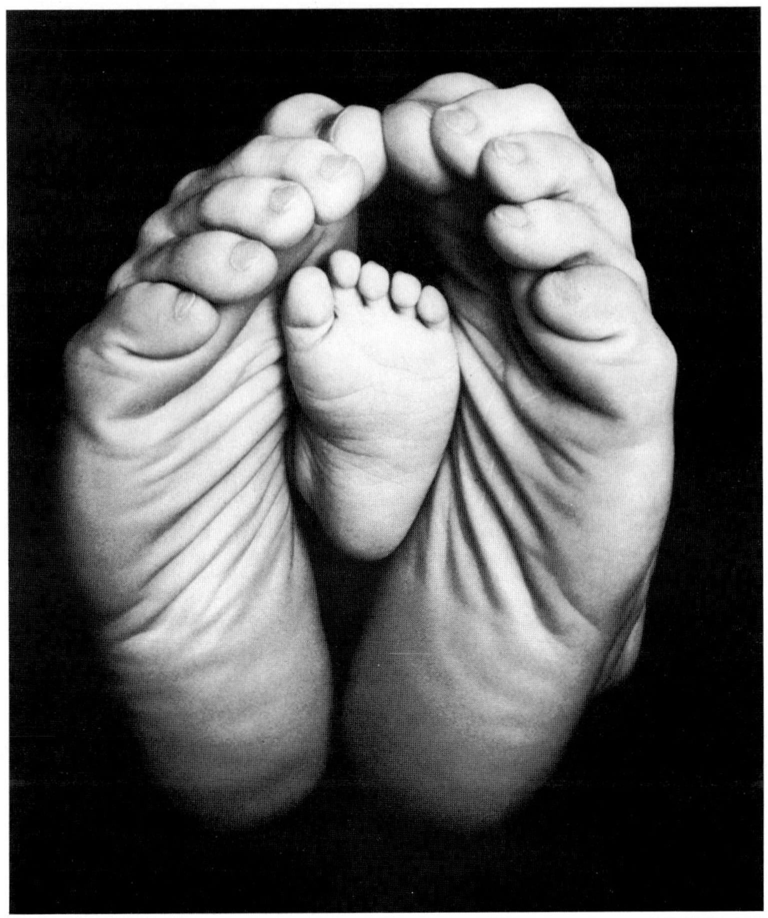

KODAK TRI-X Pan Film, electronic flash, 1/60 second *f*/16 CRAIG STEWART

Storing professional color films at normal room temperatures for short periods will not cause any noticeable changes. For example, two weeks at room temperature would not cause any significant shift in color balance or contrast. You do not have to rush professional color film from cold storage to the camera and then on to processing within a few hours. Just exercise reasonable care and judgment. Typically, a roll of professional color film will be exposed within a week of being removed from refrigerated storage and processed within the next week.

Under normal temperature conditions, 70°F (21°C) or below, Kodak color films for general use and most Kodak black-and-white films do not require refrigeration. Storage instructions for each kind of Kodak film are printed on the film carton. A few special-purpose films require storage temperatures of 0 to −10°F (−18 to −23°C). Storage recommendations for Kodak films that require refrigerated storage are also given in the Data Sheets in this book.

During extended periods of temperatures above 70°F (21°C), we recommend refrigerated storage to keep all Kodak films cool, provided they are in vapor-tight packages or in sealed cans or jars. To avoid moisture condensation, allow film that's been refrigerated to warm up to room temperature before you open the package. When the ambient temperature returns to normal, 70°F (21°C) or below, remove Kodak color films for general use from refrigerated storage so that they can age normally.

If after testing some rolls of film, you want to maintain more film of the same emulsion number at that specific color balance for an extended period, you can store it in a refrigerator or freezer. The emulsion number is printed on the film carton.

When you're traveling in a car, don't leave your film in a closed car parked in the sun on a warm or hot day. The temperature inside the car can quickly reach 140°F (60°C) or more. If you must leave film in a car, keep it in an insulated container, such as an ice chest or an insulated picnic bag. If you use ice or cold packs, keep the film packages dry. With a light-colored car, the trunk is usually somewhat cooler and is a better storage area for the insulated container than the hot passenger compartment. With a dark-colored car, the passenger compartment is usually slightly cooler than the trunk.

The coolest area for protecting your film from heat in a moving car is in the passenger compartment with the air conditioner on or the windows open. The best location is on the car floor in the shade, away from areas over the exhaust system or transmission.

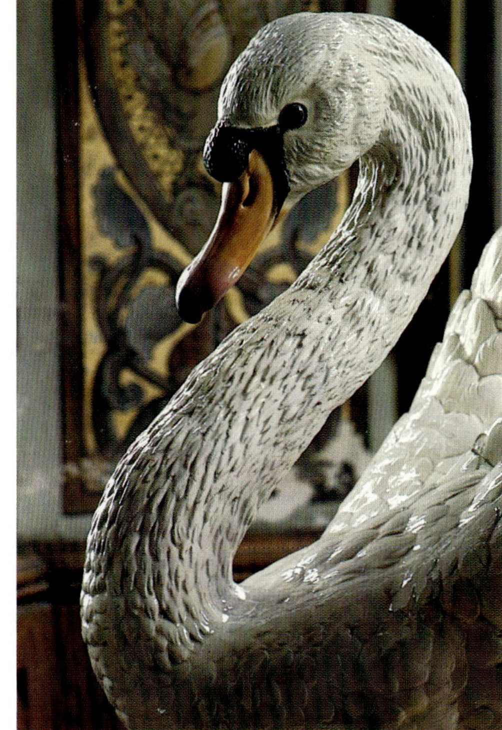

KODAK EKTACHROME 200 Film (Daylight) GARY WHELPLEY

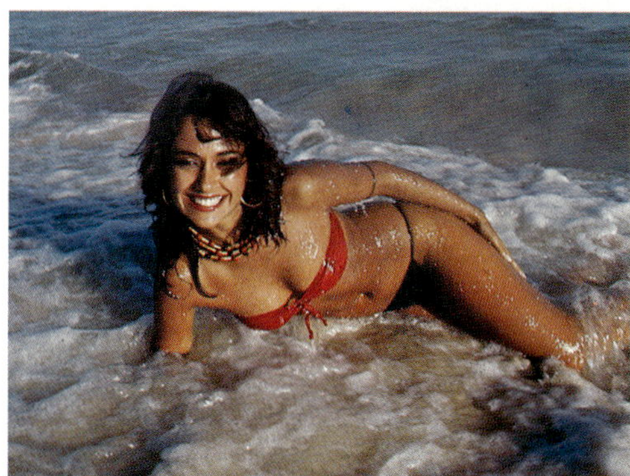

KODACHROME 25 Film (Daylight), 1/250 second *f*/5.6 NEIL MONTANUS

### Expiration Date

*Use film promptly.* Expose and process each roll of Kodak film before the "Process before" date printed on the carton. Films kept beyond this date may give unsatisfactory results due to changes in speed, contrast, and color balance; fog; and stain. The extent of changes depends largely on storage conditions. Proper storage conditions decrease the rate of change in films, but won't prevent changes entirely.

In general, we do not recommend refrigeration to extend film life. Refrigeration may be somewhat successful with Kodak black-and-white films, but the risks of detrimental effects is higher with color films. This is especially so with high-speed color films, such as

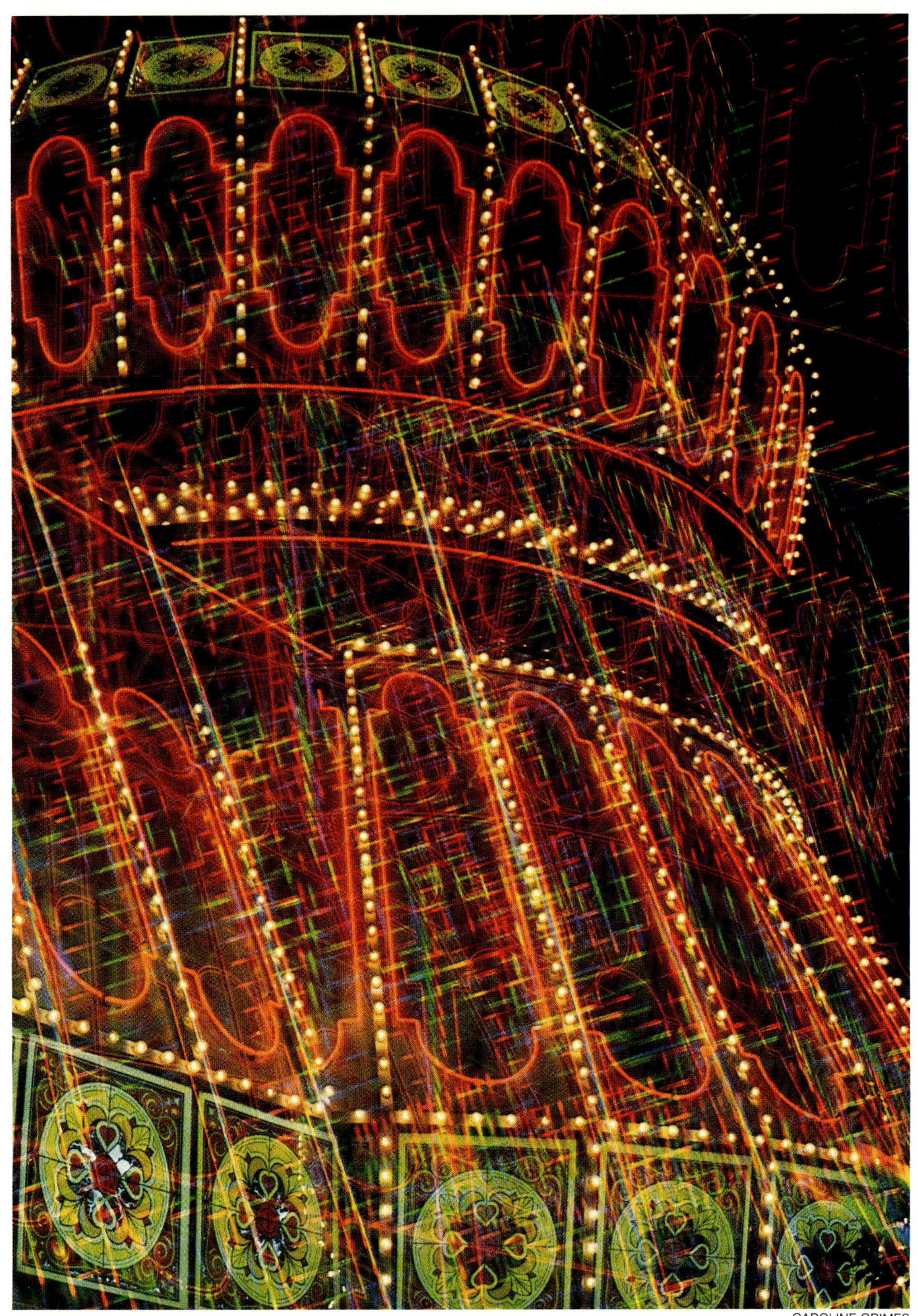

KODAK EKTACHROME 160 Film (Tungsten), exposed through diffraction grating, 1/30 second *f*/4

CAROLINE GRIMES

KODACOLOR GOLD 1600 Film. Do not attempt to extend the life of these films beyond their normal "Process before" dates by storing them in a refrigerator or freezer. High-speed films used after the date printed on the carton may show excessive graininess from the effects of cosmic and gamma radiation that's naturally present in the environment. Neither refrigeration nor freezing will prevent this effect. Storage in lead containers such as lead-foil bags also does little to prevent radiation effects. Avoid the effects of environmental radiation by exposing and processing the film before the date on the carton.

### Protection from X-Rays

X-ray equipment can fog unprocessed film when the radiation level is high or the film receives several low-level doses. The effect of exposure to x-rays is cumulative. Processed film is not affected by x-rays.

If you travel by commercial airline, your luggage may be subjected to x-ray examination each time you prepare to board an aircraft. All carry-on luggage is x-rayed unless you can obtain a visual inspection instead. Checked luggage may also be x-rayed. Although film can tolerate some x-ray exposure, excessive amounts may cause fog and shadow images on film. X-rays are particularly damaging to fast films such as KODACOLOR GOLD 1600 Film. You can usually avoid damage to unprocessed film by packing it in carry-on luggage and requesting a *visual* rather than an x-ray inspection. Carrying your film in a clear plastic bag will speed up and simplify visual inspection. The walk-through and hand-held electronic devices used at many airports to check passengers have no effect on film.

At airport boarding gates for domestic airline flights in the United States, federal regulations require that only low-output devices be used. These subject luggage to less than 1 milliroentgen of x-ray exposure per inspection, which should not perceptibly fog most camera films. But if you are carrying a very-high-speed film, it's best to request a visual inspection. Because the effects of x-rays on film are cumulative, films can be significantly fogged by repeated low-output exposures.

Visual inspection of film is particularly important when you pass through airports abroad (and international air terminals in the United States). You may encounter a wide variety of luggage-inspection systems for checked and carry-on luggage. Some of these systems may operate at relatively high x-ray levels. If you are unable to obtain a visual inspection, ask airline authorities whether or not the equipment will damage film. If you're in doubt about the safety of the equipment in use, or if your luggage will be examined more than five times, you can minimize the possibility of damage to your film in the following ways:

- Carry your film in a clear plastic bag in hand luggage, arrive early, and ask airport authorities for a visual inspection at each checkpoint. Stress the fact that the sensitive photo material you're carrying might be ruined by x-rays. Not all inspectors will cooperate; however, those who do will help reduce the possibility of film damage.
- Each time you pack your bag, arrange the contents so that the film is oriented in a different way. Or you can orient your bag differently each time it passes through x-ray inspection.
- Carry photofinishing mailers on your trip, and mail each roll of film for processing after you expose it. (Sometimes mailed packages are also x-rayed or fluoroscoped, so if you include unprocessed film in a package, label the package "Undeveloped Photographic Film. Please Do Not X-Ray.") Film mailed in processing mailers and clearly marked as film usually is not subject to x-ray or fluoroscope inspection.

- If your trip is from one city to another in the United States and back again, there's probably little need for concern unless you're carrying very-high-speed film. But the 12-countries-in-10-days whirlwind tour may present a problem to your film.

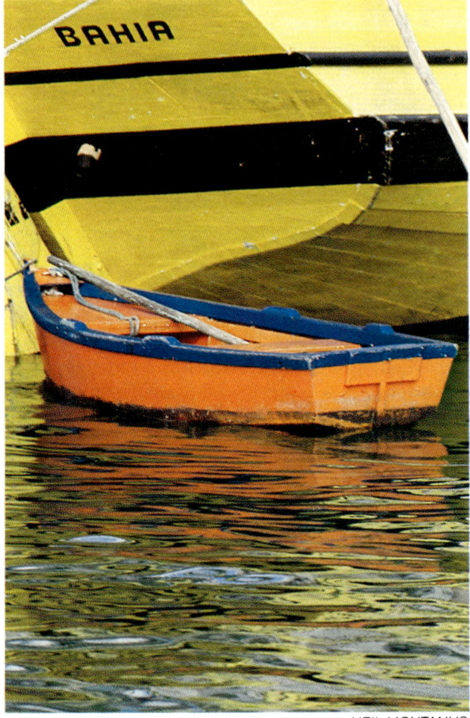


NEIL MONTANUS

KODAK EKTACHROME 200 Film (Daylight)

## PROTECTION OF FILMS AFTER YOU OPEN THE PACKAGE

When you open the vapor-tight film can, the film is no longer protected from high humidity and harmful gases. *So expose and process your films promptly after you open the package.* Kodak builds a small manufacturing bias into non-professional film to compensate for changes that occur between purchase and processing. You'll get best results, however, when you have your exposed film processed promptly. Process professional films soon after exposure. If you can't process professional film promptly, keep it refrigerated between exposure and processing.

High relative humidity and high temperature often cause changes in the latent image—the undeveloped image on exposed film. Under these conditions, it's particularly important to have your exposed films processed as soon as possible. Do not deposit film in an outdoor metal mailbox in the sun.

Under high heat or humidity, don't keep film in your camera any longer than necessary. Protect film by keeping it in a carrying case away from direct sunlight; otherwise, the temperature inside the case may become extremely high even in a temperate area. Don't leave your film in a closed car parked in the sun on a warm day. (See the recommendations on page 103 under "Protection from Heat.") Putting 135 films back into the plastic film cans will protect them from additional exposure to humidity or harmful gases.

Don't store opened packages of film in damp basements, ice chests, refrigerators, or other places where the relative humidity is high. A moderate temperature and moderate relative humidity, such as 60°F (16°C) and 40 percent RH, are better than a low temperature with high relative humidity, such as 40°F (4°C) and 80 percent RH. The ideal relative humidity for storage of opened packages of film is between 40 and 50 percent.

When you can't avoid humid storage locations, or when you must store your film in a refrigerator to keep it cool, you can put it back into the plastic film can, or store it in the special storage envelopes described on page 112. (You can use these envelopes for unprocessed as well as processed film.) Or you can use three wraps of aluminum foil, each tightly sealed with tape, to protect the film from moisture. See page 112.

If the prevailing relative humidity is above 60 percent, dry your film with a desiccating agent such as activated silica

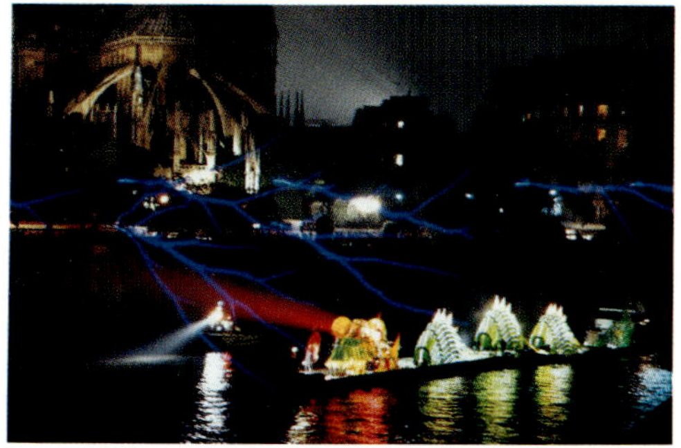

ALAIN COURTOIS

Static discharges occur most often in low relative humidity when film is advanced or rewound too rapidly.

gel before storing it in cans, jars, storage envelopes, or aluminum foil. Silica gel is available from chemical-supply companies and many photo dealers.

*Keep opened packages of film away from chemical fumes, such as industrial gases, motor exhausts, mothballs and moth repellents, formaldehyde, paints, solvents, cleaners, mildew and fungus preventives, chipboard, glues, foam insulation, insecticides, sulfides, and fabric treatments such as permanent press and stain inhibitors.* Do not store films or cameras in drawers of furniture that are made from chipboard or that may be contaminated with photographically harmful fumes from mothballs, mildew inhibitors, wood preservatives, paints, varnishes, or wood glues. Since clothes closets often contain moth repellents or mildew and fungus preventives, check carefully before storing films and cameras in such locations.

### Static

Advancing and rewinding film too rapidly and other careless handling can produce discharges of static electricity, which produce marks on processed film. Static discharges occur most often when the relative humidity is low, such as indoors during winter months. Marks produced by static can appear as lightning streaks, small dots, or fogging. High-speed films are more susceptible to the effects of static than medium- or low-speed films.

When the humidity is low, you can minimize static discharges by slowly advancing the film for each picture, slowly rewinding it after the last exposure, and handling it carefully. After film has been processed, static won't produce marks on it.

## STORAGE AND CARE OF PROCESSED FILMS AND PRINTS

Some photographs are used for only brief periods to satisfy immediate needs; other photographs are used or stored for extended periods. This section gives some suggestions for storage and care of negatives, slides, and prints.

### Black-and-White Materials

Storage conditions for processed black-and-white films and prints are less demanding than those for color photographs. You can store black-and-white negatives (or black-and-white slides) and black-and-white prints at normal temperatures—about 70°F (21°C) or below. Store black-and-white negatives and prints where the relative humidity is between 30 and 50 percent. Avoid relative humidities below 30 percent, which can cause excessive brittleness. High relative humidities (above 60 percent) are also harmful because they can encourage mold or fungus growth. Constant temperature and humidity are better than varying conditions. If the temperature is moderately higher temporarily, this should cause no harm as long as the relative humidity is below 40 percent. Temperatures above 75°F (24°C) with relative humidity above 60 percent are the most damaging; they can cause accelerated growth of mold or fungus, deterioration of the image, and sticking together or glazing of film surfaces.

Because the oxidizing gases in a polluted atmosphere may attack silver images, protect your negatives and prints from fumes of sulfur compounds such as hydrogen sulfide and coal gas, and from fumes of oxides of nitrogen, peroxides, formaldehydes, ozone, and other harmful gases. Fumes from oil-base paints can cause serious discoloration of black-and-white images. Do not return black-and-white prints and negatives to an area painted with oil-base paint for at least 4 weeks after painting. No adverse effects have been found with latex paints.

For long-term keeping of processed black-and-white films and papers, follow the most recent processing recommendations very closely. Incorrect processing procedures such as excessive times in certain solutions, insufficient fixing, and inadequate or excessive washing can cause defects during long-term storage. For example, inadequate washing of papers can leave chemical residues that will later stain the prints.

Black-and-white prints that have been toned by one of the processes that convert metallic silver to silver sulfide or silver selenide are generally more stable than untoned prints. For information on toning prints, see KODAK Publication No. G-23, *Toning KODAK Black-and-White Materials*.

When black-and-white negatives and prints are processed properly and are stored under optimum conditions, they will last for a very long time. For additional protection, you can put your negatives and prints in special storage envelopes for processed film. Although these envelopes are recommended for cold storage of processed color films, you can use them for long-term storage of black-and-white photographs as well. Do not mix black-and-white materials with color materials in the same envelope. Recommendations for using storage envelopes are on page 112.

### Color Materials

Requirements for long-term storage and care of color negatives, slides, and prints are somewhat different from those for black-and-white materials. The images in color photographs are formed by dyes;

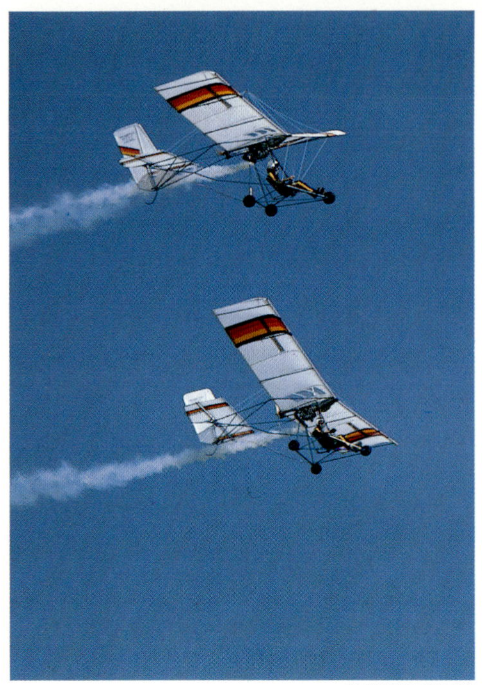

CAROLINE GRIMES

KODAK EKTACHROME 200 Film (Daylight), 210 mm telephoto lens, 1/800 second *f*/8

those in most black-and-white photographs are formed by metallic silver. In time, all dyes may change. The dyes in Kodak color films and color photographic papers provide the best possible stability while meeting other essential requirements.

The primary factors that affect the stability of color photographs are heat, humidity, light, and cleanliness of storage conditions. Store processed color films and color prints where it's dark, dry, cool, and free of contamination. You can store processed color films and color prints for extended periods under normal room conditions—e.g., in many areas on the main floors of buildings—but never store them in damp basements or hot attics. For color slides, negatives, and prints, a relative humidity between 30 and 50 percent and a temperature of about 70°F (21°C) or lower are satisfactory. Cooler temperatures are even better. Again, constant temperature and humidity are preferable to varying conditions. Avoid a relative humidity below 30 percent, because excessive brittleness may result. High relative humidities (above 60 percent) are also harmful because of the increased possibility of fungus growth or color changes. Keep the storage container for your photographs away from sources of heat, like radiators, warm-air registers, walls that contain hot-air ducts or chimneys, and windows where sunlight can strike the container.

Dye images can deteriorate when they are exposed to bright light or to normal light levels for long periods. Therefore, dark storage is best for color materials. Providing dark storage for color negatives and color slides is easy, because these images are normally exposed to light for only brief periods and then returned to storage. You can store color negatives and color slides in the dark by using metal containers such as file boxes or drawers. Wood or plastic may contain preservatives or volatile substances that can harm negatives and slides.

You can print color negatives many times without causing perceptible fading. Use a heat-absorbing glass in the enlarger between the lamp and the negative (many enlargers have a built-in heat-rejection device). Return the negatives to dark storage after printing. Properly processed and stored, Kodak color-negative films will give good results for extended periods.

Color-slide films are intended for projection. The use and storage of color slides is similar to that of color negatives; slides are usually projected on a screen with a bright light for several seconds and then returned to storage.

Kodak color-slide films are remarkably stable. As discussed earlier, many factors influence your choice of a color-slide film. But if long life in dark storage is the most important factor, perhaps the best choice is a KODACHROME Film. KODAK EKTACHROME Films withstand the effects of projection somewhat better than KODACHROME Films do. If you project your slides frequently or project them for long periods of time, it's wise to have duplicate slides made on KODAK EKTACHROME Slide Duplicating Film. Then you can project the duplicates and preserve your original slides.

Color prints are viewed in many ways—in albums, on walls, in wallets, and on desks or tables. In most cases, you can have replacement prints made from your negatives or slides if prints fade or are damaged. If you don't have the negative or slide, care of the print is very important.

Storage recommendations for color prints are the same as those for color negatives and color slides. Most prints, though, are exposed to light for much longer periods. Whenever possible, display prints in subdued light, such as the light from household tungsten lamps, as far from the light source as possible, and away from direct sunlight and fluorescent lamps. Avoid temperatures above 70°F (21°C), humidities above 50 percent, and damaging chemicals and fumes. If you can't avoid less-than-ideal conditions, keep in mind that the prints will change faster. A color print on continuous display, even under the best conditions, is likely to change in time because light, heat, humidity, and contaminants in the air will affect it. If you display your prints, store the original negatives or slides properly so that you can have new prints made if necessary.

A convenient way to store your prints for easy viewing and good long-term storage is to put them in photo albums. Make sure that all materials in the photo album are recommended for archival, or long-term, storage. See the next page for standards that specify storage materials. Of course, it's important to keep the album in a place that's free of contaminants, out of direct sunlight, and where the temperature and humidity are not high.

### Extended Storage of Color Materials

You can keep color photographs under normal room conditions for extended periods of time; but to keep fading to a minimum, store them in the dark under refrigeration at 0°F (−18°C) with a relative humidity between 30 and 35 percent.

Because refrigerators and freezers usually have high relative humidity, put your color negatives, slides, or prints into special storage envelopes before refrigerating them. These moistureproof envelopes, sold by photo dealers, are made of laminated polyethylene, aluminum, and paper. Before putting them into the envelopes, condition negatives and slides for an hour, and condition prints for 2 days in a room or cabinet at 70°F (21°C) or lower and 25 to 30 percent RH. The room or cabinet should be free of dust and fumes. Then insert the negatives, slides, or prints into the envelopes under these temperature and humidity conditions. Segregate the different types of films or prints and put them in individual storage envelopes.

If special envelopes are not available, use three wraps of aluminum foil and seal the folds and seams with moistureproof tape such as freezer tape or plastic electrical tape (not "friction" tape). Do not store black-and-white and color materials in the same envelope. Remove excess air from the package in the low-humidity atmosphere by flattening the package as much as possible before you seal it. To avoid excessive pressure on stored materials, don't pack the envelopes tightly or stack them.

If you store several negatives, slides, or prints in the same envelope, separate them with sheets of paper. Be sure that the paper is of archival quality and that it's free of harmful chemicals. See the standards reference for storage materials below.

Power failures should not cause a humidity problem in a refrigerator if color photographs are sealed in special storage envelopes. The humidity inside the envelopes is established at the time of sealing will remain stable as long as the seal is not broken. A power failure is more serious with a freezer, because puddles of water can form from melting ice and frost. Remove the storage envelopes from the freezer until power is restored. It's a good idea to keep the storage envelopes away from the bottom of the freezer to avoid moisture that can form there.

The elaborate care discussed in this section is needed only for color photographs that you want to store for a very long time.

For long-term keeping of extremely valuable images, you can have three color-separation negatives of the image made on black-and-white film. Since these separation negatives have silver images, you can expect the negatives to last as long as other properly processed black-and-white negatives stored under the best conditions. You can then have color images made from the separation negatives at any time. Custom laboratories do this type of work. The procedure, though, is expensive and requires a lot of skill.

For a more thorough discussion of long-term keeping of photographs, see KODAK Publication No. E-30, *Storage and Care of KODAK Films and Papers Before and After Processing*, or No. F-40, *Conservation of Photographs*. You can obtain a single copy of E-30 from the address given on page 50.

## Protection from Physical Damage

Keep slides and negatives as clean and dust-free as possible. A good rule is to handle the film only by the edges. The best way to protect negatives is to store them in envelopes with side seams. The paper or plastic and adhesive should meet the requirements of *American National Standard* PH1.53-1986, *Processed Films, Plates, and Papers—Filing Enclosures and Containers for Storage*. Other ANSI publications that you might find helpful are PH1.43-1985, *Processed Safety Film—Storage*, and PH1.48-1982 (R1987), *Practice for Storage of Black-and-White Photographic Paper Prints*.

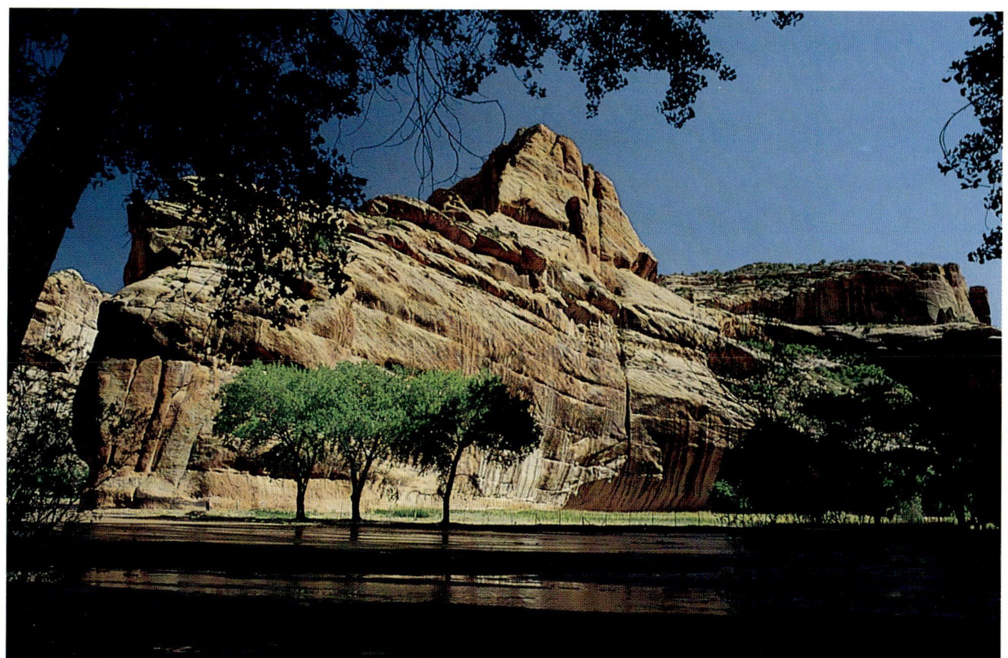

KODAK EKTACHROME Film — CAROLINE GRIMES

You can purchase American National Standards from the American National Standards Institute, Inc., 1430 Broadway, New York, New York 10018. Stores that sell photo products usually offer a variety of containers for storing slides.

Don't store color negatives or slides near moth-preventive chemicals, which tend to crystallize on the films and damage the adhesive used in slide mounts. Exposure to nitrogen oxides, hydrogen sulfide, or sulfur dioxide gas may cause slow fading of color dyes. The solvents and chemicals used in insecticides and fungicide sprays may be harmful to processed films and slide mounts. Keep films away from chemical dust; alkaline dust particles and hypo particles on the emulsion may cause dye fading after prolonged storage. Protect your film from insects, because some species will eat the gelatin emulsion or the film base.

**Care of Slides During Projection—** Your slides will stay in good condition for many years if you care for them properly. However, light and heat from prolonged projection with high-wattage lamps will shorten the life of slides and may even distort them. Avoid projection times longer than 1 minute. Never remove the heat-absorbing glass from your projector or use a lamp of higher wattage than recommended. Do not obstruct the air intake or outlet for cooling the projector.

Binding slides in glass will protect them from physical damage such as dirt and scratches. When you use glass-mounted slides in high-wattage projectors, moisture may condense inside the glass. You can usually eliminate the moisture by storing slides with activated silica gel.

**Treating Films Damaged by Water—** Water from floods, firefighting, sprinkler systems, overflowing sinks, burst pipes, backed-up sewers, and leaky roofs can cause serious damage to stored negatives and slides. Other situations, such as poor humidity control in areas where your processed film is stored, can make film unusable. Water damage may also take the following forms:

- Films sticking together because of water absorption. Separating the films may pull the emulsion from the film surfaces.
- Transfer of paper fibers or coatings from storage sleeves caused by film sticking to the sleeves.
- Ferrotyping of film surfaces in contact with plastic sleeves; i.e., shiny, glazed areas on the film.
- Embedded material from dirt or foreign matter in water.
- Uneven drying when the film dries before being treated as described below.
- Biological growth.

*Treatment*—It's important to treat the films immediately or as soon as practical to keep the damage to a minimum. The first thing to remember is to keep the water-soaked negatives and slides and their enclosures (slide mounts, envelopes, or sleeves) wet. Never let water-damaged photographic materials dry out before treatment. If you can't treat the immersed films within a few days, freeze them to retard deterioration.

Use a plastic container. Dissolve the following chemicals in a litre of water at 70°F (21°C). (To make larger or smaller volumes, increase or decrease the amounts of the chemicals proportionately.)

| Solution A* | |
|---|---|
| Quadrafos† | 0.6 grams |
| Sodium Acid Sulfate ($NaHSO_4$) | 7.0 grams |
| Sodium Tetraborate—Borax ($Na_2B_4O_7/10H_2O$) | 15.0 grams |
| Sodium Sulfate ($Na_2SO_4$) | 195.0 grams |
| Formalin (37.5% solution) | 20.0 mL |

*Before mixing any chemicals, read the precautions on the chemical labels and in the Material Safety Data Sheets (MSDS) for the chemicals, available from the manufacturer.

†Sodium hexametaphosphate.

If these chemicals are not readily available, you can substitute Alternate Solution B, below. Keep the temperature at 65°F (18°C) or below. If necessary, use ice to keep the temperature of the solution down. The cold water and the formaldehyde will help prevent swelling and softening of the gelatin emulsion, which are the major causes of damage, and the growth of bacteria.

| Alternate Solution B* | |
|---|---|
| Formalin (37.5% solution) | 15.0 mL per litre of water |

*Before mixing any chemicals, read the precautions on the chemical labels and in the Material Safety Data Sheets (MSDS) for the chemicals, available from the manufacturer.

Solution A is better because it hardens the emulsion to help minimize damage.

Immerse the films in the solution. As soon as possible during soaking, carefully separate the negatives and slides from the sleeves, envelopes, and each other. Use extreme care because the wet emulsion is very susceptible to physical damage. To remove traces of mud, silt, paper, or other foreign particles, soak the films for approximately 30 minutes in the solution. When necessary, you can clean the films by gently swabbing the surfaces with a tuft of cotton or a soft foam-rubber brush *under the surface of the solution*. Again use extreme care to minimize damage. Avoid any sudden temperature changes in the solution or wash water. For water-damaged films with little or no foreign particles, soak for 10 to 15 minutes in the solution.

After treatment in Solution A, wash the films in running water for 10 minutes at 70°F (21°) or below; after treatment in Solution B, wash the films in running water for 10 to 15 minutes at 65°F (18°C) or below. *Never* use warm water for washing, because it may cause frilling or even melting of the emulsion.

**Note:** Never use water warmer than 67°F (19°C) for washing after using Solution B.

After washing, treat the films as follows:

- For Kodak black-and-white films and for slides on KODACHROME Films—rinse for 1 minute in diluted KODAK PHOTO-FLO Solution at 65°F (18°C).
- For color slides on KODAK EKTACHROME Films—rinse for 10 to 15 seconds in a working solution of KODAK Stabilizer, Process E-6, at 65°F (18°C).
- For Kodak color-negative films—rinse for 1 minute in a working solution of KODAK FLEXICOLOR Stabilizer and Replenisher at 65°F (18°C).
- Dry in a dust-free place.

If exposed film is water-soaked before processing, keep it wet and process it as soon as possible.

You can treat water-damaged prints as described above, but salvage only those prints for which negatives are not available.

*Prevention*—Whenever possible, store film—

- Above the anticipated water level of flooding that could occur.
- In areas away from water pipes and plumbing.
- In waterproof or water-resistant containers, such as special storage envelopes.

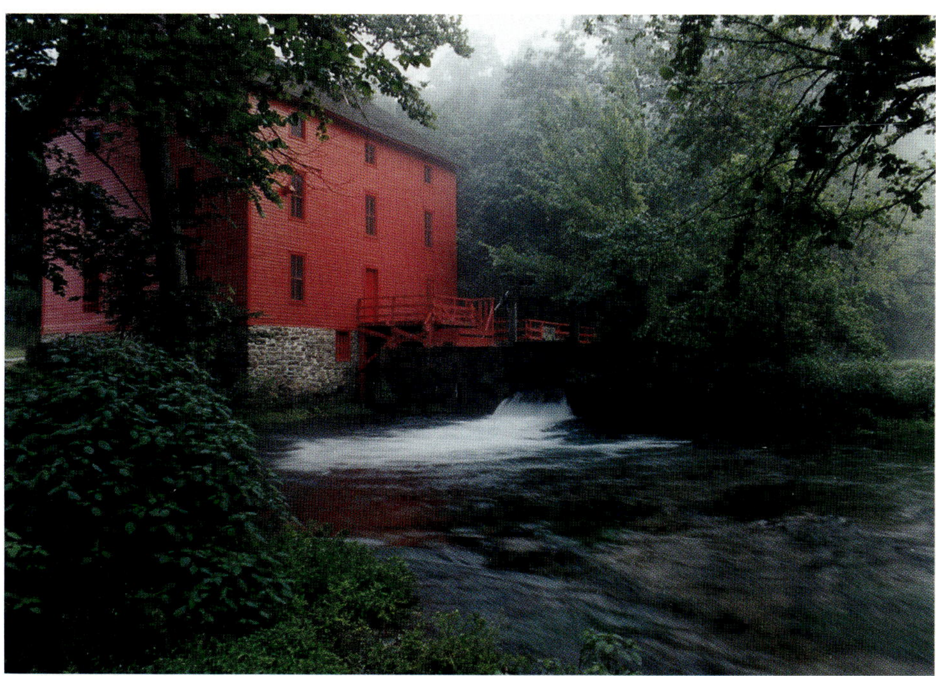

KODACOLOR GOLD 100 Film WILLIAM FLETCHER

## *KODAK* COLOR FILMS FOR 35 mm CAMERAS

| Kodak Film (Film Code) | Description | To Produce | Use with | ISO Film Speed and Filter | | | Number of Exposures Available |
|---|---|---|---|---|---|---|---|
| | | | | Daylight | Photolamps 3400 K | Tungsten 3200 K | |
| **Color Negative Films** | | | | | | | |
| Kodak Ektar 25 (CK) | SLR cameras only. This is Kodak's sharpest and finest grain color-negative film. Use it when you want to obtain outstanding big enlargements. Expose it carefully since it has less latitude than Kodacolor Gold Films. | Color prints | Daylight or Electronic Flash | 25 | 8<br>No. 80B | 6<br>No. 80A | 135-12<br>135-24<br>135-36* |
| Kodacolor Gold 100 (GA) | This film features extremely high sharpness and extremely fine grain to allow for a high degree of enlargement and wide exposure latitude. It is an excellent film for use in general lighting conditions. | Color prints | Daylight or Electronic Flash | 100 | 32<br>No. 80B | 25<br>No. 80A | 135-12<br>135-24<br>135-36 |
| Kodak Ektar 125 (CW) | With micro-fine grain and extremely high sharpness, this medium-speed film makes an excellent film for users requiring high-quality prints. | Color prints | Daylight or Electronic Flash | 125 | 40<br>No. 80B | 32<br>No. 80A | 135-24<br>135-36 |
| Kodacolor Gold 200 (GB) | With high sharpness and the same extremely fine grain as Kodacolor Gold 100 Film, this film provides twice the speed. It is a good choice for general lighting conditions when higher shutter speeds for capturing action or smaller apertures for increased depth of field are desired. | Color prints | Daylight or Electronic Flash | 200 | 64<br>No. 80B | 50<br>No. 80A | 135-12<br>135-24<br>135-36 |
| Kodacolor Gold 400 (GC) | A high-speed film for existing-light situations, fast action, great depth of field, and extended flash-distance ranges. Medium sharpness and extremely fine grain offer good quality. | Color prints | Existing Light, Daylight, or Electronic Flash | 400 | 125<br>No. 80B | 100<br>No. 80A | 135-12<br>135-24<br>135-36 |
| Kodak Ektar 1000 (CJ) | This high-speed film offers very fine grain. Use it in dim lighting when you want to make enlargements and don't need the extra speed of Kodacolor Gold 1600 Film. | Color prints | Existing Light, Daylight, or Electronic Flash | 1000 | 320<br>No. 80B | 250<br>No. 80A | 135-12<br>135-24 |
| Kodacolor Gold 1600 (GF) | Very high speed with very fine grain and medium sharpness. Use it in very dim lighting or for very fast action subjects. | Color prints | Existing Light, Daylight, or Electronic Flash | 1600 | 500<br>No. 80B | 400<br>No. 80A | 135-12<br>135-24<br>135-36 |
| **Color Slide Films** | | | | | | | |
| Kodachrome 25 (Daylight) (KM) | A popular film noted for excellent color and extremely high sharpness. It has extremely fine grain and good exposure latitude. | Color slides | Daylight or Electronic Flash | 25 | 8<br>No. 80B | 6<br>No. 80A | 135-24<br>135-36* |
| Kodachrome 40 5070 (Type A) (KPA) | A film designed for use with 3400 K photolamps. This film is excellent for informal portraits, close-ups, title slides, and for copying color originals. | Color slides | Photolamps 3400 K | 25<br>No. 85 | 40 | 32<br>No. 82A | 135-36 |
| Kodachrome 64 (Daylight) (KR) | A medium-speed, general-purpose film. Exhibits extremely high sharpness and freedom from graininess. Color rendition of this film is excellent. | Color slides | Daylight or Electronic Flash | 64 | 20<br>No. 80B | 16<br>No. 80A | 135-24<br>135-36* |

| | | | | | | | |
|---|---|---|---|---|---|---|---|
| KODACHROME 200 (Daylight) (KL) | This film features very high sharpness and fine grain. Allows faster shutter speeds for hand-holding longer lenses, smaller lens openings for increased depth of field, and use in low-light situations. | Color slides | Existing Daylight, Daylight, or Electronic Flash | 200 | 64 No. 80B | 50 No. 80A | 135-24 135-36 |
| EKTACHROME 50 HC (EM) | This new film offers very high sharpness and very fine grain, and produces vibrant colors similar to KODAK EKTACHROME 100 HC Film at a lower ISO speed. | Color slides | Daylight or Electronic Flash | 50 | 16 No. 80B | 12 No. 80A | 135-24 135-36 |
| EKTACHROME 100 HC (Daylight) (EC) | A medium-speed film for general all-around use. It has sufficient speed to let you use higher shutter speeds or smaller lens openings in normal lighting. This film produces rich color rendition and has excellent sharpness and graininess characteristics. | Color slides | Daylight or Electronic Flash | 100 | 32 No. 80B | 25 No. 80A | 135-24 135-36* |
| EKTACHROME 200 (Daylight) (ED) | A medium-speed film for existing light, fast action, subjects requiring good depth of field or high shutter speeds, and for extending the flash-distance range. It has very fine grain and high sharpness. This film can be push-processed to double the speed. | Color slides | Existing Daylight, Daylight, or Electronic Flash | 200 | 64 No. 80B | 50 No. 80A | 135-24 135-36* |
| | | | | 400† | 125† No. 80B | 100† No. 80A | |
| EKTACHROME 160 (Tungsten) (ET) | A medium-speed film for use with 3200 K tungsten lamps and existing tungsten light. It features the same very fine grain and high sharpness as the 200-speed daylight film. This film can be push-processed to double the speed. | Color slides | Tungsten Lamps 3200 K or Existing Tungsten Light | 100 No. 85B | 125 No. 81A | 160 | 135-24 135-36* |
| | | | | 200† No. 85B | 250† No. 81A | 320† | |
| EKTACHROME 400 (Daylight) (EL) | A high-speed film for existing light, fast action, subjects requiring good depth of field and high shutter speeds, and for extending the flash-distance range. It has fine grain and high sharpness and can be push-processed to double the speed. | Color slides | Existing Daylight, Daylight, or Electronic Flash | 400 | 125 No. 80B | 100 No. 80A | 135-24 135-36* |
| | | | | 800† | 250† No. 80B | 200† No. 80A | |
| EKTACHROME P800/1600 Professional Film (Daylight) (EES) | A very high-speed film for existing light and fast action. This film exposed at EI 800 or EI 1600 provides good results in adverse lighting conditions. It can be push-processed as high as EI 3200. | Color slides | Existing Daylight, Daylight, or Electronic Flash | EI 800‡ | 250‡ No. 80B | 200‡ No. 80A | 135-36 |
| | | | | EI 1600§ | 500§ No. 80B | 400§ No. 80A | |

*Professional versions of these films are available in 35 mm and 120 sizes. KODACHROME 25 Professional Film is available only in 35 mm size.

†Use these speed settings to expose these films when you want your film push processed one stop.

‡Use these speed settings to expose EKTACHROME P800/1600 Film for push processing in Process E-6P, Push 1.

§Use these speed settings to expose EKTACHROME P800/1600 Film for push processing in Process E-6P, Push 2.

## *KODAK* BLACK-AND-WHITE FILMS FOR 35 mm CAMERAS

| Kodak Film (Film Code) | Description | ISO Film Speed | Number of Exposures Available |
|---|---|---|---|
| T-Max 100 Professional (TMX) | A medium-speed panchromatic film with extremely fine grain and nearly the same speed as Kodak Plus-X Pan Film. Particularly good for detailed subjects, film also features extremely high sharpness and very high resolving power, and allows a very high degree of enlargement. | EI 100 | 135-24<br>135-36 |
| Plus-X Pan (PX) | An excellent general-purpose panchromatic film that offers medium speed and extremely fine grain. | 125 | 135-24<br>135-36 |
| Tri-X Pan (TX) | A high-speed panchromatic film especially useful for photographing existing light subjects, fast action, subjects requiring good depth of field and high shutter speeds, and for extending the flash-distance range. This film has fine grain and excellent quality for such a high speed. | 400 | 135-24<br>135-36 |
| T-Max 400 Professional (TMY) | A panchromatic film that is especially useful for photographing subjects in low light, stopping action, or expanding depth of field; this film allows a high degree of enlargement. It can be exposed at speeds of EI 800 and EI 1600 with very acceptable results. | EI 400 | 135-24<br>135-36 |
| T-MAX P3200 Professional (TMZ) | An extremely high speed, panchromatic film for use in existing light, such as sports stadiums and night events. This film is specially designed to be used as a multi-speed film. The nominal speed is EI 1000 when it is processed in Kodak T-Max Developer or Kodak T-Max RS Developer and Replenisher, or EI 800 when processed in other Kodak black-and-white developers. | EI 800–1000* | 135-36 |
| High Speed Infrared (HIE) | An infrared-sensitive film which produces striking and unusual results. With a red filter, blue sky photographs almost black and clouds look white. With this film and filter, live grass and trees will appear as though they are covered by snow. This film has fine grain. | 125 tungsten† | 135-36 |
| Technical Pan (TP) | A panchromatic film with extremely fine grain and extremely high resolving power that gives large-format performance with 35 mm convenience. Great enlargeability is possible. It is suitable for a wide number of general and scientific applications, such as photomicrography, precision copying, titling, and pictorial photography, depending on the exposure and processing used. | EI 25‡ | 135-36 |

*To expose this film at speeds higher than EI 6400 (up to EI 25,000), it is critical that you make tests to determine if the results are appropriate for your needs.

†Use this speed as a basis for determining your exposures with tungsten light when you expose the film through a No. 25 filter. In daylight, follow the exposure suggestions on the film instruction sheet.

‡Use this speed for daylight pictorial photography only when processed in Kodak Technidol Developer, or the equivalent. Other speeds for different applications require alternative developers and give appropriate results. See the instructions packaged with the film.

**Note:** Panchromatic means that the film is sensitive to all visible colors.

# FILM DATA SHEETS

## *KODAK* FILMS FOR GENERAL USE

The following Data Sheets provide detailed information to help you obtain the best possible results with each film. Because recommendations may change, whenever these Data Sheets do not agree with the instructions included with the film, follow the film instructions. The instructions in the film package are updated more frequently.

The film-code letters are given in the Data Sheets. The code letter is printed on the film carton and on 135 magazines to identify the kind of film. For example, KODACHROME 64 Film (Daylight) is identified by the letters "KR." KR135-24 is the designation for 24-exposure 135 magazines.

## *KODAK* COLOR FILMS



## *KODAK* BLACK-AND-WHITE FILMS

**For Color Prints**
The extremely fine grain and extremely high sharpness of this film provide excellent reproduction of fine detail. The film speed—ISO 100—is adequate for most general picture-taking situations, and wide exposure latitude helps maintain bright, vivid colors with over- and underexposure.

You can use this film in daylight or with electronic flash. It is designed for producing color prints, but you can also have color slides and black-and-white prints made from the negatives.

**Film Code:** GA

**Sizes Available:** 135-12, 135-24, 135-36, 120

**Adjustments for Long or Short Exposures:**
No filter or exposure adjustments are needed for exposure times of 1/10,000 to 1/10 second. For a 1-second exposure, use a KODAK Color Compensating Filter CC20Y and increase exposure by 1 stop. We do not recommend using exposure times longer than 1 second with this film.

**Definition:**

| Granularity | Resolving Power | Sharpness | Degree of Enlargement* |
|---|---|---|---|
| Extremely Fine | High<br>100 lines per mm | Extremely High | High |

*For good-quality negatives

**For Color Prints**
An ideal general-purpose color-negative film that has excellent color rendition, high sharpness, and extremely fine grain. Its characteristics are similar to those of KODACOLOR GOLD 100 Film, but the higher speed of KODACOLOR GOLD 200 Film makes it more versatile. Its speed of ISO 200 allows you to use faster shutter speeds (to stop action) or smaller apertures (for increased depth of field). You can also use this film to take pictures in some existing-light situations if your camera has an *f*/2.8 or faster lens.

KODACOLOR GOLD 200 Film is intended for use with daylight or electronic flash. Its definition characteristics are excellent for enlargements. The film is primarily for color prints, but you can also have color slides or black-and-white prints made from the negatives.

**Film Code:** GB

**Sizes Available:** 135-12, 135-24, 135-36, 110-12, 110-24, 126-12, 126-24

**Existing Light:**
Use an exposure meter or a camera with a built-in meter if you have one. If you don't have a meter, try the settings in the table. These exposures are *guides;* bracket your exposures by ±1 stop.

| Picture Subject | Shutter Speed (second) | Lens Opening |
|---|---|---|
| Interiors with Bright Fluorescent Light | 1/30* | *f*/4 |
| Indoor, Outdoor Christmas Lighting at Night | 1† | *f*/5.6 |
| Brightly Lighted Street Scenes at Night | 1/30 | *f*/2.8 |
| Brightly Lighted Theatre Districts—Las Vegas or Times Square | 1/30 | *f*/4 |
| Neon and Other Lighted Signs | 1/60 | *f*/4 |
| Store Windows at Night | 1/30 | *f*/4 |
| Floodlighted Buildings, Fountains, Monuments | 1/2† | *f*/4 |
| Distant View of City Skyline at Night | 1† | *f*/2 |
| Skylines—10 minutes after sunset | 1/60 | *f*/4 |
| Fairs, Amusement Parks | 1/30 | *f*/2 |
| Aerial Fireworks Displays—Keep camera shutter open on BULB for several bursts | Bulb† | *f*/11 |
| Night Football, Soccer, Baseball, Racetracks | 1/60 | *f*/2.8 |
| Basketball, Hockey, Bowling | 1/60 | *f*/2 |
| Boxing, Wrestling | 1/125 | *f*/2 |
| Stage Shows—Average light<br>—Bright light | 1/30<br>1/60 | *f*/2.8<br>*f*/4 |
| Circuses—Floodlighted acts | 1/30 | *f*/2.8 |
| Ice Shows—Floodlighted acts | 1/60 | *f*/2.8 |
| Ice Shows, Circuses—Spotlighted acts (carbon arc) | 1/125 | *f*/2.8 |
| Swimming Pool—Indoors, tungsten lights above water | 1/30 | *f*/2 |

*Use shutter speeds of 1/60 second or longer with fluorescent light.
†Use a tripod or other firm camera support.

**Adjustments for Long or Short Exposures:**
No filter or exposure adjustments are needed for exposure times of 1/10,000 to 1/10 second. For a 1-second exposure, use a KODAK Color Compensating Filter CC20Y and increase exposure by 1 stop. We do not recommend using exposure times longer than 1 second with this film.

**Definition:**

| Granularity | Resolving Power | Sharpness | Degree of Enlargement* |
|---|---|---|---|
| Extremely Fine | High<br>100 lines per mm | High | High |

*For good-quality negatives

### For Color Prints

This improved color-negative film provides the richest, most saturated colors, and best color accuracy of any 400-speed color-print film. KODAK T-GRAIN Emulsions allow this film to feature both high speed and extremely fine grain. It is a good choice for photographing dimly lighted subjects, fast action, and subjects that require both extensive depth of field and high shutter speeds; for using telephoto lenses with high shutter speeds; and for extending the flash distance range.

KODACOLOR GOLD 400 Film is color-balanced for daylight or electronic flash. It also has special sensitizing characteristics that give you pleasing results when you expose it with other light sources, such as household light bulbs and fluorescent lamps, without using filters over your camera lens. The wide exposure latitude of this film lets you use it for subjects ranging from bright sunlit scenes to subjects in relatively dim existing light.

**Film Code:** GC

**Sizes Available:** 135-12, 135-24, 135-36, and 110-24

**Existing Light:**
Use an exposure meter or a camera with a built-in meter if you have one. If you don't have a meter, try the settings in the table. These exposures are *guides;* bracket your exposures by ±1 stop.

| Picture Subject | Shutter Speed (second) | Lens Opening |
|---|---|---|
| Home Interiors at Night—<br>Areas with average light<br>Areas with bright light | <br>1/30<br>1/30 | <br>*f*/2<br>*f*/2.8 |
| Interiors with Bright Fluorescent Light | 1/60* | *f*/4 |
| Candlelighted Close-Ups | 1/15† | *f*/2 |
| Indoor, Outdoor Christmas Lighting at Night | 1/15† | *f*/2 |
| Brightly Lighted Street Scenes at Night | 1/60 | *f*/2.8 |
| Brightly Lighted Theatre Districts—Las Vegas or Times Square | 1/60 | *f*/4 |
| Neon and Other Lighted Signs | 1/125 | *f*/4 |
| Store Windows at Night | 1/60 | *f*/4 |
| Floodlighted Buildings, Fountains, Monuments | 1/15† | *f*/2 |
| Distant View of City Skyline at Night | 1† | *f*/2.8 |
| Skylines—10 minutes after sunset | 1/60 | *f*/5.6 |
| Fairs, Amusement Parks | 1/30 | *f*/2.8 |
| Aerial Fireworks Displays—Keep camera shutter open on BULB for several bursts | Bulb† | *f*/16 |
| Night Football, Soccer, Baseball, Racetracks | 1/125 | *f*/2.8 |
| Basketball, Hockey, Bowling | 1/125 | *f*/2 |
| Boxing, Wrestling | 1/250 | *f*/2 |
| Stage Shows—Average light<br>—Bright light | 1/60<br>1/125 | *f*/2.8<br>*f*/4 |
| Circuses—Floodlighted acts | 1/60 | *f*/2.8 |
| Ice Shows—Floodlighted acts | 1/125 | *f*/2.8 |
| Ice Shows, Circuses—Spotlighted acts (carbon arc) | 1/250 | *f*/2.8 |
| School—Stage and Auditorium | 1/30 | *f*/2 |
| Swimming Pool—Indoors, tungsten lights above water | 1/60 | *f*/2 |
| Church Interiors—Tungsten lights | 1/30 | *f*/2 |

*Use shutter speeds of 1/60 second or longer with fluorescent light.
†Use a tripod or other firm camera support.

**Adjustments for Long or Short Exposures:**
You do not need to make any exposure or filter adjustments for exposure times from 1/10,000 to 1/10 second. Increase exposure by ⅓ stop for a 1-second exposure and by 1 stop for a 10-second exposure. We do not recommend using exposure times longer than 10 seconds.

**Definition:**

| Granularity | Resolving Power | Sharpness | Degree of Enlargement* |
|---|---|---|---|
| Extremely Fine | High<br>100 lines per mm | Medium | Moderate |

*For good-quality negatives

**For Color Prints**

This very-high-speed film features the best color saturation of any 1600-speed color print film. KODACOLOR GOLD 1600 Film is the fastest KODACOLOR GOLD Film. Designed for low-light and fast-action situations, it is also an excellent choice for hand-holding telephoto lenses, or for subjects that require extensive depth of field and high shutter speeds.

This film is balanced for exposure with daylight or electronic flash. You can also use it for scenes that are lighted by mixed light sources. It features better color reproduction under tungsten illumination than other comparable-speed films.

**Film Code:** GF

**Sizes Available:** 135-12, 135-24, and 135-36

**Existing Light:**

Use an exposure meter or a camera with a built-in meter if you have one. If you don't have a meter, try the settings in the table. These exposures are *guides;* bracket your exposures by ±1 stop.

| Picture Subject | Shutter Speed (second) | Lens Opening |
|---|---|---|
| Home Interiors at Night—<br>Areas with average light<br>Areas with bright light | <br>1/30<br>1/60 | <br>f/4<br>f/4 |
| Candlelighted Close-Ups | 1/30 | f/2.8 |
| Interiors with Bright Fluorescent Light | 1/60* | f/8 |
| Indoor, Outdoor Christmas Lighting at Night | 1/30 | f/2.8 |
| Brightly Lighted Street Scenes at Night | 1/125 | f/4 |
| Brightly Lighted Theatre Districts—Las Vegas or Times Square | 1/125 | f/5.6 |
| Neon and Other Lighted Signs | 1/125 | f/8 |
| Store Windows at Night | 1/60 | f/8 |
| Floodlighted Buildings, Fountains, Monuments | 1/30 | f/2.8 |
| Distant View of City Skyline at Night | 1† | f/5.6 |
| Skylines—10 minutes after sunset | 1/125 | f/8 |
| Fairs, Amusement Parks | 1/60 | f/4 |
| Aerial Fireworks Displays—Keep camera shutter open on BULB for several bursts | Bulb† | f/32 |
| Night Football, Soccer, Baseball, Racetracks | 1/250 | f/4 |
| Basketball, Hockey, Bowling | 1/250 | f/2.8 |
| Boxing, Wrestling | 1/250 | f/4 |
| Stage Shows—Average light<br>—Bright light | 1/125<br>1/250 | f/4<br>f/5.6 |
| Circuses—Floodlighted acts | 1/250 | f/2.8 |
| Ice Shows—Floodlighted acts | 1/250 | f/4 |
| Ice Shows, Circuses—Spotlighted acts (carbon arc) | 1/250 | f/5.6 |
| School—Stage and Auditorium | 1/60 | f/2.8 |
| Swimming Pool—Indoors, tungsten lights above water | 1/60 | f/4 |
| Church Interiors—Tungsten lights | 1/30 | f/4 |

*Use shutter speeds of 1/60 second or longer with fluorescent light.
†Use a tripod or other firm camera support.

**Adjustments for Long or Short Exposures:**

You do not need to make any exposure or filter adjustments for exposure times from 1/10,000 to 1 second. For an exposure time of 10 seconds, increase exposure by 1 stop. We do not recommend using exposure times longer than 10 seconds with this film.

**Definition:**

| Granularity | Resolving Power | Sharpness | Degree of Enlargement* |
|---|---|---|---|
| Very Fine | Medium<br>80 lines per mm | Medium | Moderately Low |

*For good-quality negatives

## KODAK EKTAR 25 Film

**For Color Prints**

KODAK EKTAR 25 Film is a technically advanced 35 mm color-negative film. It offers micro-fine grain, extremely high sharpness, and very high resolving power, all of which allow an extremely high degree of enlargement. It is designed for exposure with daylight or electronic flash, and is intended for printing on KODAK EKTACOLOR Papers.

The ability of this film to produce enlargements of superb clarity will allow you to realize your full photographic potential. Use KODAK EKTAR 25 Film in cameras that allow you to set the film speed manually or that will set it automatically from the DX code on the magazine. (Some automatic 35 mm cameras do not read the DX code for ISO 25 film and will underexpose it. Check your camera manual.) This film requires more precise exposure control than general-purpose films.

KODAK EKTAR 25 Professional Film is available in 135 and 120 size.

**Film Code:** CK

**Sizes Available:** 135-12, 135-24, and 135-36

**Adjustments for Long or Short Exposures:**

You do not need to make any exposure or filter adjustments for exposure times from 1/10,000 second to 10 seconds. We do not recommend using exposure times longer than 10 seconds with this film.

**Definition:**

| Granularity | Resolving Power | Sharpness | Degree of Enlargement* |
|---|---|---|---|
| Micro-Fine | Very High<br>200 lines per mm | Extremely High | Extremely High |

*For good-quality negatives.

## KODAK EKTAR 125 Film

**For Color Prints**

Like KODAK EKTAR 25 and 1000 Films, KODAK EKTAR 125 Film is a technically advanced 35 mm color-negative film. KODAK EKTAR Films have been designed and produced to meet the needs of knowledgeable and discriminating photographers who want more from photographs than general-purpose films can provide.

KODAK EKTAR 125 Film is balanced for exposure with daylight or electronic flash. You can also obtain pleasing results under existing-light sources without filters. This medium-speed film offers finer grain and higher sharpness than any other comparable-speed color print film, and yields enlargements of extremely high quality.

**Film Code:** CW

**Sizes Available:** 135-24 and 135-36

**Adjustments for Long or Short Exposures:**

You do not need to make any exposure or filter adjustments for exposure times from 1/10,000 second to 10 seconds. We do not recommend using exposure times longer than 10 seconds.

**Definition:**

| Granularity | Resolving Power | Sharpness | Degree of Enlargement* |
|---|---|---|---|
| Micro-Fine | Very High<br>160 lines per mm | Extremely High | Very High |

*For good-quality negatives.

## For Color Prints

KODAK EKTAR 1000 Film offers more saturated colors than other color-negative film in its speed range. With its very high speed, it is excellent for low-light situations or subjects that require higher shutter speeds to stop action. It also allows you to use high shutter speeds for hand-holding telephoto lenses or small apertures for increased depth of field. Its improved sensitivity to tungsten light will provide pleasing results in situations where the lighting is difficult to meter. This film is designed for exposure with daylight or electronic flash and is intended for printing on KODAK EKTACOLOR Papers. It has very fine grain, medium sharpness, and medium resolving power.

**Film Code:** CJ

**Sizes Available:** 135-12 and 135-24

**Existing Light:**
Use an exposure meter or a camera with a built-in meter if you have one. If you don't have a meter, try the settings in the table. These exposures are *guides;* bracket your exposures by ± 1 stop.

| Picture Subject | Shutter Speed (second) | Lens Opening |
|---|---|---|
| Home Interiors at Night—<br>Areas with average light<br>Areas with bright light | <br>1/30<br>1/30 | <br>f/2.8<br>f/4 |
| Candlelighted Close-Ups | 1/30 | f/2 |
| Interiors with Bright Fluorescent Light | 1/60* | f/5.6 |
| Indoor, Outdoor Christmas Lighting at Night | 1/30 | f/2 |
| Brightly Lighted Street Scenes at Night | 1/60 | f/4 |
| Brightly Lighted Theatre Districts—Las Vegas or Times Square | 1/125 | f/4 |
| Neon and Other Lighted Signs | 1/125 | f/5.6 |
| Store Windows at Night | 1/60 | f/5.6 |
| Floodlighted Buildings, Fountains, Monuments | 1/30 | f/2 |
| Distant View of City Skyline at Night | 1† | f/4 |
| Skylines—10 minutes after sunset | 1/125 | f/5.6 |
| Fairs, Amusement Parks | 1/60 | f/2.8 |
| Aerial Fireworks Displays—Keep camera shutter open on BULB for several bursts | Bulb† | f/22 |
| Night Football, Soccer, Baseball, Racetracks | 1/250 | f/2.8 |
| Basketball, Hockey, Bowling | 1/125 | f/2.8 |
| Boxing, Wrestling | 1/250 | f/2.8 |
| Stage Shows—Average light<br>—Bright light | 1/125<br>1/250 | f/2.8<br>f/4 |
| Circuses—Floodlighted acts | 1/125 | f/2.8 |
| Ice Shows—Floodlighted acts | 1/250 | f/2.8 |
| Ice Shows, Circuses—Spotlighted acts (carbon arc) | 1/250 | f/4 |
| School—Stage and Auditorium | 1/30 | f/2.8 |
| Swimming Pool—Indoors, tungsten lights above water | 1/60 | f/2.8 |
| Church Interiors—Tungsten lights | 1/30 | f/2.8 |

*Use shutter speeds of 1/60 second or longer with fluorescent light.
†Use a tripod or other firm camera support.

**Adjustments for Long or Short Exposures:**
You do not need to make any exposure or filter adjustments for exposure times from 1/10,000 to 1 second. For an exposure time of 10 seconds, increase exposure by 1 stop. We do not recommend using exposure times longer than 10 seconds with this film.

**Definition:**

| Granularity | Resolving Power | Sharpness | Degree of Enlargement* |
|---|---|---|---|
| Very Fine | Medium<br>80 lines per mm | Medium | Moderately Low |

*For good-quality negatives

# KODACHROME 25 Film (Daylight)

**For Color Slides**
KODACHROME 25 Film is a favorite for color slides because of its excellent color quality, extremely high sharpness, and extremely fine grain. Use this film under bright lighting conditions when you want slides with the best possible image quality. The film produces rich color saturation and superb flesh tones while retaining good detail in both highlights and shadows. Its speed is adequate for many picture-taking situations. This film is designed for use in daylight or with electronic flash. It's also sold in a professional version, KODACHROME 25 Professional Film.

**Film Code:** KM

**Sizes Available:** 135-24 and 135-36

**Adjustments for Long or Short Exposures:**
You do not need to make any exposure or filter adjustments for exposure times from 1/10,000 to 1/10 second. For a 1-second exposure, increase exposure by ½ stop. We do not recommend using exposure times longer than 1 second with this film.

**Definition:**

| Granularity | Resolving Power | Sharpness |
|---|---|---|
| Extremely Fine | High<br>100 lines per mm | Extremely High |

### For Color Slides

KODACHROME 40 Film is for use with 3400 K photolamps. It has extremely fine grain, extremely high sharpness, and superior color quality. It has the exceptional definition for which KODACHROME Films are noted. Its speed is sufficient for photolamp illumination. KODACHROME 40 Film is excellent for informal portraits, close-ups, and title slides, and for copying color originals. You can also take pictures in daylight or with electronic flash if you use a No. 85 filter over your camera lens.

**Film Code:** KPA

**Size Available:** 135-36

### EXPOSURE

**Speed:**

| Light Source | ISO Speed* | KODAK WRATTEN Gelatin Filter |
|---|---|---|
| Photolamp (3400 K) | 40/17° | None |
| Tungsten (3200 K) | 32/16° | No. 82A |
| Daylight or Electronic Flash | 25/15° | No. 85 |

*Recommended for meters marked for ISO, ASA, or DIN speeds or exposure indexes.

**Photolamps (3400 K):** The following table is based on the use of two new 500-watt reflector-type photolamps (3400 K), such as General Electric DXC and Sylvania DXC reflector floodlamps. Use one lamp as the main light on one side of the camera, 2 to 4 feet (0.6 to 1.2 metres) above the level of the camera and at a 45-degree angle to the camera-subject axis. Use the other lamp as a fill-in light close to the camera at lens level, on the side opposite the main light. Position both lights at the same distance from the subject.

| Exposure for 500-Watt Reflector-Type Photolamps (3400 K) | | | |
|---|---|---|---|
| Set Shutter Speed at 1/60 Second | | | |
| Lamp-to-Subject Distance | 4½ ft (1.4 m) | 6 ft (1.8 m) | 9 ft (2.7 m) |
| Lens Opening | *f*/4 | *f*/2.8 | *f*/2 |

**Note:** Use these camera settings as guides. The lamp-to-subject distances give a lighting ratio of 2:1. For a 3:1 ratio, place the fill-in light at a distance from the subject 1.4 times the distance for the main light and use a lens opening ½ stop larger.

This table is based on the use of new lamps. After the lamps have burned for 1 hour, use a lens opening ½ stop larger; after 2 hours, use a lens opening 1 stop larger.

**Adjustments for Long or Short Exposures:**

Use the adjustments in the table to compensate for the reciprocity characteristics of the film.

| Adjustment | Exposure Time (seconds) | | | | | | | |
|---|---|---|---|---|---|---|---|---|
| | 1/10,000 | 1/1000 | 1/100 | 1/10 | 1 | 5 | 10 | 100 |
| Exposure Increase | None | None | None | None | ½ stop | 1 stop | NR | NR |
| Filter Correction | None | None | None | None | None | None | NR | NR |

NR=not recommended

**Definition:**

| Granularity | Resolving Power | Sharpness |
|---|---|---|
| Extremely Fine | High 100 lines per mm | Extremely High |

## KODACHROME 64 Film (Daylight)

**For Color Slides**
This film is an excellent choice for "all-around" picture-taking when you want color slides. Its medium speed of ISO 64 (2½ times as fast as KODACHROME 25 Film) lets you use higher shutter speeds or smaller lens openings under normal lighting conditions, and extends picture-taking capability on overcast days, in the shade, or in subdued lighting. The film features excellent color rendition—bright reds and yellows; clean whites; vivid blue skies; and pleasing flesh tones. It also features good highlight and shadow detail.

KODACHROME 64 Film is almost as sharp and fine-grained as KODACHROME 25 Film. It is designed for use in daylight or with electronic flash. A professional version, KODACHROME 64 Professional Film, is also available.

**Film Code:** KR

**Sizes Available:** 135-24, 135-36, and 126-20

**Adjustments for Long or Short Exposures:**
You do not need to make any exposure or filter adjustments for exposure times from 1/10,000 to 1/10 second. For a 1-second exposure, use a KODAK Color Compensating Filter CC10R and increase exposure by 1 stop. We do not recommend using exposure times longer than 1 second with this film.

**Definition:**

| Granularity | Resolving Power | Sharpness |
|---|---|---|
| Extremely Fine | High<br>100 lines per mm | Extremely High |

## KODACHROME 200 Film (Daylight)

**For Color Slides**
This is the fastest of the KODACHROME Films. It is a medium-speed color-reversal film that features fine grain, very high sharpness, and high resolving power. This film is designed for exposure with daylight or electronic flash, but you can also expose it with photolamps (3400 K) or tungsten illumination (3200 K) with filters.

The speed of KODACHROME 200 Film allows you to use smaller apertures for increased depth of field or higher shutter speeds for stopping action or hand-holding telephoto lenses. It gives excellent results in many low-light situations.

A professional version, KODACHROME 200 Professional Film, is also available.

**Film Code:** KL

**Sizes Available:** 135-24 and 135-36

**Adjustments for Long or Short Exposures:**
You do not need to make any exposure or filter adjustments for exposure times from 1/10,000 to 1/10 second. We do not recommend using exposure times longer than 1/10 second.

**Definition:**

| Granularity | Resolving Power | Sharpness |
|---|---|---|
| Fine | High<br>100 lines per mm | Very High |

**Existing Light:**
Use an exposure meter or a camera with a built-in meter if you have one. If you don't have a meter, try the settings in the table. These exposures are *guides;* bracket your exposures by ±1 stop.

| Picture Subject | Shutter Speed (second) | Lens Opening |
|---|---|---|
| Skylines—10 minutes after sunset | 1/60 | *f*/4 |
| Interiors with Bright Fluorescent Light | 1/30* | *f*/4 |
| Ice Shows, Circuses—Spotlighted acts (carbon arc) | 1/125 | *f*/2.8 |
| Brightly Lighted Street Scenes at Night | 1/30 | *f*/2.8 |
| Brightly Lighted Nightclub or Theatre Districts at Night—Las Vegas or Times Square | 1/30 | *f*/4 |
| Store Window Displays at Night | 1/30 | *f*/4 |
| Neon and Other Lighted Signs | 1/60 | *f*/4 |
| Floodlighted Buildings, Fountains, Monuments | 1/2† | *f*/4 |
| Christmas Lighting, Trees—Indoors and outdoors at night | 1† | *f*/5.6 |
| Fairs, Amusement Parks at Night | 1/30 | *f*/2 |
| Night Football, Soccer, Baseball, Racetracks | 1/60 | *f*/2.8 |

*Use shutter speeds of 1/60 second or longer with fluorescent light.
†Use a tripod or other camera support.

## Kodak Ektachrome 50 HC Film

**For Color Slides**
Kodak Ektachrome 50 HC Film is the newest member of the family of Kodak Ektachrome Films. It offers very high sharpness and very fine grain, and produces vibrant colors similar to Kodak Ektachrome 100 HC Film at a lower ISO speed. This film is designed for exposure with daylight or electronic flash. You can also expose it with photolamps (3400 K) or tungsten illumination (3200 K) with filters.

Ektachrome 50 HC Film is a good choice for scenic photos, informal portraits, and colorful close-ups that show fine detail. It can be processed with other films in Process E-6 with no changes to the process.

**Film Code:** EM

**Sizes Available:** 135-24 and 135-36

**Adjustments for Long or Short Exposures:**
You do not need to make any exposure or filter adjustments for exposure times from 1/10,000 to 1/10 second. For a 1-second exposure, use a CC05R filter and increase exposure by ½ stop. We do not recommend using exposure times longer than 1 second with this film.

**Definition:**

| Granularity | Resolving Power | Sharpness |
|---|---|---|
| Very Fine | High<br>125 lines per mm | Very High |

## Kodak Ektachrome 100 HC Film

**For Color Slides**
This is a medium-speed film with high color saturation. An excellent choice for both daylight and electronic-flash photography, it features very fine grain, very high sharpness, and high resolving power. It accurately records neutral colors while maintaining pleasing flesh tones. The professional version of this film, Kodak Ektachrome 100 Plus Professional Film, is available in 135, 120, and sheet sizes.

**Film Code:** EC

**Sizes Available:** 135-24 and 135-36

**Adjustments for Long or Short Exposures:**
No filter corrections or exposure adjustments are required for exposure times from 1/10,000 to 1/10 second. For a 1-second exposure, use a CC05R filter and increase exposure by ½ stop. We do not recommend using exposure times longer than 1 second with this film.

**Definition:**

| Granularity | Resolving Power | Sharpness |
|---|---|---|
| Very Fine | High<br>100 lines per mm | Very High |

### For Color Slides

This is a medium-speed film for exposure with tungsten lamps (3200 K) or existing tungsten light, such as the light from household lamps and other general-purpose tungsten lamps. Outdoors at night, you can use it for pictures of illuminated buildings, fountains, statues, signs, street scenes, and similar subjects. It has a speed of ISO 160, and features very fine grain, high sharpness, and high resolving power. You can take pictures in daylight or with electronic flash if you use a No. 85B filter over your camera lens. With special processing, you can expose this film at speeds higher than its normal rated speed. KODAK EKTACHROME 160T Professional Film is also available.

**Film Code:** ET

**Sizes Available:** 135-24 and 135-36

### EXPOSURE

**Speed:**

| Light Source | ISO Speed* | KODAK WRATTEN Gelatin Filter |
|---|---|---|
| Tungsten (3200 K) | 160/23° | None |
| Photolamp (3400 K) | 125/22° | No. 81A |
| Daylight or Electronic Flash | 100/21° | No. 85B |

*Recommended for meters marked for ISO, ASA, or DIN speeds or exposure indexes.

**Tungsten Lamps (3200 K):**
The following table is based on the use of two reflector-type photolamps (3200 K). Use one lamp as the main light on one side of the camera, 2 to 4 feet (0.6 to 1.2 metres) above the level of the camera and at a 45-degree angle to the camera-subject axis. Use the other lamp as a fill-in light close to the camera at lens level, on the side opposite the main light. Position both lights at the same distance from the subject.

**Daylight Exposure Table (with a No. 85B Filter):**
Use these settings for average subjects in daylight from 2 hours after sunrise to 2 hours before sunset.

| Lighting Conditions | Shutter Speed (second) | Lens Opening |
|---|---|---|
| Bright or Hazy Sun on Light Sand or Snow | 1/250 | *f*/16 |
| Bright or Hazy Sun (Distinct Shadows) | 1/125 | *f*/16* |
| Weak, Hazy Sun (Soft Shadows) | 1/125 | *f*/11 |
| Cloudy Bright (No Shadows) | 1/125 | *f*/8 |
| Heavy Overcast or Open Shade† | 1/125 | *f*/5.6 |

*Use *f*/8 for backlighted close-up subjects.
†Subject shaded from the sun but lighted by a large area of sky.

| Lamp | Lamp-to-Subject Distance in Feet (Metres) (Set Shutter at 1/60 Second) | | | |
|---|---|---|---|---|
| | *f*/8 | *f*/5.6 | *f*/4 | *f*/2.8 |
| General Electric EAL, Type R-40 (500-watt) | | | | |
| Main light | 4 ft (1.2 m) | 5½ ft (1.7 m) | 8 ft (2.4 m) | 11 ft (3.4 m) |
| Fill light | 5½ ft (1.7 m) | 8 ft (2.4 m) | 11 ft (3.4 m) | 16 ft (4.9 m) |
| Sylvania DXH, Type R-32 (375-watt) | | | | |
| Main light | 5 ft (1.5 m) | 7 ft (2.1 m) | 10 ft (3 m) | 14 ft (4.3 m) |
| Fill light | 7 ft (2.1 m) | 10 ft (3 m) | 14 ft (4.3 m) | 20 ft (6 m) |

**Note:** Use these camera settings as guides. The lamp-to-subject distances give a lighting ratio of about 3:1. For a 2:1 ratio, place the fill-in light at the same distance from the subject as the main light and use a lens opening ½ stop smaller. This table is based on the use of new lamps. After the lamps have burned for 1 hour, use a lens opening ½ stop larger; after 2 hours, use a lens opening 1 stop larger.

**Existing Light:**
Use an exposure meter or a camera with a built-in meter if you have one. If you don't have a meter, try the settings in the table. These exposures are *guides;* bracket your exposures by ±1 stop.

| Picture Subject | Shutter Speed (second) | Lens Opening |
|---|---|---|
| Home Interiors at Night—<br>Areas with average light<br>Areas with bright light | <br>1/15*<br>1/30 | <br>f/2<br>f/2 |
| Candlelighted Close-Ups | 1/8* | f/2 |
| Indoor, Outdoor Christmas Lighting at Night | 1* | f/5.6 |
| Brightly Lighted Street Scenes at Night | 1/30 | f/2.8 |
| Brightly Lighted Theatre Districts—Las Vegas or Times Square | 1/30 | f/4 |
| Neon and Other Lighted Signs | 1/60 | f/4 |
| Store Windows at Night | 1/30 | f/4 |
| Floodlighted Buildings, Fountains, Monuments | 1/2* | f/4 |
| Distant View of City Skyline at Night | 1* | f/2 |
| Fairs, Amusement Parks | 1/30 | f/2 |
| Aerial Fireworks Displays—Keep camera shutter open on BULB for several bursts | Bulb* | f/11 |
| Night Football, Soccer, Baseball, Racetracks | 1/60 | f/2.8 |
| Basketball, Hockey, Bowling | 1/60 | f/2 |
| Boxing, Wrestling | 1/125 | f/2 |
| Stage Shows—Average light<br>—Bright light | 1/30<br>1/60 | f/2.8<br>f/4 |
| Circuses—Floodlighted acts | 1/30 | f/2.8 |
| Ice Shows—Floodlighted acts | 1/60 | f/2.8 |
| School—Stage and Auditorium | 1/15* | f/2 |
| Swimming Pool—Indoors, tungsten lights above water | 1/30 | f/2 |
| Church Interiors—Tungsten lights | 1/15* | f/2 |

*Use a tripod or other firm camera support.

**Adjustments for Long or Short Exposures:**
No filter corrections or exposure adjustments are required for exposure times from 1/10,000 to 1/10 second. For a 1-second exposure, use a CC05R filter and increase exposure by ½ stop. We do not recommend using exposure times longer than 1 second with this film.

**Definition:**

| Granularity | Resolving Power | Sharpness |
|---|---|---|
| Very Fine | High<br>100 lines per mm | High |

## KODAK EKTACHROME 200 Film (Daylight)

**For Color Slides**
KODAK EKTACHROME 200 Film is a versatile film that you can use under lighting conditions ranging from bright sunlight to existing light. It is an excellent choice for photographing fast action, for subjects that require extensive depth of field and high shutter speeds, and for extending the distance range for flash pictures. This film combines medium speed with excellent definition characteristics—very fine grain and high sharpness. It gives pleasing color quality with good separation between similar colors. It is designed for use with daylight or electronic flash, and also gives good results under carbon-arc spotlights or indoors in existing daylight. With special processing, you can expose the film at speeds higher than its normal speed. KODAK EKTACHROME 200 Professional Film (Daylight) is available in 135, 120, and sheet sizes.

**Film Code:** ED

**Sizes Available:** 135-24 and 135-36

**Existing Light:**
Use an exposure meter or a camera with a built-in meter if you have one. If you don't have a meter, try the settings in the table. These exposures are *guides;* bracket your exposures by ±1 stop.

| Picture Subject | Shutter Speed (second) | Lens Opening |
|---|---|---|
| Skylines—10 minutes after sunset | 1/60 | *f*/4 |
| Interiors with Bright Fluorescent Light | 1/30* | *f*/4 |
| Ice Shows, Circuses—Spotlighted Acts (carbon arc) | 1/125 | *f*/2.8 |
| Brightly Lighted Street Scenes at Night | 1/30 | *f*/2.8 |
| Brightly Lighted Theatre Districts—Las Vegas or Times Square | 1/30 | *f*/4 |
| Neon and Other Lighted Signs | 1/60 | *f*/4 |
| Floodlighted Buildings, Fountains, Monuments | 1/2† | *f*/4 |
| Christmas Lighting, Trees—Indoors and outdoors at night | 1† | *f*/5.6 |
| Fairs, Amusement Parks at Night | 1/30 | *f*/2 |
| Night Football, Soccer, Baseball, Racetracks | 1/60 | *f*/2.8 |

*Use shutter speeds of 1/60 second or longer with fluorescent light.
†Use a tripod or other firm camera support.

**Adjustments for Long or Short Exposures:**
No filter corrections or exposure adjustments are required for exposure times from 1/10,000 to 1/10 second. For a 1-second exposure, use a CC05M filter and increase exposure by ½ stop. We do not recommend using exposure times longer than 1 second with this film.

**Definition:**

| Granularity | Resolving Power | Sharpness |
|---|---|---|
| Very Fine | High<br>100 lines per mm | High |

# KODAK EKTACHROME 400 Film (Daylight)

**For Color Slides**
KODAK EKTACHROME 400 Film is a high-speed film for photographing dimly lighted subjects that require both good depth of field and high shutter speeds. It lets you take flash pictures at greater distances than slower films. The film is color-balanced for daylight or electronic flash, but you can also use it to photograph performers illuminated by carbon-arc spotlights and for indoor scenes illuminated by existing daylight. KODAK EKTACHROME 400 Film has fine grain and high sharpness in addition to a high speed of ISO 400. With special processing, you can expose it at higher speeds.

**Film Code:** EL

**Sizes Available:** 135-24, 135-36, and 120

**Existing Light:**
Use an exposure meter or a camera with a built-in meter if you have one. If you don't have a meter, try the settings in the table. These exposures are *guides;* bracket your exposures by ±1 stop.

| Picture Subject | Shutter Speed (second) | Lens Opening |
|---|---|---|
| Skylines—10 minutes after sunset | 1/60 | *f*/5.6 |
| Distant View of City Skyline at Night | 1* | *f*/2.8 |
| Interiors with Bright Fluorescent Light | 1/60† | *f*/4 |
| Ice Shows, Circuses—Spotlighted Acts (carbon arc) | 1/250 | *f*/2.8 |
| Brightly Lighted Street Scenes at Night | 1/60 | *f*/2.8 |
| Brightly Lighted Theatre Districts—Las Vegas or Times Square | 1/60 | *f*/4 |
| Neon and Other Lighted Signs | 1/125 | *f*/4 |
| Floodlighted Buildings, Fountains, Monuments | 1/15* | *f*/2 |
| Christmas Lighting, Trees—Indoors and outdoors at night | 1/15* | *f*/2 |
| Fairs, Amusement Parks at Night | 1/30 | *f*/2.8 |
| Night Football, Soccer, Baseball, Racetracks | 1/125 | *f*/2.8 |
| Stage Shows—Average light<br>—Bright light | 1/60<br>1/125 | *f*/2.8<br>*f*/4 |

*Use a tripod or other firm camera support.
†Use shutter speeds of 1/60 second or longer with fluorescent light.

**Adjustments for Long or Short Exposures:**
No filter corrections or exposure adjustments are required for exposure times from 1/10,000 to 1/10 second. For a 1-second exposure, use a CC10Y filter and increase exposure by ½ stop. We do not recommend using exposure times longer than 1 second with this film.

**Definition:**

| Granularity | Resolving Power | Sharpness |
|---|---|---|
| Fine | Medium<br>80 lines per mm | High |

# KODAK EKTACHROME P800/1600 Professional Film (Daylight)

**For Color Slides**
This film is an excellent choice whenever you need a color-slide film with maximum speed for photography in dim existing light; for action or sports photography in poor light; for hand-holding telephoto lenses; for increasing depth of field with small lens openings under adverse lighting conditions; or for extending flash distance range.

KODAK EKTACHROME P800/1600 Professional Film is specifically designed for push processing to various speeds. It produces the best picture quality at EI 800 or EI 1600; however, you can obtain acceptable results with some loss of quality at EI 400 or EI 3200 with adjustments in the development time. Use a KODAK Color Compensating Filter CC10Y if you expose the film at EI 400.

KODAK EKTACHROME P800/1600 Film is color balanced for daylight or electronic flash, but it also produces very good results with carbon-arc spotlights. It features high sharpness and has medium to moderately coarse graininess (depending on the speed used for exposure).

**Film Code:** EES

**Size Available:** 135-36

**Electronic-Flash Guide Numbers:**
If your flash unit does not have settings for high-speed films, use this table as a starting point for determining the correct guide number. Divide the proper guide number by the flash-to-subject distance in feet or metres to determine the *f*-number for average subjects.

### EI 800

| **Output of Unit (BCPS*)** | | | | | | | | | |
|---|---|---|---|---|---|---|---|---|---|
| **350** | **500** | **700** | **1000** | **1400** | **2000** | **2800** | **4000** | **5600** | **8000** |
| **Guide Number** (for Distance in Feet) | | | | | | | | | |
| 120 | 140 | 170 | 200 | 240 | 280 | 330 | 400 | 470 | 560 |
| **Guide Number** (for Distance in Metres) | | | | | | | | | |
| 36 | 42 | 50 | 60 | 70 | 85 | 100 | 120 | 143 | 170 |

*BCPS=beam candlepower seconds

### EI 1600

| **Output of Unit (BCPS*)** | | | | | | | | | |
|---|---|---|---|---|---|---|---|---|---|
| **350** | **500** | **700** | **1000** | **1400** | **2000** | **2800** | **4000** | **5600** | **8000** |
| **Guide Number** (for Distance in Feet) | | | | | | | | | |
| 170 | 200 | 240 | 280 | 340 | 400 | 480 | 560 | 670 | 800 |
| **Guide Number** (for Distance in Metres) | | | | | | | | | |
| 50 | 60 | 70 | 85 | 105 | 120 | 145 | 170 | 205 | 244 |

*BCPS=beam candlepower seconds

**Existing Light:**
Use an exposure meter or a camera with a built-in meter if you have one. If you don't have a meter, try the settings in the table. These exposures are *guides;* bracket your exposures by ±1 stop.

| Picture Subject | Shutter Speed (second) and Lens Opening | |
|---|---|---|
| | EI 800 | EI 1600 |
| Skylines—10 minutes after sunset | 1/125 at *f*/5.6 | 1/125 at *f*/8 |
| Distant View of City Skyline at Night | 1* at *f*/4 | 1* at *f*/5.6 |
| Interiors with Bright Fluorescent Light | 1/60† at *f*/5.6 | 1/60† at *f*/8 |
| Ice Shows, Circuses—Spotlighted Acts (carbon arc) | 1/250 at *f*/4 | 1/250 at *f*/5.6 |
| Brightly Lighted Street Scenes at Night | 1/60 at *f*/4 | 1/125 at *f*/4 |
| Brightly Lighted Theatre Districts—Las Vegas or Times Square | 1/125 at *f*/4 | 1/125 at *f*/5.6 |
| Neon and Other Lighted Signs | 1/125 at *f*/5.6 | 1/125 at *f*/8 |
| Floodlighted Buildings, Fountains, Monuments | 1/30 at *f*/2 | 1/30 at *f*/2.8 |
| Christmas Lighting, Trees—Indoors and outdoors at Night | 1/30 at *f*/2 | 1/30 at *f*/2.8 |
| Fairs, Amusement Parks at Night | 1/60 at *f*/2.8 | 1/60 at *f*/4 |
| Night Football, Soccer, Baseball, Racetracks | 1/250 at *f*/2.8 | 1/250 at *f*/4 |
| Stage Shows—Average light<br>—Bright light | 1/125 at *f*/2.8<br>1/250 at *f*/4 | 1/125 at *f*/4<br>1/250 at *f*/5.6 |

*Use a tripod or other firm camera support.
†Use shutter speeds of 1/60 second or longer with fluorescent light.

**Adjustments for Long or Short Exposures:**
No filter corrections or exposure adjustments are required for exposure times from 1/10,000 to 1/10 second. For a 1-second exposure, use a CC10Y filter and increase exposure by ½ stop. We do not recommend using exposure times longer than 1 second with this film.

## PROCESSING
This film requires special processing. The film magazine has a space for you to circle the speed you used to expose the film. The speeds printed on the magazine are 400 (normal Process E-6); 800 (Push 1); 1600 (Push 2); and 3200 (Push 3).

You can have your film processed by a processing lab by returning the film to your photo dealer. Be sure to indicate the speed at which you exposed the film. Your dealer can also have duplicate slides, color prints, or enlargements made from your slides.

To process the film yourself, use the KODAK HOBBY-PAC™ Color Slide Kit or the KODAK EKTACHROME Film Processing Kit, Process E-6 (1 Gallon), sold by photo dealers. Changing the first development time changes the speed of the film up to EI 3200. See page 51. Detailed instructions are provided with the kits.

**Definition:**

| Film Speed | Granularity | Resolving Power | Sharpness |
|---|---|---|---|
| EI 800 | Medium | Medium<br>80 lines per mm | High |
| EI 1600 | Moderately Coarse | Medium<br>63 lines per mm | High |

# KODAK EKTACHROME Slide Duplicating Film
# KODAK EKTACHROME SE Duplicating Film SO-366

**For Color Slides**
These films are intended for making duplicate color slides from original slides made on KODACHROME or KODAK EKTACHROME Films. EKTACHROME Slide Duplicating Film is designed for relatively long exposure times with tungsten illumination (3200 K). EKTACHROME SE Duplicating Film SO-366 is intended for short exposure times with electronic flash.

These films produce excellent color-slide duplicates. However, because a duplicate slide is a copy of another photograph, you may be able to see a slight reduction in quality when you apply critical quality standards.

**Size Available:** 135-36. You can order SO-366 Film from your photo dealer.

## EXPOSURE

You can expose these films with enlargers or contact-printing equipment. You will have fewer problems with dust and scratches if you use a diffusion enlarger.

You will find filter-pack data for individual emulsions on the film carton. Use this data, along with the "Starting-Point Data," for your initial setup.

The exposure index for these films ranges from 4 to 20. Make an exposure series in 1-stop increments to determine the exposure index for a particular emulsion.

**Camera Exposure:** You can make duplicate slides by using a single-lens reflex camera with a through-the-lens exposure meter and a suitable slide-duplicating attachment.

As a starting point, set the camera ISO or ASA speed indicator to the exposure index provided with the film. Set the shutter speed at 1 second for exposure with tungsten illumination (3200 K). You can also use 1 second as a starting-point exposure with a standard illuminator (5000 K) or direct sunlight (reflected off a sheet of white paper) with correction filters. Start with the *filter-pack data* provided with the film. Then add any necessary filters listed in the table on page D19 (for the type of transparency you are duplicating) and the KODAK Color Compensating Filter or KODAK WRATTEN Gelatin Filter given in the table below (for your light source).

| Light Source | Filter Adjustment |
|---|---|
| 3200 K | Use only the starting-point data |
| 5000 K | Use the starting-point data for tungsten (3200 K) plus a KODAK Color Compensating Filter CC30R |
| Daylight | Use the starting-point data for tungsten (3200 K) plus a KODAK WRATTEN Gelatin Filter No. 85B |

Place the filters between the transparency you are duplicating and the light source. Use through-the-lens metering and adjust the aperture to the proper exposure.

Make an exposure series in 1-stop increments to determine the best exposure for your film and exposing equipment. If the lowest speed setting on your camera is 25, set the speed indicator at 25 and adjust your camera as follows:

| Exposure Index provided with the film | Increase the lens aperture by |
|---|---|
| 12 | 1 stop |
| 6 | 2 stops |
| 3 | 3 stops |

With SO-366 Film, use the starting-point data and make a trial exposure with the camera ISO or ASA indicator set at the exposure index provided with the film.

If you use SO-366 Film with daylight, start with the filters given in the table on page D19 and add 10R + 10Y. Set the ISO or ASA indicator at the exposure index provided with the film, and use an exposure time of 1/10 second.

## STARTING-POINT DATA

For a starting filter pack, use the basic *filter pack* given in the instruction sheet or on the film carton. Then see the following table for exposure and filter adjustments for the type of originals you are duplicating. Include a KODAK WRATTEN Gelatin Filter No. 2B in the filter packs listed in the table.

| KODAK Film (originals to be duplicated) | EKTACHROME Slide Duplicating Film with tungsten (3200 K) illumination | SO-366 Film with electronic flash (5600 K) illumination |
|---|---|---|
| KODACHROME (Process K-12)<br>EKTRACHROME (Process E-6) | *Filter Pack*<br>1 second at<br>*f*/11 to *f*/16 | *Filter Pack*<br>*f*/11 to *f*/16 |
| KODACHROME (Process K-14) | *Filter Pack*<br>+CC10C<br>1 second at<br>*f*/11 to *f*/16 | *Filter Pack*<br>+CC10C<br>*f*/11 to *f*/16 |
| EKTRACHROME (Process E-4) | *Filter Pack*<br>−CC15C<br>1 second at<br>*f*/11 to *f*/16 | *Filter Pack*<br>−CC15C<br>*f*/11 to *f*/16 |

**Adjusting the Filter Pack:** Judge the color balance of duplicate transparencies made for projection by viewing the projected images. When you view a duplicate transparency, you may find that you want to change the color balance. Usually you'll want to change the overall hue of the duplicate. To adjust the filter pack, subtract a filter of the same color as the overall hue, or add a filter that is complementary to the overall hue. Use the information in the table to determine the filter adjustment:

| If the overall color balance is too | Subtract this filter(s) OR | Add this filter(s) |
|---|---|---|
| Yellow | Yellow | Magenta + Cyan (or Blue) |
| Magenta | Magenta | Yellow + Cyan (or Green) |
| Cyan | Cyan | Yellow + Magenta (or Red) |
| Blue | Magenta + Cyan (or Blue) | Yellow |
| Green | Yellow + Cyan (or Green) | Magenta |
| Red | Magenta + Yellow (or Red) | Cyan |

If you use filters between the transparency and the duplicating film, keep the number of filters in the filter pack to a minimum. Using more than three CC filters will result in a significant loss in sharpness. If all three subtractive colors are in the pack, remove equivalent filters of all three colors. For example, if the pack contains 40C + 40M + 20Y, remove the lowest-value filter and reduce the other two by the same amount as follows:

| | |
|---|---|
| Filter Pack | 40C + 40M + 20Y |
| Subtract* | −20C 20M 20Y |
| Adjusted Filter Pack | 20C + 20M |

*This removes the neutral density

You can reduce the 20C + 20M further by substituting 20B. When you change the filter pack, you must adjust the exposure, or the density of the new duplicate will differ from the density of the previous duplicate.

**Adjustment for Emulsion-Number Changes:** Each box of film has an emulsion number, which is printed on the film carton. When you change to a new film emulsion number, you may have to change the exposure and filter pack.

To change from one emulsion number to a new one, start with the filter pack you are currently using. Then subtract the *recommended* filter pack for the old emulsion from the filter pack you're using. This calculation will give you the difference between the filter pack that you're using and the pack that was recommended. Finally, add the recommended filter pack for the new emulsion to this difference to obtain your new filter pack.

Example:

| | | |
|---|---|---|
| Current filter pack | 50C | 40Y |
| Subtract the recommended pack for *old* emulsion | −30C | 25Y |
| Difference | 20C | 15Y |
| Add the recommended pack for *new* emulsion | +35C | 30Y |
| | 55C | 45Y |

If the filter pack doesn't contain enough cyan or yellow filtration for you to remove the required amount, add the complementary filter. Then make any necessary adjustments to the exposure. For small changes in density (±1 stop), a change in exposure time is acceptable; for larger exposure compensations, change the aperture if possible.

**Definition*:**

| Granularity | Resolving Power | Sharpness |
|---|---|---|
| Extremely Fine | High 125 lines per mm | Very High |

*These classifications apply to EKTACHROME Slide and EKTACHROME SE Duplicating Films only. The definition of duplicate slides is a function of the originals and the quality of the duplicating equipment.

**For Black-and-White Prints**
KODAK T-MAX 100 Professional Film is a medium-speed panchromatic film with extremely fine grain and extremely high sharpness. It is ideally suited for detailed subjects that require maximum image quality. Its rich gradation and wide exposure latitude make it an excellent choice for general use in daylight or artificial light. You can push-process this film to a speed of EI 800.

**Film Code:** TMX

**Sizes Available:** 135-24, 135-36, 120, and sheet sizes

## EXPOSURE

**Nominal Speed:** EI 100

The speed numbers for this film are expressed as Exposure Indexes (EI). The developer you use to process this film affects the exposure index. Set your camera or meter (marked for ISO/ASA or ISO/DIN speeds) at the speed for your developer given in the table.

| KODAK Developer or Developer and Replenisher | Exposure Index (EI) |
|---|---|
| **T-MAX** | **100/21°** |
| **T-MAX RS** | **100/21°** |
| **D-76** | **100/21°** |
| **D-76 (1:1)** | **100/21°** |
| HC-110 (Dil B) | 100/21° |
| MICRODOL-X | 50/18° |
| MICRODOL-X (1:3) | 100/21° |
| **DURAFLO RT** | **80/20°** |

**Note:** The developers and exposure indexes in **bold type** are the primary recommendations.

**Filter Factors:** If you are using a handheld meter, adjust the indicated exposure according to the table below. However, if your camera has a built-in exposure meter that makes the reading through a filter used over the lens, see your camera manual for instructions on exposure with filters.

Also see page 94.

| KODAK WRATTEN Gelatin Filter | Daylight | | Tungsten | |
|---|---|---|---|---|
| | Increase lens aperture by (*f*-stops) OR | Increase exposure by (filter factor) | Increase lens aperture by (*f*-stops) OR | Increase exposure by (filter factor) |
| No. 8 (yellow) | ⅔ | 1.5 | ⅓ | 1.2 |
| No. 11 (yellowish green) | 1⅔ | 3 | 1⅔ | 3 |
| No. 12 (deep yellow) | 1 | 2 | ⅓ | 1.2 |
| No. 15 (deep yellow) | 1 | 2 | ⅔ | 1.5 |
| No. 25 (red) | 3 | 8 | 2 | 4 |
| No. 47 (blue) | 3 | 8 | 4⅔ | 25 |
| No. 58 (green) | 2⅔ | 6 | 2⅔ | 6 |
| Polarizing Filter | 1⅓ | 2.5 | 1⅓ | 2.5 |

**Adjustments for Long or Short Exposures:** To compensate for the reciprocity of this film, increase the exposure as shown in the table below.

| If indicated exposure time is (seconds) | Use this lens-aperture adjustment OR | This adjusted exposure time (seconds) |
|---|---|---|
| 1/10,000 | +⅓ stop | Change aperture |
| 1/1,000 | None | None |
| 1/100 | None | None |
| 1/10 | None | None |
| 1 | +⅓ stop | Change aperture |
| 10 | +½ stop | 15 |
| 100 | +1 stop | 200 |

## PROCESSING

**Processing Services:** You can have your film developed and printed by a processing lab by returning the film to your photo dealer. You can also order enlargements made from your negatives.

**Processing the Film Yourself:** You can develop your film in your own darkroom; see the instructions that follow.

**Darkroom Recommendations:** *Handle unprocessed film in total darkness.*

**Development Times** are for small roll-film tanks with agitation for 5 seconds at 30-second intervals throughout development. See page 75 for the method of agitation. The most widely used time and temperature are in heavy type. If your negatives are consistently too low in contrast, increase the development time; if too high in contrast, decrease the development time.

| KODAK Developer or Developer and Replenisher | Development Times in Minutes:Seconds* (for small roll-film tanks) | | | | |
|---|---|---|---|---|---|
| | 65°F (18°C) | 68°F (20°C) | 70°F (21°C) | 72°F (22°C) | 75°F (24°C) |
| T-MAX | NR | 8:00 | 7:30 | 7:00 | **6:30** |
| T-MAX RS | NR | 8:00 | 7:00 | 7:00 | **6:00** |
| D-76 | 10:30 | **9:00** | 8:00 | 7:00 | 6:00 |
| D-76 (1:1) | 14:30 | **12:00** | 11:00 | 10:00 | 8:30 |
| HC-110 (Dilution B) | 8:00 | **7:00** | 6:30 | 6:00 | 5:00 |
| MICRODOL-X | 16:00 | **13:30** | 12:00 | 10:30 | 8:30 |
| MICRODOL-X (1:3) | NR | NR | 20:00 | 18:30 | **16:00** |

*Development times shorter than 5 minutes may produce unsatisfactory uniformity.
NR = Not recommended

**Rinse** at 65 to 75°F (18 to 24°C) with agitation in KODAK Indicator Stop Bath or running water for 30 seconds.

**Fix** at 65 to 75°F (18 to 24°C) with agitation in KODAK Fixer or KODAFIX Solution for 5 to 10 minutes or in KODAK Rapid Fixer for 3 to 5 minutes.

**Note:** Your fixer may exhaust more rapidly with this film than with other films.

**Wash** the film for 20 to 30 minutes in running water at 65 to 75°F (18 to 24°C) with a flow rate that provides at least one complete change of water in 5 minutes. You can wash long rolls on the processing reel. To save time and conserve water, use KODAK Hypo Clearing Agent.

**Note:** Keep the temperatures of the rinse, fix, and wash close to the developer temperature.

**Dry** in a dust-free place. To minimize drying marks, treat the film in KODAK PHOTO-FLO Solution after washing, or wipe the surfaces carefully with a KODAK Photo Chamois or a soft viscose sponge.

Also see pages 73–80.

**Definition:**

| Granularity | Resolving Power | Sharpness | Degree of Enlargement* |
|---|---|---|---|
| Extremely Fine | Very High 200 lines per mm | Extremely High | Very High |

*For good-quality negatives

# KODAK T-MAX 400 Professional Film

**For Black-and-White Prints**
KODAK T-MAX 400 Film is a high-speed panchromatic film with extremely fine grain and very high sharpness. Its high speed makes it especially useful for photographing dimly lighted subjects, stopping action, increasing depth of field while using high shutter speeds, and for extending the distance range for flash pictures. You can use this very versatile film to photograph subjects under a wide variety of lighting conditions. You can expose this film at EI 400 or 800 with normal processing or at EI 1600 with push processing. If you push-process it in KODAK T-MAX Developer, you can expose the film at EI 3200.

**Film Code:** TMY

**Sizes Available:** 135-24, 135-36, 120, and sheet sizes

## EXPOSURE

**Nominal Speed:** EI 400

| KODAK Developer or Developer and Replenisher | Exposure Index (EI) |
|---|---|
| **T-MAX** | **400/27°** |
| **T-MAX RS** | **400/27°** |
| **D-76** | **400/27°** |
| **D-76 (1:1)** | **400/27°** |
| HC-110 (Dil B) | 320/26° |
| MICRODOL-X | 200/24° |
| MICRODOL-X (1:3) | 320/26° |
| **DURAFLO RT** | **400/27°** |

**Note:** The developers and exposure indexes in **bold type** are the primary recommendations.

**Filter Factors:** If you are using a handheld meter, adjust the indicated exposure according to the table below. However, if your camera has a built-in exposure meter that makes the reading through a filter used over the lens, see your camera manual for instructions on exposure with filters.

Also, see page 94.

| KODAK WRATTEN Gelatin Filter | Daylight | | Tungsten | |
|---|---|---|---|---|
| | Increase lens aperture by (*f*-stops) OR | Increase exposure by (filter factor) | Increase lens aperture by (*f*-stops) OR | Increase exposure by (filter factor) |
| No. 8 (yellow) | ⅔ | 1.5 | ⅓ | 1.2 |
| No. 11 (yellowish green) | 1⅔ | 3 | 1⅔ | 3 |
| No. 12 (deep yellow) | 1 | 2 | ⅓ | 1.2 |
| No. 15 (deep yellow) | 1 | 2 | ⅔ | 1.5 |
| No. 25 (red) | 3 | 8 | 2 | 4 |
| No. 47 (blue) | 3 | 8 | 4⅔ | 25 |
| No. 58 (green) | 2⅔ | 6 | 2⅔ | 6 |
| Polarizing Filter | 1⅓ | 2.5 | 1⅓ | 2.5 |

**Existing-Light Exposures:** Use an exposure meter or an automatic camera if you have one. For cameras without exposure meters, try the settings in the table. These exposures are *guides;* bracket your exposures by ±1 or 2 stops.

| Picture Subject | Shutter Speed (second) | Lens Opening |
|---|---|---|
| Home Interiors at Night—<br>Areas with average light<br>Areas with bright light | <br>1/30<br>1/30 | <br>*f*/2<br>*f*/2.8 |
| Interiors with Bright Fluorescent Light | 1/60* | *f*/4 |
| Candlelighted Close-Ups | 1/15† | *f*/2 |
| Indoor, Outdoor Christmas Lighting at Night | 1/15† | *f*/2 |
| Brightly Lighted Street Scenes at Night | 1/60 | *f*/2.8 |
| Brightly Lighted Theatre Districts—Las Vegas or Times Square | 1/60 | *f*/4 |
| Neon and Other Lighted Signs | 1/125 | *f*/4 |
| Store Windows at Night | 1/60 | *f*/4 |
| Floodlighted Buildings, Fountains, Monuments | 1/15† | *f*/2 |
| Distant View of City Skyline at Night | 1† | *f*/2.8 |
| Skylines—10 minutes after sunset | 1/60 | *f*/5.6 |
| Fairs, Amusement Parks | 1/30 | *f*/2.8 |
| Aerial Fireworks Displays—Keep camera shutter open on BULB for several bursts | Bulb† | *f*/16 |
| Night Football, Soccer, Baseball, Racetracks | 1/125 | *f*/2.8 |
| Basketball, Hockey, Bowling | 1/125 | *f*/2 |
| Boxing, Wrestling | 1/250 | *f*/2 |
| Stage Shows—Average light<br>—Bright light | 1/60<br>1/125 | *f*/2.8<br>*f*/4 |
| Circuses—Floodlighted acts | 1/60 | *f*/2.8 |
| Ice Shows—Floodlighted acts | 1/125 | *f*/2.8 |
| Ice Shows, Circuses—Spotlighted acts (carbon arc) | 1/250 | *f*/2.8 |
| School—Stage and Auditorium | 1/30 | *f*/2 |
| Swimming Pool—Indoors, tungsten lights above water | 1/60 | *f*/2 |
| Church Interiors—Tungsten lights | 1/30 | *f*/2 |

*Use shutter speeds of 1/60 second or longer with fluorescent light.
†Use a tripod or other firm camera support.

**Adjustments for Long or Short Exposures:** The following table gives the exposure compensation for different exposure times. No development adjustment is necessary.

| If indicated exposure time is (seconds) | Use this lens-aperture adjustment | OR This adjusted exposure time (seconds) |
|---|---|---|
| 1/10,000 | None | None |
| 1/1,000 | None | None |
| 1/100 | None | None |
| 1/10 | None | None |
| 1 | +⅓ stop | Change aperture |
| 10 | +½ stop | 15 |
| 100 | +1½ stops | 300 |

## PROCESSING

**Processing Services:** You can have your film developed and printed by a processing lab by returning the film to your photo dealer. You can also order enlargements made from your negatives.

**Processing the Film Yourself:** You can develop your film in your own darkroom by following the steps below.

**Darkroom Recommendations:** *Handle unprocessed film in total darkness.*

**Development Times** are for small roll-film tanks with agitation for 5 seconds at 30-second intervals throughout development. See page 75 for the method of agitation. The most widely used time and temperature are in heavy type. If your negatives are consistently too low in contrast, increase the development time; if too high in contrast, decrease the development time.

| KODAK Developer or Developer and Replenisher | Development Times in Minutes:Seconds* (for small roll-film tanks) | | | | |
|---|---|---|---|---|---|
| | 65°F (18°C) | 68°F (20°C) | 70°F (21°C) | 72°F (22°C) | 75°F (24°C) |
| T-MAX | NR | 7:00 | 6:30 | 6:30 | **6:00** |
| T-MAX RS | NR | 7:00 | 6:00 | 6:00 | **5:00** |
| D-76 | 9:00 | **8:00** | 7:00 | 6:30 | 5:30 |
| D-76 (1:1)† | 14:30 | **12:30** | 11:00 | 10:00 | 9:00 |
| HC-110 (Dilution B) | 6:30 | **6:00** | 5:30 | 5:00 | 4:30 |
| MICRODOL-X | 12:00 | **10:30** | 9:00 | 8:30 | 7:30 |
| MICRODOL-X (1:3)† | NR | NR | 20:00 | 18:30 | **16:00** |

*Development times shorter than 5 minutes may result in unsatisfactory uniformity.
NR = Not recommended

**Rinse** in KODAK Indicator Stop Bath at 65 to 75°F (18 to 24°C) for 30 seconds with agitation. You can use a running-water rinse if an acid stop bath is not available.

**Fix** at 65 to 75°F (18 to 24°C) with agitation in KODAK Fixer or KODAFIX Solution for 5 to 10 minutes or in KODAK Rapid Fixer for 3 to 5 minutes.

**Note:** Your fixer may exhaust more rapidly with this film than with other films.

**Wash** the film for 20 to 30 minutes in running water at 65 to 75°F (18 to 24°C) with a flow rate that provides at least one complete change of water in 5 minutes. You can wash long rolls on the processing reel. To save time and conserve water, use KODAK Hypo Clearing Agent.

**Note:** Keep the temperatures of the rinse, fix, and wash close to the developer temperature.

**Dry** in a dust-free place. To minimize drying marks, treat the film in KODAK PHOTO-FLO Solution after washing, or wipe the surfaces carefully with a KODAK Photo Chamois or a soft viscose sponge.

Also, see pages 73-80.

### Definition:

| Granularity | Resolving Power | Sharpness | Degree of Enlargement* |
|---|---|---|---|
| Extremely Fine | High 125 lines per mm | Very High | High |

*For good-quality negatives

**For Black-and-White Prints**
A multi-speed panchromatic film that combines high to ultra-high film speeds with finer grain than that of other fast black-and-white films, KODAK T-MAX P3200 Professional Film is an excellent choice for available-light applications that require exposure indexes of 3200 to 25,000.

The nominal speed is EI 1000 when the film is processed in KODAK T-MAX Developer or T-MAX RS Developer and Replenisher, or EI 800 when it is processed in other Kodak black-and-white developers. Because of its great latitude, you can expose it at EI 1600 and obtain negatives of high quality. There will be no change in the grain of the final print, but there may be a slight loss of shadow detail. When you need a higher speed, you can expose this film at EI 3200 or 6400 with an increase in development time. At these higher speeds, there will be an increase in contrast and graininess with a loss of shadow detail. If you expose films at speeds higher than EI 6400, it is critical that you make tests to determine if the results are appropriate for your needs.

**Film Code:** TMZ

**Size Available:** 135-36

## EXPOSURE

**Filter Factors:** Increase exposure by the filter factor or the number of stops indicated when you use filters. For greatest exposure accuracy with a through-the-lens meter, take the meter reading without the filter over the lens, and then increase your exposure as shown in the table. See page 94.

| KODAK WRATTEN Gelatin Filter | Daylight | | Tungsten | |
|---|---|---|---|---|
| | Increase lens aperture by (*f*-stops) OR | Increase exposure by (filter factor) | Increase lens aperture by (*f*-stops) OR | Increase exposure by (filter factor) |
| No. 8 (yellow) | 2/3 | 1.5 | 1/3 | 1.2 |
| No. 11 (yellowish green) | 1 2/3 | 3 | 1 2/3 | 3 |
| No. 12 (deep yellow) | 2/3 | 1.5 | 1/3 | 1.2 |
| No. 15 (deep yellow) | 2/3 | 1.5 | 2/3 | 1.5 |
| No. 25 (red) | 2 2/3 | 6 | 2 | 4 |
| No. 47 (blue) | 3 1/3 | 9.5 | 4 1/3 | 19 |
| No. 58 (green) | 2 2/3 | 6 | 2 2/3 | 6 |
| Polarizing Filter | 1 1/3 | 2.5 | 1 1/3 | 2.5 |

**Existing-Light Exposures:** Use an exposure meter or an automatic camera if you have one. For cameras without working exposure meters, or for scenes that are difficult to meter, try the settings suggested in the table. These exposures are *guides;* for more assurance, bracket your exposures ± 1 stop.

| Picture Subject | Shutter Speed (second) | Lens Opening |
|---|---|---|
| Home Interiors at Night—<br>Areas with average light<br>Areas with bright light | <br>1/30<br>1/30 | <br>*f*/2.8<br>*f*/4 |
| Candlelighted Close-Ups | 1/30 | *f*/2 |
| Interiors with Bright Fluorescent Light | 1/60* | *f*/5.6 |
| Indoor, Outdoor Christmas Lighting at Night | 1/30 | *f*/2 |
| Brightly Lighted Street Scenes at Night | 1/60 | *f*/4 |
| Brightly Lighted Theatre Districts—Las Vegas or Times Square | 1/125 | *f*/4 |
| Neon and Other Lighted Signs | 1/125 | *f*/5.6 |
| Store Windows at Night | 1/60 | *f*/5.6 |
| Floodlighted Buildings, Fountains, Monuments | 1/30 | *f*/2 |
| Distant View of City Skyline at Night | 1† | *f*/4 |
| Skylines—10 minutes after sunset | 1/125 | *f*/5.6 |
| Fairs, Amusement Parks | 1/60 | *f*/2.8 |

| Picture Subject | Shutter Speed (second) | Lens Opening |
|---|---|---|
| Aerial Fireworks Displays—Keep camera shutter open on BULB for several bursts | Bulb† | *f*/22‡ |
| Night Football, Soccer, Baseball, Racetracks | 1/250 | *f*/2.8 |
| Basketball, Hockey, Bowling | 1/125 | *f*/2.8 |
| Boxing, Wrestling | 1/250 | *f*/2.8 |
| Stage Shows—Average light<br>—Bright light | 1/125<br>1/250 | *f*/2.8<br>*f*/4 |
| Circuses—Floodlighted acts | 1/125 | *f*/2.8 |
| Ice Shows—Floodlighted acts | 1/250 | *f*/2.8 |
| Ice Shows, Circuses—Spotlighted acts (carbon arc) | 1/250 | *f*/4 |
| School—Stage and auditorium | 1/30 | *f*/2.8 |
| Swimming Pool—Indoors, tungsten lights above water | 1/60 | *f*/2.8 |
| Church Interiors—Tungsten lights | 1/30 | *f*/2.8 |

*Use shutter speeds of 1/60 second or longer with fluorescent light.
†Use a tripod or other firm camera support.
‡If *f*/22 is not available on your camera, you can use *f*/16.

**Adjustments for Long or Short Exposures:** You do not need to make any exposure or filter adjustments for exposure times from 1/10,000 second to 1 second. At an exposure time of 10 seconds, increase exposure by ⅔ stop.

## PROCESSING

**Processing Services:** You can have your film developed and printed by a processing lab by returning the film to your photo dealer. You can also order enlargements made from your negatives.

**Processing the Film Yourself:** You can develop your film in your own darkroom by following the steps below.

**Safelight:** *Total darkness is required.*

**Development Times** are for small roll-film tanks with agitation for 5 seconds at 30-second intervals throughout development. See page 75 for the method of agitation. These times are starting-point recommendations. If your negatives are consistently too low in contrast, increase the development time; if too high in contrast, decrease the development time.

| KODAK Developer or Developer and Replenisher | Exposed at EI | Development Times in Minutes:Seconds* (for small roll-film tanks) | | | |
|---|---|---|---|---|---|
| | | 70°F (21°C) | 75°F (24°C) | 80°F (27°C) | 85°F (29°C) |
| T-MAX | 400/27° | 7:00 | 6:00 | 5:00 | 4:00 |
| | 800/30° | 7:30 | 6:30 | 5:30 | 4:30 |
| | 1600/33° | 8:00 | 7:00 | 6:00 | 5:00 |
| | 3200/36° | 11:00 | 9:30 | 8:00 | 6:30 |
| | 6400/39° | 13:00 | 11:00 | 9:30 | 8:00 |
| | 12,500/42°* | 15:30 | 12:30 | 10:30 | 9:00 |
| | 25,000/45°* | 17:30 | 14:00 | 12:00 | 10:00 |
| T-MAX RS | 400/27° | 7:00 | 6:00 | 5:30 | 5:00 |
| | 800/30° | 8:30 | 6:30 | 6:00 | 5:30 |
| | 1600/33° | 9:30 | 7:30 | 7:00 | 6:00 |
| | 3200/36° | 12:00 | 10:00 | 9:00 | 8:00 |
| | 6400/39° | 14:00 | 11:00 | 10:00 | 9:00 |
| | 12,500/42°* | 16:00 | 12:00 | 11:00 | 10:00 |
| | 25,000/45°* | NR | 14:00 | 13:00 | 11:00 |
| D-76 | 400/27° | 9:30 | 7:30 | 6:00 | 4:30 |
| | 800/30° | 10:00 | 8:00 | 6:30 | 5:00 |
| | 1600/33° | 10:30 | 8:30 | 7:00 | 5:30 |
| | 3200/36° | 13:30 | 11:00 | 8:30 | 7:30 |
| | 6400/39° | 16:00 | 12:30 | 10:30 | 9:00 |
| HC-110 (Dilution B) | 400/27° | 6:30 | 5:00 | 4:30 | 3:30 |
| | 800/30° | 7:00 | 5:30 | 4:45 | 4:00 |
| | 1600/33° | 7:30 | 6:00 | 5:00 | 4:30 |
| | 3200/36° | 10:00 | 7:30 | 6:30 | 5:45 |
| | 6400/39° | 12:00 | 9:30 | 8:00 | 6:45 |

*Expose and process a test roll to determine if results at these exposure indexes are acceptable for your needs. For general use, it is best to expose film at EI 3200 or EI 6400.

**Note:** Tank developing times shorter than 5 minutes may produce unsatisfactory uniformity.

**Rinse** at 70 to 85°F (21 to 29°C) with agitation in KODAK Indicator Stop Bath or running water for 30 seconds.

**Fix** at 70 to 85°F (21 to 29°C) for 3 to 5 minutes with vigorous agitation in KODAK Rapid Fixer. Be sure to agitate the film frequently during fixing.

**Note:** To keep fixing times as short as possible, we strongly recommend using KODAK Rapid fixer. If you use another fixer, such as KODAK Fixer or KODAFIX Solution, fix for 5 to 10 minutes or twice the time it takes for the film to clear. You can check the film for clearing after 3 minutes in KODAK Rapid Fixer or 5 minutes in KODAK Fixer or KODAFIX Solution.

**Important:** Your fixer may exhaust more rapidly with this film than with other films.

**Wash** the film for 20 to 30 minutes in running water at 70 to 85°F (21 to 29°C) with a flow rate that provides at least one complete change of water in 5 minutes. To save time and conserve water, use KODAK Hypo Clearing Agent.

**Note:** Keep the temperatures of the rinse, fix, and wash close to the developer temperature.

**Dry** in a dust-free place. To minimize drying marks, treat the film in KODAK PHOTO-FLO Solution after washing, or wipe the surfaces carefully with a KODAK Photo Chamois or soft viscose sponge.

Also, see pages 73–80.

**Definition:**

| Granularity | Resolving Power | Sharpness | Degree of Enlargement* |
|---|---|---|---|
| Fine | High 125 lines per mm | High | Moderate |

*For good-quality negatives

**For Black-and-White Prints**
KODAK PLUS-X Pan Film is a general-purpose panchromatic film that offers medium speed, extremely fine grain, and very high sharpness even at high degrees of enlargement. It produces high-quality results with excellent rendering of a wide tonal range. Its speed is adequate for average or bright lighting conditions. The professional version of this film, KODAK PLUS-X Pan Professional Film, is also available. See page 57.

**Film Code:** PX

**Sizes Available:** 135-24, 135-36, 120, and long rolls.

## EXPOSURE

**Filter Factors:** If you are using a handheld meter, adjust the indicated exposure according to the table below. However, if your camera has a built-in exposure meter that makes the reading through a filter used over the lens, see your camera manual for instructions on exposure with filters.

Also, see page 94.

| | KODAK WRATTEN Gelatin Filter | | | | | | |
|---|---|---|---|---|---|---|---|
| Light Source | No. 8 | No. 11 | No. 15 | No. 25 | No. 47 | No. 58 | Polarizing Screen |
| Daylight | 2 | 4 | 2.5 | 6 | 6 | 8 | 2.5 |
| Tungsten | 1.5 | 4 | 1.5 | 4 | 12 | 8 | 2.5 |

**Adjustments for Long or Short Exposures:** The following table gives the exposure and development compensation for different exposure times.

| If indicated exposure time is (seconds) | Use this lens-aperture adjustment | OR This adjusted exposure time (seconds) | AND This development adjustment |
|---|---|---|---|
| 1/100,000 | +1 stop | Change aperture | +20% |
| 1/10,000 | +½ stop | Change aperture | +15% |
| 1/1,000 | None | None | +10% |
| 1/100 | None | None | None |
| 1/10 | None | None | None |
| 1 | +1 stop | 2 | −10% |
| 10 | +2 stops | 50 | −20% |
| 100 | +3 stops | 1200 | −30% |

**Note:** Make exposure corrections for long or short exposure times as indicated in the table. Make the development correction only if you want the whole roll of film processed for the corrected development time. If correcting the development is not practical because of significantly different exposure times used for different pictures on the roll, develop the film for the normal development time. Usually you can make the contrast correction by using higher- or lower-contrast photographic paper when you make the prints.

## PROCESSING

**Processing Services:** You can have your film developed and printed by a processing lab by returning the film to your photo dealer. You can also order enlargements made from your negatives.

**Processing the Film Yourself:** You can develop your film in your own darkroom by following the steps below.

**Darkroom Recommendations:** *Handle this film in total darkness.* However, when development is half completed, you can use a KODAK 3 Safelight Filter (dark green) in a suitable safelight lamp with a 15-watt bulb for a few seconds only. Keep the film at least 4 feet (1.2 metres) from the lamp.

**Development Times** are for small roll-film tanks with agitation for 5 seconds at 30-second intervals. See page 75 for the method of agitation. The most widely used time and temperature are in heavy type. If your negatives are consistently too low in contrast, increase the development time; if too high in contrast, decrease the development time.

| KODAK Developer or Developer and Replenisher | Development Times in Minutes:Seconds* (for small roll-film tanks) | | | | |
|---|---|---|---|---|---|
| | 65°F (18°C) | 68°F (20°C) | 70°F (21°C) | 72°F (22°C) | 75°F (24°C) |
| T-MAX | 6:30 | 5:30 | 5:30 | 5:00 | **5:00** |
| T-MAX RS | 6:30 | **5:30** | 4:30 | 4:00 | 3:30 |
| HC-110 (Dilution B) | 6:00 | **5:00** | 4:30 | 4:00 | 3:30 |
| D-76 | 6:30 | **5:30** | 5:00 | 4:30 | 3:45 |
| D-76 (1:1) | 8:00 | **7:00** | 6:30 | 6:00 | 5:00 |
| MICRODOL-X | 8:00 | **7:00** | 6:30 | 6:00 | 5:30 |
| MICRODOL-X (1:3) | NR | NR | 11:00 | 10:00 | **9:30** |

*Development times shorter than 5 minutes may produce unsatisfactory uniformity.
NR = Not recommended

**Rinse** in KODAK Indicator Stop Bath at 65 to 75°F (18 to 24°C) for 30 seconds with agitation. You can use a running-water rinse if an acid stop bath is not available.

**Fix** at 65 to 75°F (18 to 24°C) with agitation in KODAK Fixer for 5 to 10 minutes or in KODAK Rapid Fixer or KODAFIX Solution for 2 to 4 minutes.

**Wash** the film for 20 to 30 minutes in running water at 65 to 75°F (18 to 24°C). To minimize drying marks, treat the film in KODAK PHOTO-FLO Solution after washing, or wipe the surfaces carefully with a KODAK Photo Chamois or a soft viscose sponge.

**Note:** Keep the temperatures of the rinse, fix, and wash close to the developer temperature.

**Dry** in a dust-free place.

Also, see pages 73-80.

**Definition:**

| Granularity | Resolving Power | Sharpness | Degree of Enlargement* |
|---|---|---|---|
| Extremely Fine | High 125 lines per mm | Very High | High |

*For good-quality negatives

**For Black-and-White Prints**

KODAK TRI-X Pan Film is an all-purpose film for use in a wide range of subject and lighting conditions. It is a good choice for photographing dimly lighted subjects, fast action, and subjects requiring good depth of field and high shutter speeds, and for extending the distance range for flash pictures. It features high speed, high sharpness, fine grain, high resolving power, and a moderate degree of enlargement capability. It has excellent tone reproduction and excellent quality for existing-light pictures. A professional version is also available.

**Film Code:** TX

**Sizes Available:** 135-24, 135-36, 120, and long rolls

## EXPOSURE

**Filter Factors:** If you are using a handheld meter, adjust the indicated exposure according to the table below. However, if your camera has a built-in exposure meter that makes the reading through a filter used over the lens, see your camera manual for instructions on exposure with filters.

Also, see page 94.

| | KODAK WRATTEN Gelatin Filter | | | | | | | |
|---|---|---|---|---|---|---|---|---|
| **Light Source** | **No. 8** | **No. 11** | **No. 12** | **No. 15** | **No. 25** | **No. 47** | **No. 58** | **Polarizing Filter** |
| Daylight | 2 | 4 | 2.5 | 2.5 | 8 | 6 | 6 | 2.5 |
| Tungsten | 1.5 | 3 | — | 1.5 | 5 | 12 | 6 | 2.5 |

**Existing-Light Exposures:** Use an exposure meter or an automatic camera if you have one. For cameras without working exposure meters, or for scenes that are difficult to meter, try the settings suggested in the table. These exposures are *guides;* for more assurance, bracket your exposures ±1 stop.

| Picture Subject | Shutter Speed (second) | Lens Opening |
|---|---|---|
| Home Interiors at Night—<br>Areas with average light<br>Areas with bright light | <br>1/30<br>1/30 | <br>*f*/2<br>*f*/2.8 |
| Interiors with Bright Fluorescent Light | 1/60* | *f*/4 |
| Candlelighted Close-Ups | 1/15† | *f*/2 |
| Indoor, Outdoor Christmas Lighting at Night | 1/15† | *f*/2 |
| Brightly Lighted Street Scenes at Night | 1/60 | *f*/2.8 |
| Brightly Lighted Theatre Districts—Las Vegas or Times Square | 1/60 | *f*/4 |
| Neon and Other Lighted Signs | 1/125 | *f*/4 |
| Store Windows at Night | 1/60 | *f*/4 |
| Floodlighted Buildings, Fountains, Monuments | 1/15† | *f*/2 |
| Distant View of City Skyline at Night | 1† | *f*/2.8 |
| Skylines—10 minutes after sunset | 1/60 | *f*/5.6 |

| Picture Subject | Shutter Speed (second) | Lens Opening |
|---|---|---|
| Fairs, Amusement Parks | 1/30 | *f*/2.8 |
| Aerial Fireworks Displays—Keep camera shutter open on BULB for several bursts | Bulb† | *f*/16 |
| Night Football, Soccer, Baseball, Racetracks | 1/125 | *f*/2.8 |
| Basketball, Hockey, Bowling | 1/125 | *f*/2 |
| Boxing, Wrestling | 1/250 | *f*/2 |
| Stage Shows—Average light<br>—Bright lighting | 1/60<br>1/125 | *f*/2.8<br>*f*/4 |
| Circuses—Floodlighted acts | 1/60 | *f*/2.8 |
| Ice Shows—Floodlighted acts | 1/125 | *f*/2.8 |
| Ice Shows, Circuses—Spotlighted acts (carbon arc) | 1/250 | *f*/2.8 |
| School—Stage and auditorium | 1/30 | *f*/2 |
| Swimming Pool—Indoors, tungsten lights above water | 1/60 | *f*/2 |
| Church Interiors—Tungsten lights | 1/30 | *f*/2 |

*Use shutter speeds of 1/60 second or longer with fluorescent light.
†Use a tripod or other firm camera support.

**Adjustments for Long or Short Exposures:** The following table gives the exposure and development compensation for different exposure times.

| If indicated exposure time is (seconds) | Use this lens-aperture adjustment | OR This adjusted exposure time (seconds) | AND This development adjustment |
|---|---|---|---|
| 1/100,000 | +1 stop | Change aperture | +20% |
| 1/10,000 | +½ stop | Change aperture | +15% |
| 1/1,000 | None | None | +10% |
| 1/100 | None | None | None |
| 1/10 | None | None | None |
| 1 | +1 stop | 2 | −10% |
| 10 | +2 stops | 50 | −20% |
| 100 | +3 stops | 1200 | −30% |

**Note:** Make exposure corrections for long or short exposure times as indicated in the table. Make the development correction only if you want the whole roll of film processed for the corrected development time. If correcting the development is not practical because of significantly different exposure times used for different pictures on the roll, develop the film for the normal development time. Usually you can make the contrast correction by using higher- or lower-contrast photographic paper when you make the prints.

## PROCESSING

**Processing Services:** You can have your film developed and printed by a processing lab by returning the film to your photo dealer. You can also order enlargements made from your negatives.

**Processing the Film Yourself:** You can develop your film in your own darkroom by following the steps below.

**Safelight:** *Total darkness is required.* However, when development is half completed, you can use a KODAK 3 Safelight Filter (dark green) in a suitable safelight lamp with a 15-watt bulb *for a few seconds only*. Keep the film at least 4 feet (1.2 metres) from the lamp.

**Development Times** are for small roll-film tanks with agitation for 5 seconds at 30-second intervals throughout development. See page 75 for the method of agitation. The most widely used time and temperature are in heavy type. If your negatives are consistently too low in contrast, increase the development time; if too high in contrast, decrease the development time.

| KODAK Developer or Developer and Replenisher | Development Times in Minutes:Seconds* (for small roll-film tanks) | | | | |
|---|---|---|---|---|---|
| | 65°F (18°C) | **68°F (20°C)** | 70°F (21°C) | 72°F (22°C) | 75°F (24°C) |
| T-MAX | 7:00 | 6:00 | 6:00 | 5:30 | **5:30** |
| T-MAX RS | 7:00 | 6:00 | 5:30 | 5:30 | **5:00** |
| HC-110 (Dilution B) | 8:30 | **7:30** | 6:30 | 6:00 | 5:00 |
| D-76 | 9:00 | **8:00** | 7:30 | 6:30 | 5:30 |
| D-76 (1:1)† | 11:00 | **10:00** | 9:30 | 9:00 | 8:00 |
| MICRODOL-X | 11:00 | **10:00** | 9:30 | 9:00 | 8:00 |
| MICRODOL-X (1:3)† | NR | NR | 15:00 | 14:00 | **13:00** |
| DK-50 (1:1) | 7:00 | **6:00** | 5:30 | 5:00 | 4:30 |

*Development times shorter than 5 minutes may produce unsatisfactory uniformity.
†For greater sharpness.
NR = Not recommended

**Rinse** in KODAK Indicator Stop Bath at 65 to 75°F (18 to 24°C) for 30 seconds with agitation. You can use a running-water rinse if an acid stop bath is not available.

**Fix** at 65 to 75°F (18 to 24°C) with agitation in KODAK Fixer or KODAFIX Solution for 5 to 10 minutes or in KODAK Rapid Fixer for 4 minutes.

**Wash** the film for 20 to 30 minutes in running water at 65 to 75°F (18 to 24°C). You can use KODAK Hypo Clearing Agent to save time and conserve water.

**Note:** Keep the temperatures of the rinse, fix, and wash close to the developer temperature.

**Dry** in a dust-free place. To minimize drying marks, treat the film in KODAK PHOTO-FLO Solution after washing, or wipe the surfaces carefully with a KODAK Photo Chamois or a soft viscose sponge.

Also, see pages 73–80.

**Definition:**

| Granularity | Resolving Power | Sharpness | Degree of Enlargement* |
|---|---|---|---|
| Fine | High<br>100 lines per mm | High | Moderate |

*For good-quality negatives

**For Black-and-White Prints**
This is a variable-contrast panchromatic film with extended red sensitivity and superb definition useful for several applications. Technical Pan Film, when processed in special low-contrast developer, is a superior pictorial film for making giant-size enlargements of 25X and more with little perceptible grain. The film features micro-fine grain and extremely high resolving power and sharpness to obtain its high quality.

For other applications, you can use Technical Pan Film to make reduced copy negatives of printed matter, such as books, newspapers, maps, engineering drawings, documents, and similar originals, and of color and black-and-white continuous-tone originals. The film produces good quality in copies of originals that contain both line and halftone material. You can vary the contrast by your choice of developer. The film's moderate to very high contrast combined with excellent definition characteristics meet the requirements for various copying purposes. The film speed varies with development and type of use. See the table below.

This film is also useful in photomicrography and other scientific and industrial applications that require high-definition photographic records. You can also use it for making reverse-text title slides with a black background and light type when you photograph white artwork with black type.

**Film Code**: TP

**Sizes Available**: 135-36 and 120

## EXPOSURE

**Speed:** Film speeds are for exposure meters marked for ISO/ASA speeds or Exposure Indexes and recommended development. For copying, use the film speeds below for determining trial exposures. For more assurance, bracket the estimated exposure by 1 or 2 stops using half-stop increments.

| Use | Contrast Required | Film Speed | | KODAK Developer | Development Time (minutes) 68°F (20°C) |
|---|---|---|---|---|---|
| **Pictorial** | Low | EI 25 | | TECHNIDOL Liquid*<br>TECHNIDOL LC* | 9<br>15 |
| **Copy Applications: Type of Original** | | **Gray Card†** | **White Card‡** | | |
| Printed matter; line drawings | Maximum—Very High | EI 320 | EI 64 | D-19 | 4 |
| Continuous-tone photographs | Moderate<br>Low | EI 32<br>EI 25 | EI 6<br>EI 5 | HC-110 (Dilution F)§<br>TECHNIDOL Liquid | 6<br>5 |
| Printed matter for reverse-text slides‖ | Maximum—Very High | EI 200 | EI 40 | DEKTOL | 3 |

*KODAK TECHNIDOL Liquid Developer is recommended for both 135 and 120 sizes of Technical Pan Film. KODAK TECHNIDOL LC Developer (powder) is recommended only for the 135-size film.

†For reflected-light meter readings, including in-camera meter readings, of an 18-percent reflectance gray card, such as the KODAK Gray Card, or for incident-light meter readings at the copyboard.

‡For reflected-light exposure meter readings, including readings with in-camera meters, from a matte white card of 90-percent reflectance at the copyboard.

§You can prepare HC-110 Developer, Dilution F, by diluting one part stock solution with 19 parts water. Mix Dilution F fresh and discard frequently rather than replenish.

‖After photographing white artwork with black type, mount the processed negatives made on this film in slide mounts for projection.

**Illumination:** The recommended lighting setup for copying consists of two light sources, one on either side of the copy material, with the lights placed so that they are at an angle of 45 degrees to the material. Use a sheet of clean plate glass to hold the original flat.

**Exposure Examples:** With two No. 2 photoflood lamps in matte surfaced reflectors 4 feet (1.2 metres) from the copy, use an exposure of about 1/60 second at *f*/8. With No. 1 photoflood lamps the same distance from the copy, use about 1/30 second at *f*/8. These exposures are based on development for maximum contrast in KODAK Developer D-19.

**Filter Factors:** *Pictorial*— Due to the extended red sensitivity of Technical Pan Film, flesh tones and shades of red may reproduce lighter in prints than with typical panchromatic black-and-white films. You can compensate for this effect by using a CC40C or CC50C filter over the camera lens.

*Copying*— Usually, a filter is not required to achieve the desired contrast between background and subject matter. In special cases, such as in copying old newspapers or books with yellowed paper, use a No. 8 yellow filter or a No. 15 deep-yellow filter. For copying blueprints, use a No. 25 red filter. Increase the normal exposure by the filter factor in the table. However, if your camera has a built-in exposure meter that makes the reading through a filter used over the lens, see your camera instructions for exposure with filters. Also, see page 94.

| Light Source | KODAK WRATTEN Gelatin Filter | | | | | |
|---|---|---|---|---|---|---|
| | No. 8 | No. 11 | No. 15 | No. 25 | No. 47 | No. 58 |
| Daylight* | 1.5* | — | 2 | 3 | — | — |
| Tungsten† | 1.2 | 5 | 1.2 | 2 | 25 | 12 |

*Filter factors are based on a 1/25-second daylight exposure and development in KODAK TECHNIDOL Liquid Developer for 9 minutes at 68°F (20°C).
†Filter factors are based on a 1-second exposure with tungsten light and development in KODAK HC-110 Developer (Dilution D) for 8 minutes at 68°F (20°C).

**Adjustments for Long or Short Exposures:** The following table gives the exposure and development compensation for different exposure times for development in KODAK TECHNIDOL LC Developer.

| If indicated exposure time is (seconds) | Use this lens-aperture adjustment | OR This adjusted exposure time (seconds) | AND this development adjustment |
|---|---|---|---|
| 1/10,000 | None | None | +30% |
| 1/1000 | None | None | +20% |
| 1/100 | None | None | None |
| 1/10 | None | None | None |
| 1 | None | None | −10% |
| 10 | +½ stop | 15 | −10% |
| 100 | +1½ stops | Not recommended | None |

**Note:** Make exposure corrections for long exposure times as indicated in the table. Make the development correction only if you want the whole roll of film processed for the corrected development time. If correcting the development is not practical because of significantly different exposure times used for different pictures on the roll, develop the film for the normal development time. Usually you can make the contrast correction for reciprocity effect by using higher- or lower-contrast photographic paper when you make the prints.

## PROCESSING

You can develop your film in your own darkroom by following the steps below.

**Darkroom Recommendations:** Handle unprocessed film in total darkness. After development is half completed, you can use a KODAK 3 Safelight Filter (dark green) in a suitable safelight lamp with a 15-watt bulb for a few seconds only. Keep the safelight at least 4 feet (1.2 metres) from the film.

**Development Times** are for small roll-film tanks with agitation for 5 seconds at 30-second intervals throughout development. (See the table under "Exposure" for development times.) See page 75 for method of agitation. For development in KODAK TECHNIDOL Developers, see the recommendations on the next page for agitation interval and method of agitation. If your negatives are consistently too low in contrast, increase the development time; if too high in contrast, decrease the development time.

**Agitation:** The recommended agitation procedures for processing Technical Pan Film in TECHNIDOL Developers differ from those recommended for other Kodak films. It's important to carefully follow the agitation instructions given below.

*KODAK TECHNIDOL Liquid Developer.* In total darkness, drop the loaded film reel into a full tank of developer solution smoothly; dislodge any air bubbles from the film or reel by tapping the bottom of the tank on the work surface from a height of about 1 inch. Immediately agitate by shaking the tank vigorously up and down 10 to 12 times for two seconds. *Do not rotate the tank.* Let the tank sit for 28 seconds and then start the next 2-second agitation. Repeat every 30 seconds for the remainder of the development time.

*KODAK TECHNIDOL LC Developer.* In total darkness, drop the loaded film reel into a full tank of developer solution, smoothly and without hesitation. Attach the top to the tank.

Then promptly dislodge any air bubbles from the film or reel by tapping the bottom of the tank on the work surface from a height of about 1 inch. Immediately agitate the film tank as follows. Extend your arm and rotate the tank 180° at the wrist with no lateral arm movement. *Do not shake the tank vigorously.* Use an initial agitation of 4 inversion cycles by rotating the tank down and up for each cycle. Let the tank sit for the remainder of the first 30 seconds. After 30 seconds, start agitating for 5 seconds at 30-second intervals for the remainder of the development time, using 2 to 5 inversion cycles each time.

**Rinse** in KODAK Indicator Stop Bath at 65 to 70°F (18 to 21°C) for 15 to 30 seconds with agitation. You can use a running-water rinse for 30 seconds if an acid stop bath is not available.

**Fix** in KODAK Fixer for 2 to 4 minutes or in KODAK Rapid Fixer for 1½ to 3 minutes at 65 to 70°F (18 to 21°C) with frequent agitation.

**Wash** the film for 5 to 15 minutes in running water at 65 to 70°F (18 to 21°C). You can use KODAK Hypo Clearing Agent to save time and conserve water.

**Note:** Keep the temperatures of the rinse, fix, and wash close to the developer temperature.

**Dry** in a dust-free place. To minimize drying marks, treat the film in KODAK PHOTO-FLO Solution after washing. Do not squeegee or sponge the film.

Also, see pages 73-80.

**Definition:**

| Granularity | Resolving Power | Sharpness | Degree of Enlargement* |
|---|---|---|---|
| Micro Fine† | Extremely High<br>320 lines per mm | Extremely High | Extremely High |
| Extremely Fine‡ | Extremely High<br>320 lines per mm | Extremely High | Extremely High |

*The degree of enlargement usually will be limited by camera and subject conditions rather than by film characteristics.
†For negatives developed in KODAK TECHNIDOL Liquid Developer.
‡For negatives developed in KODAK TECHNIDOL LC Developer, or KODAK HC-110 Developer, Dilution D, for 8 minutes at 68°F (20°C).

**For Black-and-White Prints**
KODAK High Speed Infrared Film is a moderately high-contrast, infrared-sensitive film that features abstract tone reproduction. With a red filter, it gives striking and unusual effects. The film is often used for pictorial landscape photographs to create an eerie, dream-like quality with light foliage and dark skies. High Speed Infrared Film is useful to show detail ordinarily obscured by atmospheric haze in distant landscapes. It is also useful in aerial, scientific, medical, industrial, legal, and documentary photography and in photomicrography.

**Film Code:** HIE

**Size Available:** 135-36

**Storage and Handling:** Film magazines must be handled in *total darkness* when the magazines are outside the film cans. Load and unload your camera only in total darkness. You may want to use a changing bag on location for loading your camera. See your photo dealer for the one that's opaque to infrared rays. Store unexposed 135 magazines of this film in a refrigerator at 55°F (13°C) or lower in the original sealed package. It's important to store unexposed film in total darkness, such as in the tightly closed film cans. Allow film to warm up to room temperature (approximately 4 hours) before opening the package to avoid moisture condensation on film surfaces. Have your film processed promptly after exposure.

If you have to postpone processing of the film, store exposed unprocessed film in the tightly closed film cans under refrigeration below 40°F (4°C). Before opening the film cans and processing exposed film, allow the film to warm up to room temperature.

Do not load or unload your camera or process the film in rooms that have fluorescent lighting even with the lights off. For a short time after they have been turned off, fluorescent lamps have an afterglow that will fog this film.

**Focusing:** Camera lenses do not focus infrared rays in the same plane as visible light rays. Some camera lenses have index marks on their focusing scales for taking infrared pictures. If your lens has one, use it. Otherwise, set your lens at the smallest opening that conditions permit. If you have to use large lens openings, and your lens has no infrared focusing mark, try to focus on the near side of the main subject or make a focus test. An alternative method is to extend the lens by adding 0.25 percent of the focal length to the lens-film extension for infinity focus.

**Filters:** To obtain infrared rendition in your pictures, you must use a filter over the lens (or light source) to absorb the blue and green light to which the film is sensitive. For general photography, a No. 25 filter is recommended; you can also use a No. 29 filter. When you want to record only the infrared radiation, use a No. 87, No. 87C, or No. 89B filter.

**Speeds:** It's not possible to give exact speeds for KODAK High Speed Infrared Film, because the ratio of infrared to visible light varies and exposure meters do not respond accurately to infrared radiation. Similar levels of visible light may be vastly different in the amounts of infrared radiation they contain. Make trial exposures to determine the proper exposure for the conditions under which you take your pictures. You can use the following speeds as a basis for determining exposures under average conditions with meters marked for ISO/ASA speeds or Exposure Indexes. With cameras that have a built-in exposure meter that makes the reading through any filter used over the lens, use these film speeds and make the meter reading before you put the filter on the camera. Or, use a hand-held exposure meter.

**Film Speed***

| Light Source | KODAK WRATTEN Gelatin Filter | | | |
|---|---|---|---|---|
| | No. 25, 29, or 89B | No. 87 | No. 87C | No Filter |
| Daylight | 50 | 25 | 10 | 80 |
| Tungsten | 125 | 64 | 25 | 200 |

*With development in KODAK Developer D-76.

**Daylight Exposures:** For subjects in bright or hazy sunlight (distinct shadows), use these recommendations as the basis of your trial exposures.

| Exposed Through a No. 25 Filter | |
|---|---|
| Distant Scenes | Nearby Scenes |
| 1/125 second *f*/11 | 1/30 second *f*/11 |

**Photolamps:** The following table is based on the use of two 500-watt reflector-type photolamps with a No. 25 filter over the camera lens. Place one lamp on each side of the camera at an angle of 45 degrees to the camera-subject axis.

| Exposure for 500-Watt Reflector-Type Photolamps | | | |
|---|---|---|---|
| Set Shutter Speed at 1/30 Second | | | |
| Lamp-to-Subject Distance | 3 ft (0.9 m) | 4½ ft (1.4 m) | 6½ ft (2 m) |
| Lens Opening | *f*/11 | *f*/8 | *f*/5.6 |

**Electronic Flash Guide Numbers:** This table is intended as a starting point in determining the correct guide number for electronic flash units rated in beam candlepower seconds (BCPS) and a No. 87 filter over the camera lens. Divide the proper guide number by the flash-to-subject distance in feet to determine the *f*-number for your trial exposures.

| Output of Unit (BCPS*) | | | | | | | | | |
|---|---|---|---|---|---|---|---|---|---|
| **350** | **500** | **700** | **1000** | **1400** | **2000** | **2800** | **4000** | **5600** | **8000** |
| **Guide Number** (for Distance in Feet) | | | | | | | | | |
| 20 | 24 | 30 | 35 | 40 | 50 | 60 | 70 | 85 | 100 |
| **Guide Number** (for Distance in Metres) | | | | | | | | | |
| 6 | 7 | 9 | 11 | 12 | 15 | 18 | 24 | 26 | 30 |

**Adjustments for Long or Short Exposures:** The following table gives the exposure compensation for different exposure times. No development adjustment is necessary.

| Adjustment | Exposure Time (Seconds) | | | | | |
|---|---|---|---|---|---|---|
| | **1/1000** | **1/100** | **1/10** | **1** | **10** | **100** |
| Exposure Increase | +⅓ stop | None | None | None | None | +⅔ stop or multiply exposure time by 1.6 |

## PROCESSING

You can develop your film in your own darkroom by following the steps below.

**Safelight:** *Total darkness is required.*

**Development Times** are for small roll-film tanks with agitation for 5 seconds at 30-second intervals throughout development. See page 75 for the method of agitation. The most widely used time and temperature are in heavy type. If your negatives are consistently too low in contrast, increase the development time; if too high in contrast, decrease the development time.

| KODAK Developer | Development Times in Minutes:Seconds* (for small roll-film tanks) | | | | |
|---|---|---|---|---|---|
| | 65°F (18°C) | **68°F (20°C)** | 70°F (21°C) | 72°F (22°C) | 75°F (24°C) |
| D-76† | 13:00 | **11:00** | 10:00 | 9:30 | 8:00 |
| HC-110 (Dil B)‡ | 7:00 | **6:00** | 6:00 | 5:30 | 5:00 |
| D-19§ | 7:00 | **6:00** | 5:30 | 5:00 | 4:00 |

*Development times shorter than 5 minutes may produce unsatisfactory uniformity.
†For pictorial use.
‡For scientific use.
§For maximum contrast.

**Rinse** in KODAK Indicator Stop Bath at 65 to 75°F (18 to 24°C) for 30 seconds with agitation. You can use a running-water rinse if an acid stop bath is not available.

**Fix** at 65 to 75°F (18 to 24°C) with agitation in KODAK Fixer or KODAFIX Solution for 5 to 10 minutes or in KODAK Rapid Fixer for 2 to 4 minutes.

**Wash** the film for 20 to 30 minutes in running water at 65 to 75°F (18 to 24°C). Use KODAK Hypo Clearing Agent to save time and conserve water.

**Note:** Keep the temperatures of the rinse, fix, and wash close to the developer temperature.

**Dry** in a dust-free place. To minimize drying marks, treat the film in KODAK PHOTO-FLO Solution after washing, or wipe the surfaces carefully with a KODAK Photo Chamois or a soft viscose sponge.

Also, see pages 73–80.

**Definition:**

| Granularity | Resolving Power | Sharpness | Degree of Enlargement* |
|---|---|---|---|
| Fine | Medium 80 lines per mm | Medium | Moderately low |

*For good-quality negatives

## Selecting a Kodak Developer for Black-and-White Film

**Kodak T-Max Developer**—A moderately active liquid developer that offers enhanced shadow detail in both normally processed and push-processed films. It produces higher image quality (enhanced shadow detail) than current popular push-processing developers when you process film normally or push it one, two, or three stops. You can use T-Max Developer to process roll sizes of Kodak T-Max Professional Films and most other black-and-white continuous-tone films. This developer is intended for use in unreplenished systems. It has large capacity, allowing you to process up to 48 rolls of film per gallon.

T-Max Developer is available as a one-part concentrate in sizes to make one gallon and five gallons of working solution. You can easily mix smaller volumes by mixing one part of the concentrate with four parts water. Both the concentrate and working solution have excellent storage characteristics.

**Kodak T-Max RS Developer and Replenisher**—A moderately active liquid black-and-white film developer *and* replenisher that offers enhanced shadow detail in both normally processed and push-processed films. Like Kodak T-Max Developer, it produces higher image quality than current popular push-processing developers when you process film normally or push it one, two, or three stops. You can use T-Max RS Developer and Replenisher to process all roll and sheet sizes of Kodak T-Max Professional Films, as well as most other black-and-white continuous-tone films.

T-Max RS Developer and Replenisher are a two-part developer specially formulated for replenished systems, but you can also use them as an unreplenished developer. They are available in convenient sizes to make one gallon and ten gallons of solution; use this solution as a working-tank solution or a replenisher. Both the concentrate and working solution have excellent storage characteristics.

**Kodak T-Max 100 Direct Positive Film Developing Outfit**—Use this kit with Kodak T-Max 100 Professional Film to produce high-quality slides from continuous-tone photographs, drawings, and artwork. You can also use the kit with T-Max 100 Professional Film to produce copy negatives from black-and-white or color negatives, or duplicate black-and-white slides, or black-and-white slides from color slides.

Use this kit with Kodak Technical Pan Film to produce high-quality slides of computer-generated graphs and line art, or to produce high-contrast title slides.

**Kodak Developer D-76**—Long a favorite of pictorial photographers, it is well known for superior performance. This developer produces full emulsion speed and excellent shadow detail with normal contrast and fine grain with a wide selection of black-and-white films. It produces a long density scale, and its excellent development latitude permits push processing with relatively low fog.

For greater sharpness, but with a slight sacrifice in graininess, you can dilute the developer 1:1. You can use Kodak Replenisher D-76R, sold by photo dealers, to extend the useful life of the developer. Instructions are included with the developer and the replenisher.

**Kodak HC-110 Developer**—A highly active general-purpose developer for rapid processing of most black-and-white films, HC-110 Developer produces full film speed, excellent shadow detail, and a long tonal range. It yields a low fog level in push-processing. This developer yields sharp images and fine grain with a large variety of black-and-white films. Both developer and replenisher are conveniently supplied in highly concentrated liquid form. Dilution A is intended for short development times; Dilution B is for longer development times, which yield better development uniformity.

**Kodak Developer DK-50**—This is a popular general-purpose developer that works well with or without dilution. Moderately fast acting, it produces crisp, clean negatives with good highlight detail and medium grain. You can use Kodak Replenisher DK-50R to extend the capacity of the developer.

**Kodak Microdol-X Developer**—An excellent fine-grain developer, Microdol-X Developer is designed to produce low graininess and high sharpness with minimum speed loss. This developer is particularly suited for developing small negatives intended for making big enlargements. It is clean-working and has a long solution life. You can obtain even greater image sharpness by using Microdol-X Developer diluted 1:3, but with a slight increase in graininess. You can purchase this developer in either powder or liquid form. A powder replenisher is also available to extend the capacity.

**Kodak Technidol Liquid Developer**—This developer is produced specifically for use with Kodak Technical Pan Film for pictorial photography. It provides contrast appropriate for pictorial applications while retaining useful film speed. It enhances edge effects and apparent sharpness.

TECHNIDOL Liquid Developer produces micro-fine grain, extremely high resolving power—320 lines per mm—and extremely high sharpness. With this developer/film combination, you can make 25X and greater enlargements with little apparent grain. The developer is easy to mix in its convenient liquid form and is recommended for any size of Technical Pan Film.

**KODAK TECHNIDOL LC Developer**—This developer has characteristics similar to those of KODAK TECHNIDOL Liquid Developer. You can use it for the same pictorial applications with KODAK Technical Pan Film in the 135 size only. The developer and film provide extremely fine grain, extremely high resolving power—320 lines per mm—and extremely high sharpness. TECHNIDOL LC Developer is supplied in powder form. Mix it just before using it and discard the solution after one use.

**KODAK Developer D-19**—This is a high-capacity, rapid-working developer that yields brilliant, high-contrast negatives. It is especially suitable for copying and for technical applications that require higher-than-normal contrast.

**KODAK DEKTOL Developer**—Primarily a paper developer. DEKTOL Developer is also used for some high-contrast applications with specific films, such as KODAK Technical Pan Film. The developer is supplied in powder form.

**KODAK DURAFLO RT Developer Replenisher and Starter**—These are designed to provide rapid, fine grain results in roller transport processing machines. A hardener is incorporated into the developer to allow films to be processed in this type of equipment at higher temperatures without damage to the emulsion.

# NOTES

# NOTES

# NOTES

# INDEX